SINCE YESTERDAY

Also available in Perennial Library
by Frederick Lewis Allen:

THE BIG CHANGE: America Transforms Itself, 1900–1950
ONLY YESTERDAY: An Informal History of the 1920s

SINCE YESTERDAY

THE 1930s IN AMERICA

SEPTEMBER 3, 1929–SEPTEMBER 3, 1939

FREDERICK LEWIS ALLEN

PERENNIAL LIBRARY

Harper & Row, Publishers
New York, Cambridge, Philadelphia, San Francisco
London, Mexico City, São Paulo, Singapore, Sydney

A hardcover edition of this book was published by Harper & Row, Publishers, Inc.

SINCE YESTERDAY. Copyright 1939, 1940 by Frederick Lewis Allen. Copyright renewed 1968 by Agnes Rogers Allen. All rights reserved. Printed in the United States of America. No part of this book may be used or reproduced in any manner whatsoever without written permission except in the case of brief quotations embodied in critical articles and reviews. For information address Harper & Row, Publishers, Inc., 10 East 53rd Street, New York, N.Y. 10022. Published simultaneously in Canada by Fitzhenry & Whiteside Limited, Toronto.

First PERENNIAL LIBRARY edition published 1972. Reissued in 1986.

Library of Congress Cataloging-in-Publication Data

Allen, Frederick Lewis, 1890–1954.
  Since yesterday.

  Includes index.
    1. United States—History—1919–1933. 2. United States—Economic conditions—1918–1945. 3. United States—Social conditions—1933–1945. I. Title.
  E784.A63   1986   973.91   86-45060
  ISBN 0-06-091322-3 (pbk.)

86   87   88   89   90   MPC   10   9   8   7   6   5   4   3   2   1

To

LETITIA CUNNINGHAM ROGERS
who has a wise head and a warm heart

CONTENTS

ILLUSTRATIONS

PREFACE

EVER since, in *Only Yesterday*, I tried to tell the story of life in the United States during the nineteen-twenties I have had it in the back of my mind that some day I might make a similar attempt for the nineteen-thirties. I definitely began work on the project late in 1938 and had it three-quarters done by the latter part of the summer of 1939, though I did not yet know how the story would end. The outbreak of war in Europe provided an obvious conclusion, since it promised to end an era perhaps as definitely as the Panic of 1929 had ended one. By an odd chance, the declaration of war upon Germany by the British and French governments took place ten years to a day after that September 3, 1929, which I had already made the subject of my first chapter. It gave me a turn to realize how precisely the course of events had provided me with a decade to chronicle.

The span of time covered in *Only Yesterday* was from the Armistice of November 11, 1918, to the Panic of October-November, 1929, with a concluding chapter which recited the course of events between the Panic and the spring of 1931 and tried to suggest how the temper of the country had altered during that post-Panic interval. (The book was published in December, 1931.) When I came to plan the present volume it was clear that some overlapping would be necessary, for obviously the story of the nineteen-thirties should start before the Panic and give some idea of the high place from which the country fell during the economic collapse of 1929-32. Hence my decision to begin with a study of things as they were on September 3, 1929 (which I had written in somewhat different form as an article in *Harper's Magazine* in 1937), and in a second chapter to cover the Panic and the course of events up to the spring

of 1931. The story of the Panic itself, however, I have abbreviated in this book, since I told it in considerable detail
in *Only Yesterday*.

The problem of selection and emphasis, always difficult,
is of course doubly difficult when one is writing so close
to the event. In *Only Yesterday* I brought into sharp relief
manners and customs, fads and follies, and everyday circumstances of life. In the present volume I have done the
same thing to some degree, but not quite as much; for the
heart of the story of America in the nineteen-thirties was
obviously the enormous economic and political transformation which took place, and such trivialities as had been
of the essence of life in the United States in the nineteen-
twenties were now, it seemed to me, less significant. Future
events may make my selection and appraisal of material
look very dated; in that case I can only hope my very mis-
calculations may have a certain paradoxical value as indicating the sort of pitfall into which one readily fell in 1939,
even if one were conscientiously intent upon presenting a
fair appraisal.

F. L. A.

SINCE YESTERDAY

Chapter One

PRELUDE: SEPTEMBER 3, 1929

§ 1

D O YOU remember what you were doing on September 3, 1929?

Probably not—unless you have an altogether exceptional memory.

Let me refresh your recollection. For if we are to understand the changes in American life during the nineteen-thirties, we must first recall what things were like before this period began—before the Panic which introduced the Depression. Perhaps the most convenient way of doing this is to imagine ourselves re-living a single day in 1929: seeing what things look like, listening to the talk, glancing at the newspapers and magazines and books, noticing what are the preoccupations and assumptions and expectations in people's minds—and doing all this with the eyes and ears and intellectual perspective of today.

I have chosen September 3, 1929, as the day to re-visit, for it was then that the Big Bull Market reached its peak: that the Dow-Jones average of stock-market prices, which had been rising so long and so furiously, made its high record for all time. If there was any single day when the wave of prosperity—and of speculation—which characterized the nineteen-twenties may be said to have attained its utmost height before it curled over and crashed, September 3, 1929, was that day.

So let us go back and look about us.

§ 2

It is a very hot day, this first Tuesday in September, 1929. Not everywhere, to be sure: in the Far West and South the temperatures are moderate. But from the coast of Maine to the wheatfields of Nebraska the sun beats down implacably.

Yesterday was Labor Day; and last night, as the long holiday week end came to its close, the suburban highways approaching the larger American cities were nightmares of congestion as endless lines of cars full of sunburned, sweltering vacationists and week-enders crept cityward through the night, inch by angry inch. On the New Jersey highways leading to New York the tie-up was so complete that people by the thousands, hopeless of reaching the Holland Tunnel for hours, parked their cars in Newark or Hoboken and finished the journey to New York by tube. The railroad stations, too, were jammed with people—not only vacationists and week-enders but boy and girl campers returning to town en masse; never had Labor Day traffic been so overwhelming, or the collective discomfort of Labor Day travel been greater. (There were, of course, no air-conditioned cars.)

As you get up on Tuesday morning, September 3, after an airless night, the weather prediction in the morning paper offers you no relief. "Fair and continued warm today and tomorrow," it says. You are in for it: for a temperature of 94.2° in New York; 90° in Chicago, Detroit, and Kansas City; 92° in St. Louis; 94° in Minneapolis; 97° in Boston.

After breakfast you go out on the street. The men you see there do not look so very different from those of a decade later, though more of them are wearing starched collars and waistcoats than in subsequent years, and not nearly so many of them are going hatless. But the women are different indeed. The fashionable figure is straight up and down—no breasts, no waist, no hips; and if few of the women you see can even approximate this ideal, at least they are visibly making the effort. Not yet have Mae West's curves become a national influence. The waistline—if it can be called one—is round the hips. The skirts are short, reaching only two or three inches below the knee: shorter than they will be again until 1939. (The new evening dresses —backless and sleeveless—have panels, godets, or drapery hanging about the ankles, but the dresses themselves are still short.) Every dress has a v-neck, almost every sweater even. If this were a wintry day, instead of one of the hottest days of summer, you would see every woman hugging herself energetically to hold in place her straight wrap-around coat. The women's hats are small helmets that fit tightly right down to the nape of the neck and so closely surround the face that a profile view of a woman shows hardly more than an eye, the nose, mouth, and chin, a lock or two of hair to decorate the cheek—and the helmet. Not all women wear their hair short, but the approved style is to shingle it in the back and draw it forward over the ears.

Even in a large city you may see one or two backless dresses among the shoppers and a few pairs of stockingless legs, for the sun-tan craze is in the full flush of novelty. As the advertisements in the *Ladies Home Journal* declare, "This is a sun-worshipping year . . . all the world has gone in for sun-tan." You will have to look long and hard to detect any tinted nails, however; that style is still in the future.

The automobiles surging by you are angular; there isn't a streamline among them. Horizontal and perpendicular lines; square tops, with the upper rear angle hardly rounded at all; perpendicular or almost perpendicular windshields; perpendicular, flat radiator fronts. No pointed or rounded prows, no sloping rears, no draft ventilators.

You will not be able to go far, in the central part of any

of the big cities, without hearing the deafening clatter of riveters, for although the Florida boom went to pieces in 1926, and the boom in suburban developments—which has been filling up the open spaces in the outskirts of the cities with Cotswold Terraces and Rosemont Groves and Woodmere Drives—has been lagging a bit since 1927, the boom in apartment-house construction and particularly in office-building construction is still going full tilt. Not in the poorer districts are the riveters noisiest, but at the centers of big business and of residential wealth, for it is the holders and manipulators of securities who are the chief beneficiaries of this last speculative phase of Coolidge-Hoover prosperity. That network of steel girders which you see rising so high above the street is going to be a luxurious co-operative apartment house; that place where the sidewalk is roofed over and the steam shovels are gobbling up an immense excavation is the site for a new skyscraper for brokers' offices and investment-trust offices and mortgage-bond salesmen.

In New York they are tearing down the old Waldorf-Astoria to make room for a skyscraper to end skyscrapers, the Empire State Building. John D. Rockefeller, Jr., has architects quietly at work making preliminary plans for a big mid-town development which he hopes will have a new Opera House as its central feature (he doesn't know yet that the Opera will decline to come in and that his colossal investment will have to take new shape in a Radio City). The Chrysler Building and several other major skyscrapers are still shooting upward. Most of the other cities of America are doing their best to emulate New York's frenzy for monuments of steel and stone ever loftier, more ambitious, and more expressive of the era of confident speculative finance.

As you walk on, a man passes you whistling "Singin' in the Rain," which at the moment rivals "The Pagan Love Song" and "Vagabond Lover" in popularity.

Here is a movie theatre advertising Al Jolson in "Say It with Songs"; across the street another one advertises "Our Modern Maidens," with Joan Crawford (still in her harum-scarum phase) and Rod La Rocque. A little further Ronald Colman may be seen in "Bulldog Drummond." The fact that this is advertised as Mr. Colman's "first all-talking picture" bears witness that the invasion of the movies by sound is not yet complete. Even in the big cities there are still silent pictures competing with the talking ones. The migration of Broadway stage celebrities to Hollywood has been under way for some time, as movie producers search for actors who can speak their parts acceptably, but still the studios are fumbling uncertainly with the new medium, and still the critics regard the "talkie" as something of an awkward parvenu. When your local theatre, succumbing to the trend of the times, gets itself wired for sound, the noises which blare forth are sometimes wonderful indeed. The actors lisp absurdly; the outbursts of song, coming after "silent sequences," are often cacophonous; and as Gilbert Seldes remarks in an article in the current *Harper's*, "The tinkle of a glass, the shot of a revolver, a footfall on a hardwood floor, and the noise of a pack of cards being shuffled, are all about alike."

Steadily, however, the medium is being improved; and indeed there are many people in this era of rapid engineering advance and bold business enterprise who are wondering whether the talking picture will not soon be superseded in its turn by television. "Within twelve months—eighteen months at the latest—the talkies will have to meet the competition of the talkie-projector in the home," writes Mr. Seldes. ". . . And within another year we shall probably have the simple and comparatively inexpensive mechanisms, now being perfected, which will throw on a small screen set up beside the home radio set a moving picture projected from a central broadcasting station."

If you are to be in New York this evening, perhaps the stage will be more to your taste than the movies. "Street Scene" is having a long run there, and so is that grim reminiscence of war, "Journey's End," which you may prefer if you have liked the current best-selling novel, *All Quiet on the Western Front*. Eddie Cantor is on the stage in "Whoopee," you can see Bert Lahr in "Hold Everything!" If you enjoy opening nights, you can go to the first performance of a new musical show called "Sweet Adeline," which exemplifies a budding tendency to turn back in nostalgic mood to the sentiments of the gay nineties. If you had rather sit quietly at home on such a hot night and listen to the radio, you can hear the Fada Symphony Orchestra, the Pure Oil Band, Whiteman's Old Gold Orchestra, or the Freed Orchestradians. Not yet has the technique of the radio variety show been perfected, nor can you listen in on a world-wide broadcast, but the crooners—led by Rudy Vallee—are on the air in full force. The average price of a radio set is still as high as $135, for the low-priced small sets have not yet come on the market. In these prosperous times, however, radios are being bought in quantity despite their size and price, and already some twelve million American families own them.

§ 3

Let us look at the newspapers. They may help us to orient ourselves. What will tomorrow morning's headlines say about today's events?

They will agree that the most exciting and important events of September 3, 1929, aside from the heat wave and purely local happenings, are a speech by the Prime Minister of England, a golf tournament, and two incidents in aviation.

The Prime Minister is Ramsay MacDonald; his speech is delivered at Geneva before the Assembly of the League of

Nations. (Yes, the League, in 1929, is an important—though hardly determining—factor in international relations.) MacDonald announces in his speech that negotiations between Great Britain and the United States for the limitation of naval armaments are progressing favorably, and that full agreement seems near. He hopes shortly to visit the United States to further that agreement. (He will come, a little later, and he and President Hoover will sit and talk on a log by the Rapidan River near Hoover's rural camp.)

These armament negotiations of 1929 are incidents in the long post-war struggle for agreement—and for national advantage—in a Hitlerless world. Germany is a republic and a member of the League of Nations; the Dawes Plan of collecting reparations from Germany is about to be succeeded by the less oppressive Young Plan; France, the most powerful nation on the Continent, still occupies the Rhineland. Japan has not yet gone into Manchuria, let alone into China, nor Italy into Ethiopia; Spain is not yet torn by civil war; and Adolf Hitler is the little-regarded leader of a noisy minority of German Brown Shirts, his name quite unknown to most Americans.

There is plenty of tension, to be sure. National feelings run high, and for years past the attentive students of international affairs have been intermittently predicting a major war. At this very moment there is a grave threat of war between Russia and China. Mussolini is cherishing dreams of empire; there are Arab riots in Palestine; and Gandhi is giving trouble to the British in India. But still in the main the lines drawn at Versailles in 1919 are holding, and the democratically governed nations are on top.

Much more exciting than Ramsay MacDonald's address, to most Americans, is another front-page event of September 3: the National Amateur Golf Championship at Pebble Beach, California. The incomparable Bobby Jones is there, tying for first place with Gene Homans in the qualifying round. Will Jones go on victoriously to win his fifth American amateur title? (He will not; he will be beaten tomorrow by young Johnny Goodman, who in turn will be beaten by nineteen-year-old Lawson Little. Not till next year will Jones be able to perform the feat of taking the British amateur and open titles, and the American amateur and open, all in one season.) Meanwhile the question whether Jones will win is in millions of people's minds all over the country; for golf is in its heyday as the business man's game. For years past, aspiring executives have been drilled in the idea that afternoons spent in plus-fours provide not only enjoyment but useful business contacts, and country clubs have been becoming more palatial, more expensive, and more heavily mortgaged with membership bonds.

Of the two headlined incidents in aviation, one is a triumph, the other a disaster. The triumph belongs to the great German dirigible, the Graf Zeppelin. Having successfully circled the world, it is now on its way home across the Atlantic from Lakehurst to Friedrichshafen; by the evening of the third of September it has completed the ocean crossing, and observers in little Spanish towns see it floating overhead, its cabins brilliantly lighted against the sky. So impressive has been the Graf Zeppelin's demonstration of the possibilities of lighter-than-air flying that the designers of the Empire State Building are about to build a mooring mast on top of the skyscraper; they will announce their decision on December 11 with this somewhat premature prophecy: "The directors of Empire State, Inc., believe that in a comparatively short time the Zeppelin airships will establish transatlantic, transcontinental, and transpacific lines, and possibly a route to South America from the port of New York. Building with an eye to the future, it has been determined to erect this mooring tower."

In striking contrast to the Graf Zeppelin's triumph is the air disaster of September third: the crash of a Transcontinental Air Transport plane in New Mexico during a thunderstorm, with the loss of eight lives: a severe setback to heavier-than-air flying.

One might be misled by the word "Transcontinental." There is no coast-to-coast passenger service by air in 1929. During the summer the T.A.T., with Colonel Lindbergh as its adviser, has begun a pioneer service in conjunction with the Pennsylvania and Santa Fe railroads: passengers take an overnight train from New York to Columbus, Ohio; fly by day from Columbus to Waynoke, Oklahoma; take another overnight train to Clovis, New Mexico; and then continue by air to the Coast. In newspaper advertisements you may see Lionel Barrymore as he alights from the "Airway Limited," which has reduced the journey from New York to Los Angeles to the record-breaking time of forty-eight hours. No night flying is permitted. Yet now, before the first summer is over, one of the big Ford trimotor planes has gone smashing into Mount Taylor in New Mexico. The disaster is an ugly blow to the fledgling air-transport industry. Since Lindbergh's flight to Paris in 1927 the adventurers of the air have been crossing oceans boldly, airplane stocks have been soaring, and the Post Office Department has been successfully flying the mail across the country; but passenger flying in the United States is still in its hazardous and uncertain infancy.

The newspapers which record the events of September 3, 1929, contain other items of interest. You will learn in them that in Gastonia, North Carolina, a jury has been chosen for the trial of sixteen strikers and alleged Communists for the killing of the Chief of Police. (Yes, there is occasionally a bitter industrial conflict in the nineteen-twenties, even though unionism is weak, the membership of the American Federation of Labor has dwindled, and radicalism is almost negligible. There is, of course, no CIO.) You will learn that Commander Byrd—not yet an Admiral—is waiting in the snows of Little America for his flight over the South Pole. Babe Ruth, you will discover, is still top man in baseball: though he has made no home run on September 3, his record for the season, so far, stands at 40 home runs as against 31 for Jimmy Foxx and 29 for Lou Gehrig. Bill Tilden is expected to win the amateur tennis championship at Forest Hills (and will do so—for the seventh time), but his era of supremacy, like Bobby Jones's and Babe Ruth's, has not long to run. (His seventh championship will be his last.) From the social columns of the newspaper you may learn that Alfred E. Smith has wandered far enough from the torrid sidewalks of New York to be the guest of honor at a luncheon at fashionable Southampton. Having been defeated by Herbert Hoover in the national election of 1928, Smith is now preparing himself for a loftier if narrower Presidency— that of the Empire State Building.

§ 4

But the event for which September 3, 1929, will probably be longest remembered in the United States, you will not find recorded in the newspapers at all. No headlines will announce tonight that the Big Bull Market has reached its climax; for no headline writers—nor anybody else for that matter—can see into the future. The financial reporters will remark, to be sure, that bullish enthusiasm has resulted in "another in the long series of consecutive new high records established by the share market," but the comment will be casual. Men do not whip themselves into frenzies over the usual. None of us is aware, on September 3, 1929, that the people of the United States are crossing one of the great divides of national history. The way ahead is hidden, as always, by fog. Surely, we imagine, there is higher ground just ahead. Yet at this very moment the path under our feet is about to turn downward.

Suppose we go into a broker's office this morning. It is crowded with men and women; every seat is taken, men are standing against the walls, and during the lunch hour there will be a dense cluster at the door as business men on their way to lunch stop by to see how their fortunes are faring. All eyes are riveted on the trans-lux screen, across which runs an endless procession of letters and figures—the record of sales taking place on the New York Stock Exchange. The tickers are having a hard time to keep up with the trading today, for the volume of transactions, though not phenomenal for 1929, is large: the day's total will run to nearly four and a half million shares. Probably half the people in this room have bought stocks on margin; in the whole United States, probably well over a million people are thus speculating with borrowed money, while several millions more are keeping a hopeful eye upon the daily fluctuations in market prices. The financing of all these speculative borrowings has sucked into the stock market a huge amount of credit; at this very moment the total of loans to brokers— loans by the banks, and by business corporations acting through the banks—comes to over eight billion dollars; yet still the demand so far exceeds the supply that the interest rate for loans to brokers stands today at nine per cent.

If you can interpret the symbols as they hurry across the lighted screen, notice the prices they record. United States Steel is edging up to 261¾; Anaconda Copper is at 130⅞; American Telephone, at 302; General Electric, at 395; General Motors, at 71⅞; and Radio Corporation, which recently split its shares five for one, is quoted on the new basis at 99 (which would be 495 on the old basis). Absurdly high, these prices? Not in the opinion of most of the men in this room. Wherever men of property gather these days—in business offices, in the suburban club cars, at the downtown lunch tables, in the country-club locker rooms—you will hear that this is a new era, that the future of the blue-ribbon stocks is dazzling, that George F. Baker never sells anything, that you can't go far wrong if you are a Bull on America. "These new investment trusts are taking the best stocks out of the market; better buy them now, while they're still within reach." "Prices too high? But look at the figures that the Blue Ridge Corporation has just announced that it'll pay! Those fellows know what they're doing." "One of the biggest men in the Street told me yesterday that he expects to see General Electric go to a thousand." "I tell you, Electric Bond and Share at 183 is dirt cheap when you consider what's ahead for the public utilities."

It is not only in the places where the wealthy congregate that one hears discussion of the market. In these days when janitors have put their savings into Montgomery Ward, when cowboys have margin accounts in American Can, and when nursemaids have just bought 200 shares of Cities' Service, stock-market talk is recurrent at dinner parties, in streetcars, on commuting trains, among filling-station employees, among bookkeepers lunching at the automat. The stories about big winnings, the conjectures about foolproof methods of stock-market forecasting, the gossip about Packard's current earnings, form the leitmotif of the times.

In every era young intellectuals tend to be rebellious. Do they, in 1929, rebel against the speculative frenzy of finance capitalism? Very few of them do. If most of them look askance at American business and American business men, it is only because they regard them as vulgar and commercial-minded. The heaven of the young intellectuals of 1929 is not Moscow but Montparnasse; their gods are not radical economists or novelists of proletarian revolt, but Proust, Cézanne, Jung, Mencken, Hemingway (as a Left Bank author of terse disillusionment), and T. S. Eliot.

In Chicago, Samuel Insull is now at the summit of his career; he is watching the stock of Insull Utilities Investments—that stock which was delivered to him only a few

months ago at less than $8 a share—reach a high price for
the day of $115, a share; and he is preparing to launch yet
another super-super-corporation, and to witness the Civic
Opera's first season in the mammoth building which he
has provided for it. In Cleveland, men of vision are betting
their shirts on those wonder-boys of railroading, the brothers
Van Sweringen, who have so piled holding company upon
holding company that they now control six railroads and
are acquiring control of a seventh. In Detroit the big bankers and automobile executives, succumbing to the prevalent
fever for financial concentration, are discussing a movement
to combine dozens of Michigan banks into huge groups. On
the Pacific Coast, the current financial sensation is Amadeo
Giannini's Bank of America, which seems well on its way
to swallow up all California business, if not to dominate a
large part of American banking. Charlie Mitchell's salesmen from the National City Company in New York are
selling South American bonds to the little crossroads bank,
and Anaconda Copper stock to the bank's president. The
optimism of prosperity is everywhere.

Well, not quite everywhere. The farmers of America are
not prospering: hard times have been almost incessant on
the farms since the post-war collapse of agricultural prices
in 1921. The textile towns of New England are in a bad
way. In the deep South and the uplands of the Alleghenies,
and in the cut-over regions of northern Michigan, there is
much privation. Nor can it be denied that there is unemployment. To paraphrase the words of F. C. Mills in his
Economic Tendencies in the United States, the displacement of men by machines, the turnover of men within
industries, and the shifting of men from industry to industry, are making men less secure in their jobs, and especially
are making it harder for men past the prime of life to get
back into new jobs once they are displaced. The rewards
for employed men are often high, but mechanical improve-

ments and a faster pace of work are making it harder to hold on. And it must be admitted, too, that when one uses the word prosperity one is using a relative term. According to the Brookings estimates, even in this banner year of 1929 no less than seventy-eight per cent of the American population have family incomes of less than $3,000 or individual incomes of less than $1,500, and something like forty per cent have family incomes of less than $1,500 or individual incomes of less than $750. Certainly such a state of affairs is far from utopian. Yet by all current standards elsewhere in the world, and by all remembered standards in America, the average of well-being is high; and among the well-to-do it is glittering.

President Hoover has just returned to the blinding heat of Washington from a week end at his Rapidan camp, and this morning he meets with his Cabinet from 10:30 till 12. No record will be kept of what goes on at that meeting, but one may hazard a reasonable guess as to some of the topics under discussion The talk may turn to the armament negotiations with Great Britain, or to some thorny questions of tariff adjustment, or to the danger of a Russo-Chinese war over the Chinese Eastern Railroad. Mr. Hoover may consult his Cabinet as to whether he should denounce the shipbuilding companies which retained William B. Shearer as an "observer" at the Geneva arms conference, presumably to hinder naval reduction. (He will denounce them, three days hence.) There are also awkward questions relating to Prohibition, farm relief, and Mexican policy which may come before the meeting. Are those men gathered about the long table in the White House offices turning their attention today to the question whether prosperity can be maintained? It is possible, but unlikely.

Not that Herbert Hoover shares the widespread belief that the speculative debauch in the stock market is a happy and healthy phenomenon. On the contrary, he has been supporting the Federal Reserve Board in its unavailing efforts to check the flow of credit into speculation, and he has done his share of worrying over the possible consequences of a collapse of prices. But by this time the boom is well beyond control, except by some drastic measure which might bring on the very crash it was intended to avert. Otherwise the economic skies seem clear. Business is undeniably booming. Perhaps the speculative storm will manage to blow itself out and all will be well. Prosperity, these days, has come to be taken for granted; and busy men whose desks are piled with problems pressing for solution do not borrow trouble by debating just when and how it might come to an unimaginable end.

Besides, the maintenance of general prosperity is not, in 1929, generally regarded as a presidential responsibility. The New York *Herald Tribune* is going to press tonight with a laudatory review of Hoover's first six months in office, and nowhere in that review will there be a word about the stock market or so much as a hint that the maintenance of general economic stability is the government's affair. In every political election, of course, the party in power, as a matter of routine, takes all credit for whatever good times have been enjoyed, and the party out of power excoriates it for whatever hard times have been suffered; but the most that is really expected of the government from month to month, in relation to the progress of the national economy, is that its policies of taxation, regulation, subsidy, and the like, shall if possible be helpful to business rather than hurtful, and particularly shall be helpful to those business interests which are able to write their wishes into legislation. Otherwise the government is expected to keep its hands off. Insofar as the economic machinery does not run of its own accord, automatically, the citizens look less to the political chiefs in Washington for economic leadership than to the financial chiefs in Wall Street. Not Herbert Hoover and his

Cabinet but the bankers and industrialists and holding-company promotors are the architects and custodians of this prosperity.

§ 5

But if the maintenance of prosperity is not considered a current problem, Prohibition emphatically is. The Eighteenth Amendment is in full force, and so are the bootleggers and rumrunners. Al Capone, as it happens, is serving a year's sentence in Philadelphia for carrying a pistol, but he will be out soon; meanwhile his Chicago gang and similar gangster groups in other cities are taking an enormous toll from the illicit liquor business. Very few people believe that repeal of the Eighteenth Amendment is a reasonable possibility; any well-informed student of politics will tell you that a few dry states could block it indefinitely. Moralists are attributing the prevalence of crime to the dire influences of the speakeasy.

If your rambles this afternoon should take you through midtown New York, you may notice well-dressed men and women descending the steps to the basement entrances of certain brownstone houses. They are not calling on the cook, but making a routine entrance to a speakeasy: standing patiently at the door till Tony or Mino, within, has appraised them through a little barred window and decided to unbolt the door. The man-about-town carries in his wallet a collection of autographed speakeasy cards, certifying to membership in this or that "club," in case he should wish to go for a drink to some place where he is not already well known by sight as a patron or can identify himself as a "friend of Mr. Jones's."

President Hoover has appointed a commission to study the whole question of law enforcement and crime; and this very day its chairman, George W. Wickersham, is on a train from New York to Washington, going over the agenda for tomorrow's meeting. Prohibition is only one of the topics which this commission will investigate; indeed, though the minutes of tomorrow's meeting will cover five pages, only two lines will deal with liquor legislation. But to the general public nothing in the commission's program really matters except Prohibition. For the wet-or-dry issue is the hottest one in American politics.

§ 6

At any moment some currents in the great stream of history are diminishing, and other currents are gaining in volume and strength. At any moment there are things ending, waves of popular excitement subsiding, men moving into the twilight of their careers; and there are also things beginning, future events being quietly prepared for, men and women walking about unknown whose names will soon be on everybody's lips.

On this September day of 1929, the last surviving veteran of the Mexican War is dying. . . . Ex-President William Howard Taft, now the Chief Justice of the Supreme Court, is in declining health, and has but a few months more to live. . . . Thomas A. Edison's achievements as an inventor are behind him, for he is in his eighty-third year. On this hot day he is convalescing from an attack of pneumonia, but is sitting up in a chair and declaring that he expects to go to Dearborn in a few weeks to celebrate the fiftieth anniversary of his incandescent light. (The expectation is justified, for he still has two full years to live.) . . . Calvin Coolidge's lifework is behind him, too. Last March he left the White House for his simple duplex apartment on Massasoit Street, Northampton, where the rent is $36 a month; and although he is said to have made a hundred thousand dollars writing magazine articles since March 4, he still uses a little second-story office with a desk, two chairs, and a bookcase filled with old law books. Life is quiet for him, these days, too quiet; he longs for the days that are done. . . . In the day's news there is an echo of the oil scandal of the Administration which preceded Coolidge's: Harry F. Sinclair, serving a term in the District of Columbia jail for contempt of the Senate during the oil investigations, has been denied permission to leave the jail on errands as the jail physician's "pharmaceutical assistant."

It has been said that coming events cast their shadows before. But if this is true, the shadows are not recognized as such. On September 3, 1929, Governor Franklin D. Roosevelt of New York State, who ran for the Governorship last year at the urgent invitation of his old friend Al Smith, is awaiting replies to a questionnaire which he has just sent out to mayors and village presidents throughout the State. The questionnaire asks them on what basis their communities buy electric power—from private utilities or from municipal plants? and at what cost? This inquiry might seem prophetic, but to mortals denied the gift of prophecy it does not seem especially significant. The men who are pushing up the prices of public-utility stocks to Himalayan levels are not greatly disturbed. For anybody in Albany will tell you that Roosevelt is just collecting information which he thinks he needs in order to carry out Al Smith's power policy.

If you follow the liberal weeklies carefully, you will see occasional caustic references to that autocratic reactionary, that stubborn member of the A F of L bureaucracy, the leader of the United Mine Workers, John L. Lewis. . . . Father Coughlin of Royal Oak, outside Detroit, is well known within the range of the single broadcasting station which transmits his sermons but almost unknown beyond them. . . . In Long Beach, California, there is an elderly practicing physician named Francis E. Townsend, quite unknown save to his patients and personal friends: the time for the Townsend Pension Plan is still far away. . . . Huey Long is in the midst of a stormy term as Governor of Louisiana, but Northerners have heard little of him yet. . . . The people who are accustomed to sitting in a Greenwich Village speakeasy and occasionally hearing young Howard Scott—a none-too-successful engineer—expound his curious economic theories, would be amazed if they were told that within four years Technocracy will be the talk of the United States.

Broadcasters take a day off every week, and so on this September 3 Freeman F. Gosden and Charles J. Correll are getting a rest after their first fortnight on the NBC network as "Amos 'n' Andy." In two months their program will be changed from a late evening hour to 7 P.M., Eastern Standard Time, and within a year their popularity will be so immense that one will hardly be able to walk a block in an American town at that hour without hearing "I'se regusted" and "Dat's de propolition" issuing from open window after window. Have they any inkling of what is ahead for them? Does Garnet Carter of Lookout Mountain, Tennessee, who is today boarding a train for Miami to install the first miniature golf course in Florida, dream that by next summer miniature golf courses will be springing up by every highway all over the land? Does Walt Disney, who, after years of adversity, is at last finding a public for his Mickey Mouse pictures and has just brought out his first Silly Symphony, foresee his fame and fortune as the creator of "Three Little Pigs" and "Snow White"?

As the heat of the day begins to wane in Cazenovia, New York, a young writer named Hervey Allen sits down to work at the second chapter of a huge novel which will not be published for nearly four years: *Anthony Adverse*. . . . In the John Day publishing house in New York, the editors are making up their minds to publish a novel called *East*

Wind, West Wind, which has been declined already by so many publishers that its author has not even bothered to tell her agents that she has left China for a visit to the United States. In her mind is taking shape another novel; who guesses that this yet unwritten book, *The Good Earth,* will win for Pearl Buck the Nobel Prize? . . . Who, for that matter, would ever pick a freckle-faced, fourteen-year-old boy in Oakland, California, named Donald Budge, as the future world's tennis champion? The boy hasn't even touched a racket since he was eleven. . . . Recent graduates of Cushing Academy at Ashburnham, Massachusetts, remember well their schoolmate Ruth Elizabeth Davis, but not in connection with Hollywood; for not until 1930 will she begin her screen career. (Later they will see her often as Bette Davis.) . . . In one of the Middle Western cities, if you drop into a theatre on the Orpheum vaudeville circuit tonight, you may be amused by a young ventriloquist named Edgar Bergen talking to a dummy that he calls Charlie McCarthy. . . . If you are in New York and the heat drives you to a roof garden for the evening, and you happen to choose the Park Central Hotel, you may appreciate the nimbleness of a twenty-year-old clarinetist in the band; but his name will be as unfamiliar to you as those of Bergen and McCarthy: it is Benny Goodman. Does anybody think of him—does he think of himself—as the future King of Swing?

Everybody who follows the newspapers at all closely in 1929 can identify for you instantly Bishop Cannon, Texas Guinan, Senator Heflin, Jimmy Walker, Hugo Eckener, Legs Diamond, Mabel Walker Willebrandt, Dolly Gann, or "Doug and Mary." But even your local newspaper editor, who prides himself on knowing the names of public characters, will probably have to go to books of reference to identify General Hugh S. Johnson, Alf M. Landon, Harry Hopkins, Thomas E. Dewey, or Eleanor Roosevelt. And not in any book of reference will he find Joe Louis, Bruno Richard Hauptmann, Robert Taylor, the WPA, or the New Deal.

In all the country there is no such thing as a streamlined train, a bar operating openly and legally, or a man living on Federal relief. Shirley Temple is a baby less than five months old, and the Dionne quintuplets are unborn.

And so, for that matter, is the Depression. In fact, if you wished to be set down as the craziest of prophets by any of the men and women whom you have watched going about their affairs in the glaring sunlight of September 3, 1929, you would only have to tell them that within two months they are to witness the greatest financial panic in American history, and that it will usher in a prolonged and desperate economic crisis.

Chapter Two

EXIT PROSPERITY

§ 1

AFTER September 3, 1929, the stock market dropped sharply, surged up again, dropped again—and did not surge back. Instead, as September came to an end, it sagged lower and lower.

Even so, there was not at first much uneasiness. Again and again, during the Big Bull Market of the two preceding years, there had been sharp breaks lasting several days, thousands of injudicious and unfortunate speculators had been shaken out, and yet prices had recovered and climbed on to new heights. Why worry now? Why not take advantage of these bargain prices? And so margin traders, large and small, who had previously sold out at big profits came floating in again, staking their previous winnings on the chance that Steel would climb back from 230 to 260, or General Electric from 370 to 395, and beyond; and accordingly the volume of brokers' loans rose to a new—and final—peak of over eight and a half billion dollars. Meanwhile the chorus of financial prognosticators assuring all and sundry that nothing was amiss, and that prices were suffering only a temporary setback, rose louder than ever.

Yet still the market sagged. Foreign funds were being withdrawn from it, partly as a result of the collapse of Hatry's speculative bubble in England, partly, perhaps, because speculation in New York had seemed from the first a hazardous business to European investors and many of them were now having qualms. Some American investors, too, were prudently withdrawing as they noticed that the volume of industrial production was declining a little. All the time, as prices ebbed, insecurely margined traders were being forced to sell. As October continued and there was no smart recovery, a note of uncertainty, of urgency, of stridency even, came into the clamor that all was well. Perhaps, after all, it was not. . . . The decline became more rapid. Surely this must be the bottom, the last chance to buy cheap. Or was it the beginning of the end?

The short session of Saturday, October 19, was a bad one, such volatile stocks as Auburn and Case losing 25 points and 40 points respectively in two hours of trading, and even General Electric losing $9\frac{1}{4}$. Monday, October 21, was worse, for by this time more and more traders were reaching the end of their resources and being sold out; the volume of trading reached six million shares. Tuesday was better: did not the great Charles E. Mitchell of the National City Bank, returning from Europe, radiate assurance? But on Wednesday the storm broke anew and the losses were unprecedented: Adams Express lost 96 points during the day, Auburn lost 77, Westinghouse lost 25, and the stock-market page of the late afternoon papers showed a startling procession of minus figures down the column of "net change": $-6\frac{1}{2}$, -3, $-14\frac{3}{8}$, -7, $-2\frac{1}{2}$, $-16\frac{1}{4}$, -12, and so on. By this time the volume of selling was so great that the supposedly almost instantaneous ticker service was left far behind; at three o'clock, when the Exchange was closing for the day, the figures running across the trans-lux screens in brokers' offices all over the country were reporting transactions which had taken place at sixteen minutes past one—an hour and forty-four minutes before!

And on Thursday, October 24. . . .

That Thursday morning the selling came in a roaring and presently incredible deluge. How much of it was short selling will never be known, for no statistical record of the total was kept, but apparently the amount was not very great. Some of it, of course, was frightened selling, even at the outset: already men and women had discovered, to their great alarm, that the slow gains of weeks and months could be swept away in a few precipitous hours. But even in the first hour on Thursday the greater part of the selling was surely forced selling. In a market so honeycombed with credit, the beautifully contrived system whereby the stock gambler whose margin was exhausted by a fall in market prices was automatically sold out, became a beautifully contrived system for wrecking the price structure. In poured the selling orders by hundreds and thousands; it seemed as if nobody wanted to buy; and as prices melted away, presently the brokers in the howling melee of the Stock Exchange were fighting to sell before it was too late. The great Panic was on.

By noon that day, dismayed crowds of men and women in brokers' branch offices everywhere saw the ticker recording unbelievable prices, and realized furthermore that it was so hopelessly behind the market as to be well-nigh useless as a clue to what was actually taking place in the maelstrom of Wall Street, where Montgomery Ward was falling headlong from 83 to 50, Radio from 68¾ to 44½, even United States Steel from 205½ to 193½.

To the rescue came the big bankers. A few minutes after noon, five of them—Messrs. Lamont of J. P. Morgan & Co., Mitchell of the National City Bank, Potter of the Guaranty Trust, Wiggin of the Chase National, and Prosser of the Bankers Trust—met at the House of Morgan and formed a pool to support prices. So high was the confidence of the financial world in their sagacity and power that even before they had decided upon anything, when simply the news went about that they were meeting, prices steadied, rallied; and by the time Richard Whitney, as the representative of the bankers' pool, went on the floor of the Stock Exchange at half past one to bid for stocks, he hardly had to do more than go through the motions: when he offered to buy 10,000 shares of Steel at 205, he found only 200 shares for sale at that price. The gods of Wall Street still could make the storm to cease.

Not till eight minutes past seven that evening, when night had darkened the windows of the brokers' offices, did the tickers stop chattering out prices from the Exchange floor. Nearly thirteen million shares had changed hands. Wild rumors had been going about all day—that exchanges had been closed, that troops had been called out in New York, that eleven speculators had committed suicide. Panic this was, and no doubt about it. But the bankers, it was hoped, had saved the day.

For two more days the market, struggling, nearly held its own, while the lights burned all night in Wall Street as the brokers' clerks struggled to get their records straight, and the telegrams calling for more margin went out by hundreds and thousands. Then the avalanche began again; and this time the bankers could not conceivably have stopped it if they had tried. All they tried to do was to provide bids for stock where there were no bids at all: to give to the rout a semblance of order.

On Tuesday, October 29, came the climax. The official statistics of the day gave the volume of trading as 16,410,030 shares, but no one knows how many sales went unrecorded in the yelling scramble to sell: there are those who believe that the true volume may have been twenty or even twenty-five million. Big and small, insiders and outsiders, the high-riders of the Big Bull Market were being cleaned out: the erstwhile millionaire and his chauffeur, the all-powerful pool operator and his suckers, the chairman of the board with his two-thousand-share holding and the assistant book-keeper with his ten-share holding, the bank president and his stenographer. Here are a few of the losses for that single day in individual stocks—and remember that they came on top of a long succession of previous losses: American Telephone and General Electric, 28 points apiece; Westinghouse, 19 points; Allied Chemical, 35 points; North American, 27½ points; Auburn, 60 points; Columbian Carbon, 38¾ points—and these despite a sharp rally at the close!

Said the sober *Commercial & Financial Chronicle* in its issue of November 2, "The present week has witnessed the greatest stock-market catastrophe of all the ages."

Now at last there came a turn in the tide, as old John D. Rockefeller announced that his son and he were buying common stocks, and two big corporations declared extra dividends as a gesture of stubborn confidence. The Exchange declared a holiday and shortened the hours of trading to give the haggard brokers and sleepless clerks a chance to begin to dig themselves out from under the mass of accumulated work. Then prices went down once more, and again down. Day after day the retreat continued. Not until November 13 did prices reach their bottom for 1929.

The disaster which had taken place may be summed up in a single statistic. In a few short weeks it had blown into thin air *thirty billion dollars*—a sum almost as great as the entire cost to the United States of its participation in the World War, and nearly twice as great as the entire national debt.

§ 2

President Hoover went into action. He persuaded Secretary Mellon to announce that he would propose to the coming Congress a reduction in individual and corporate income taxes. He called to Washington groups of big bankers and industrialists, railroad and public-utility executives, labor leaders, and farm leaders, and obtained assurances that capital expenditures would go on, that wage-rates would not be cut, that no claims for increased wages other than those in negotiation would be pressed. He urged the governors and mayors of the country to expand public works in every practicable direction, and showed the way by arranging to increase the Federal public-buildings expenditure by nearly half a billion dollars (which at that time seemed like pretty heavy government spending). Hoover and his associates began at every opportunity to declare that conditions were "fundamentally sound," to predict a revival of business in the spring, to insist that there was nothing to be disturbed about.

Thereupon the bankers and brokers and investors and business men, and citizens generally, caught their breath and looked about them to take stock of the new situation. Outwardly they became aggressively confident, however they might be gnawed inwardly by worry. Why, *of course* everything was all right. The newspapers and magazines carried advertisements radiating cheer: "Wall Street may sell stocks, but Main Street is still buying goods." "All right, Mister—now that the headache is over, LET'S GO TO WORK." It was in those days soon after the Panic that a new song rose to quick popularity—a song copyrighted on November 7, 1929, when the stock market was still reeling: "Happy Days Are Here Again!"

But it was useless to declare, as many men did, that nothing more had happened than that a lot of gamblers had lost money and a preposterous price-structure had been salutarily deflated. For in the first place the individual losses, whether sustained by millionaires or clerks, had immediate repercussions. People began to economize; indeed, during the worst days of the Panic some businesses had come almost to a standstill as buyers waited for the hurricane to blow itself out. And if the rich, not the poor, had been the chief immediate victims of the crash (it was not iron-workers and sharecroppers who were throwing themselves out of windows that autumn, but brokers and promoters), nevertheless trouble spread fast as servants were discharged, as jewelry shops and high-priced dress shops and other luxury businesses found their trade ebbing and threw off now idle employees, as worried executives decided to postpone building the extension to the factory, or to abandon this or that unprofitable department, or to cut down on production till the sales prospects were clearer. Quickly the ripples of uncertainty and retrenchment widened and unemployment spread.

Moreover, the collapse in investment values had undermined the credit system of the country at innumerable points, endangering loans and mortgages and corporate structures which only a few weeks previously had seemed as safe as bedrock. The Federal Reserve officials reported to Hoover, "It will take perhaps months before readjustment is accomplished." Still more serious was the fact—not so apparent then as later—that the smash-up of the Big Bull Market had put out of business the powerful bellows of inflation which had kept industry roaring when all manner of things were awry with the national economy. The speculative boom, by continually pouring new funds into the economic bloodstream, had enabled Coolidge-Hoover prosperity to continue long after its natural time.

Finally, the Panic had come as a shock—a first shock—to the illusion that American capitalism led a charmed life. Like a man of rugged health suffering his first acute illness, the American business man suddenly realized that he too was a possible prey for forces of destruction. Nor was the shock confined to the United States. All over the world, America's apparently unbeatable prosperity had served as an advertisement of the advantages of political democracy and economic finance capitalism. Throughout Europe, where the nations were loaded down with war debts and struggling with adverse budgets and snarling at one another over their respective shares of a trade that would not expand, men looked at the news from the United States and thought, "And now, perhaps, the jig is up even there." . . .

But if business was so shaken by the Panic that during the winter of 1929-30 it responded only languidly to the faith-healing treatment being prescribed for it by the Administration, the stock market found its feet more readily. Presently the old game was going on again. Those pool operators whose resources were at least half intact were pushing stocks up again. Speculators, big and little, convinced that what had caught them was no more than a downturn in the business cycle, that the bottom had been passed, and that the prosperity band wagon was getting under way again, leaped in to recoup their losses. Prices leaped, the volume of trading became as heavy as in 1929, and a Little Bull Market was under way. That zeal for mergers and combinations and holding-company empires which had inflamed the rugged individualists of the nineteen-twenties reasserted itself: the Van Sweringers completed their purchase of the Missouri Pacific; the process of amalgamation in the aviation industry and in numerous others was resumed; the Chase National Bank in New York absorbed two of its competitors and became the biggest bank in all the world; and the investment salesmen reaped a new harvest selling to the suckers five hundred million dollars' worth of the very latest thing in investments—shares in fixed investment trusts, which would buy the very best stocks (as of 1930) and hold on to them till hell froze.

Who noticed that there was more zeal for consolidating businesses than for expanding them or initiating them? In the favorite phrase of the day, Prosperity was just around the corner.

But a new day was not dawning. This light in the economic skies was only the afterglow of the old one. What if the stock ticker—recording Steel at 198¾, Telephone at 274¼, General Motors at 103⅝, General Electric at 95⅜,

Standard Oil of New Jersey at 84⅞—promised fair weather?
Even at the height of the Little Bull Market there were
breadlines in the streets. In March Miss Frances Perkins,
Industrial Commissioner for New York State, was declaring
that unemployment was worse than it had been since that
state had begun collecting figures in 1914. In several cities,
jobless men by the hundreds or thousands were forming
pathetic processions to dramatize their plight—only to be
savagely smashed by the police. In April the business index
turned down again, and the stock market likewise. In May
and June the market broke severely. While Hoover, grimly
fastening a smile on his face, was announcing, "We have
now passed the worst and with continued unity of effort we
shall rapidly recover," and predicting that business would
be normal by fall—in this very season the long, grinding,
heart-breaking decline of American business was beginning
once more.

§ 3

Not yet, however, had the Depression sunk very deeply
into the general public consciousness. Of the well-to-do, in
particular, few were gravely disturbed in 1930. Many of
them had been grievously hurt in the Panic, but they had
tried to laugh off their losses, to grin at the jokes about
brokers and speculators which were going the rounds. ("Did
you hear about the fellow who engaged a hotel room and
the clerk asked him whether he wanted it for sleeping or
jumping?" "No—but I heard there were two men who
jumped hand-in-hand because they'd held a joint account!")
As 1930 wore on, they were aware of the Depression chiefly
as something that made business slow and uncertain and
did terrible things to the prices of securities. To business
men in "Middletown," a representative small mid-Western
city, until 1932 "the Depression was mainly something they

read about in the newspapers"—despite the fact that by 1930 every fourth factory worker in the city had lost his job. In the country at large, nearly all executive jobs still held intact; dividends were virtually as large as in 1929; few people guessed that the economic storm would be of long duration. Many men and women in the upper income brackets had never seen a visible sign of this unemployment that they kept reading about until, in the fall of 1930, the International Apple Shippers' Association, faced with an oversupply of apples, had the bright idea of selling them on credit to unemployed men, at wholesale prices, for resale at 5 cents apiece—and suddenly there were apple-salesmen shivering on every corner.

When the substantial and well-informed citizens who belonged to the National Economic League (an organization whose executive council included such notables as John Hays Hammond, James Rowland Angell, Frank O. Lowden, David Starr Jordan, Edward A. Filene, George W. Wickersham, and Nicholas Murray Butler) were polled in January, 1930, as to what they considered the "paramount problems of the United States for 1930," their vote put the following problems at the head of the list: 1. Administration of Justice; 2. Prohibition; 3. Lawlessness, Disrespect for Law; 4. Crime; 5. Law Enforcement; 6. World Peace— and they put Unemployment down in *eighteenth* place! Even a year later, in January, 1931, "Unemployment, Economic Stabilization" had moved up only to fourth place, following Prohibition, Administration of Justice, and Lawlessness.

These polls suggest not only how well insulated were the "best citizens" of the United States against the economic troubles of 1930, and how prone—as Thurman Arnold later remarked—to respond to public affairs with "a set of moral reactions," but also how deep and widespread had become the public concern over the egregious failure of Prohibition to prohibit, and over the manifest connection between the illicit liquor traffic and the gangsters and racketeers.

Certainly the Prohibition laws were being flouted more generally and more openly than ever before, even in what had formerly been comparatively sober and puritanical communities. As a "Middletown" business man told the Lynds, "Drinking increased markedly here in '27 and '28, and in '30 was heavy and open. With the Depression, there seemed to be a collapse of public morals. I don't know whether it was the Depression, but in the winter of '29-'30 and in '30-'31 things were roaring here. There was much drunkenness—people holding bathtub gin parties. There was a great increase in women's drinking and drunkenness." In Washington, in the fall of 1930, a bootlegger was discovered to have been plying his wares even in the austere precincts of the Senate Office Building. In New York, by 1931, enforcement had become such a mockery that the choice of those who wanted a drink was no longer simply between going to a speakeasy and calling up a bootlegger; there were "cordial and beverage shoppes" doing an open retail business, their only concession to appearances being that bottles were not ordinarily on display, and the show windows revealed nothing more embarrassing to the policeman on the beat than rows of little plaster figurines. By the winter of 1930-31, steamship lines operating out of New York were introducing a new attraction for the wholeheartedly bibulous—week-end cruises outside the twelve-mile limit, some of them with no destination at all except "the freedom of the seas."

With every item of gangster news—the killing of "Jake" Lengle of the Chicago *Tribune*; the repeated shootings of Legs Diamond in a New York gang war; the bloody rivalry between Dutch Schultz and Vincent Coll in the New York liquor racket; the capture of "Two-gun" Crowley (a youth who had been emulating gangster ways) after an exciting siege, by the police, of the house in which he was hiding out in New York's upper West Side; the ability of Al Capone, paroled from prison in Pennsylvania, to remain at large despite the universal knowledge that he had long been the dictator of organized crime in Chicago—with every such item of news the public was freshly reminded that the gangsters were on the rise and that it was beer-running and "alky-cooking" which provided them with their most reliable revenue. Preachers and commencement orators and after-dinner speakers inveighed against the "crime wave." District Attorney Crain of New York said the racketeers "have their hands in everything from the cradle to the grave—from babies' milk to funeral coaches"; and President Hoover said that what was needed to combat racketeering was not new laws, but enforcement of the existing ones.

Meanwhile sentiment against Prohibition was apparently rising: when the *Literary Digest*, early in 1930, took a straw vote of almost five million people, only 30½ per cent favored continuance and strict enforcement of the Eighteenth Amendment and Volstead Act; 29 per cent were for modification, and 40½ per cent for repeal. Nor was the cause of righteous enforcement aided when Bishop James Cannon, Jr., of the Methodist Episcopal Church, South, who had been one of the most active of dry leaders, was discovered—to the glee of the wets—to have been speculating in the stock market under the auspices of a New York bucket shop.

Perhaps the Wickersham Commission, when it came out of its long huddle over the law-enforcement problem, would throw a clear beam of light into this confusion? On the 19th of January, 1931, it reported upon Prohibition—and the confusion was thereby worse confounded. For, in the first place, the body of the Wickersham report contained explicit and convincing evidence that Prohibition was not working; in the second place, the eleven members of the Commission came to eleven separate conclusions, two of which were in general for repeal, four for modification, and five—less than a majority, it will be noted—for further trial of the Prohibition experiment. And in the third place, the commission *as a whole* came out, paradoxically, for further trial.

Confronted by this welter of disagreement and contradiction, the puzzled citizen could be sure of only one thing: that the supposedly enlightened device of collecting innumerable facts and trying to reason from them to an inevitable conclusion had been turned into a farce. The headache of the Prohibition problem remained to vex him.

§ 4

There were other diversions aplenty to take people's minds off the Depression. There was, for instance, the $125,000,000 boom in miniature golf. People had been saying that what the country needed was a new industry; well, here it was—in travesty. Garnet Carter's campaign to establish miniature golf in Florida during the winter of 1929-30 had been so sensationally successful that by the summer hundreds of thousands of Americans were parking their sedans by half-acre roadside courses and earnestly knocking golf balls along cottonseed greenswards, through little mouse holes in wooden barricades, over little bridges, and through drainpipes, while the proprietors of these new playgrounds listened happily to the tinkle of the cash register and decided to go in for even bigger business in 1931— to lease the field across the way and establish a driving range, with buckets of balls and a squad of local boys as retrievers (armed with beach umbrellas against the white hail of slices and hooks).

There was the incredible popularity of Amos 'n' Andy on the radio, which made the voices of Freeman F. Gosden and Charles J. Correll the most familiar accents in America, set millions of people to following, evening by evening, the fortunes of the Fresh Air Taxicab Company and the progress of Madam Queen's breach-of-promise suit against Andy —and gave the rambunctious Huey Long, running for the Senate in Louisiana, the notion of styling himself the "Kingfish" as he careened about the State with two sound-trucks to advertise him to the unterrified Democracy. (Long won the election, incidentally, though he had to kidnap and hold incommunicado on Grand Isle, till primary day was past, two men who had been threatening him with embarrassing lawsuits.)

There was Bobby Jones's quadruple triumph in golf—the British and American amateur and open championships— which inspired more words of cabled news than any other individual's exploits during 1930, and quite outshone Max Schmeling's defeat of Jack Sharkey, the World's Series victory of the Philadelphia Athletics, the success of Enterprise in defending the America's Cup at Newport against the last of Sir Thomas Lipton's Shamrocks, and the winnings of Gallant Fox, Whichone, and Equipoise on the turf. Always the fliers could command excitement: Lindbergh, the prince charming of American aviators, inaugurated the air-mail route to the Canal Zone (and soon afterward became the father of a son destined for a tragic end); in September, 1930, Costes and Bellonte made the first successful westward point-to-point flight across the Atlantic, taking off at Paris in the "Question Mark" and landing at Long Island.

There was the utterly fantastic epidemic of tree-sitting, which impelled thousands of publicity-crazy boys to roost in trees by day and night in the hope of capturing a "record," with occasional misadventures: a boy in Fort Worth fell asleep, hit the ground, and broke two ribs; the owner of a tree at Niagara Falls sued to have a boy removed from its branches, whereupon the boy's friends cut a branch from another tree, carried him to a new perch, and enabled him to continue his vigil; a boy in Manchester, New Hampshire, stayed aloft till a bolt of lightning knocked him down. To this impressive conclusion had come the mania for flagpole-sitting and Marathon-dancing which had characterized the latter nineteen-twenties.

As the winter of 1930-31 drew on, there were other things to talk about than the mounting unemployment relief prob-lem and the collapse of the speculatively managed Bank of United States in New York. Some of the new automobiles were equipped for "free wheeling." (If you pulled out a button on the dashboard, the car would coast the moment you took your foot off the throttle. When you stepped on it again there was a small whirring sound and the engine took up its labor once more without a jolt.) The device was good for endless discussions: was it a help? did it save gas? was it safe? A lively backgammon craze was bringing comfort to department-store managers: however badly things might be going otherwise in the Christmas season, at least backgam-mon boards were moving. While the head of the house sat at his desk miserably contemplating the state of his finances, his eighteen-year-old son was humming "Body and Soul" and trying to screw up his courage to fill his hip flask with the old man's gin for the evening's dance, where he dreamed of meeting a girl with platinum-blonde hair like Jean Har-low's in "Hell's Angels."

Not everybody was worrying about the Depression—yet.

§ 5

But Herbert Hoover worried, and worked doggedly at the Presidency, and saw his prestige steadily declining as the downward turn in the business index mocked his cheerful predictions, and thereupon worried and worked the harder. Things were not going well for the great economic engineer.

The London Arms Conference, despite the most careful

preparation—during which Ramsay MacDonald had come to Washington to confer—had produced a none-too-impressive agreement: it set "limitations" which the United States could not have attained without spending a billion dollars on new construction.

Congress, applying itself to tariff revision, had got out of hand and had produced, not the limited changes which Hoover had half-heartedly advocated, but a new sky-high tariff bill which (in the words of Denna Frank Fleming) was virtually "a declaration of economic war against the whole of the civilized world," giving "notice to other nations that retaliatory tariffs, quotas, and embargoes against American goods were in order . . . notice to our war debtors that the dollar exchange with which they might make their payments to us would not be available." It had been obvious to anybody beyond the infant class in economics that the United States could neither have a flourishing export trade nor collect the huge sums owing it from abroad unless it either lent foreign countries the money with which to pay (which it had been doing in the nineteen-twenties—and had now stopped doing) or else permitted imports in quantity. Over a thousand American economists, finding themselves in agreement for once (and for the last time during the nineteen-thirties) had protested against any general tariff increase. Hoover was no economic illiterate. But he was by nature and training an administrator rather than a politician, and he had been so outmaneuvered politically during the long tariff wrangle that when the Hawley-Smoot Tariff Bill was finally laid on his desk in June, 1930, he signed it—presumably with an inward groan.

His Farm Board had been trying to sustain the prices of wheat and cotton by buying them on the market, and had succeeded by the end of the 1930 season in accumulating sixty million bushels of wheat and a million and a third bales of cotton, without doing any more than slow up the price decline. As if the farm situation were not bad enough already, a terrific drought had developed during the summer in the belt of land running from Virginia and Maryland on the Eastern seaboard out to Missouri and Arkansas (a precursor of other and more dreadful droughts to come); and when wells failed and crops withered in the fields, new lamentations arose to plague the man in the White House. Nor had these lamentations ceased when it became apparent that the continuing contraction of business threatened an ugly winter for the unemployed, whose numbers, by the end of 1930, had increased from the three or four millions of the spring to some five or six millions.

Since Hoover's first fever of activity after the Panic, he had been leery of any direct governmental offensive against the Depression. He had preferred to let economic nature take its course. "Economic depression," he insisted, "cannot be cured by legislative action or executive pronouncement. Economic wounds must be healed by the action of the cells of the economic body—the producers and consumers themselves." So he stood aside and waited for the healing process to assert itself, as according to the hallowed principles of laissez-faire economics it should.

But he was not idle meanwhile. For already there was a fierce outcry for Federal aid, Federal benefits of one sort or another; and in this outcry he saw a grave threat to the Federal budget, the self-reliance of the American people, and the tradition of local self-rule and local responsibility for charitable relief. He resolved to defeat this threat. Although he set up a national committee to look after the unemployment relief situation, this committee was not to hand out Federal funds; it was simply to co-ordinate and encourage the state and local attempts to provide for the jobless out of state appropriations and local charitable drives. (Hoover was quite right, said those well-to-do people who told one another that a "dole" like the one in England would be "soul-destroying.") He hotly opposed the war veterans' claim for a Bonus—only to see the "Adjusted Compensation" bill passed over his veto. He vetoed pension bills. To meet the privation and distress caused by the drought he urged a Red Cross campaign and recommended an appropriation to enable the Department of Agriculture to loan money "for the purpose of seed and feed for animals," but fought against any handouts by the Federal government to feed human beings.

In all this Hoover was desperately sincere. He saw himself as the watchdog not only of the Treasury, but of America's "rugged individualism." "This is not an issue," he said in a statement to the press, "as to whether people shall go hungry or cold in the United States. It is solely a question of the best method by which hunger and cold shall be prevented. It is a question as to whether the American people, on one hand, will maintain the spirit of charity and mutual self-help through voluntary giving and the responsibility of local government as distinguished, on the other hand, from appropriations out of the Federal Treasury for such purposes. . . . I have . . . spent much of my life in fighting hardship and starvation both abroad and in the Southern States. I do not feel that I should be charged with lack of human sympathy for those who suffer, but I recall that in all the organizations with which I have been connected over these many years, the foundation has been to summon the maximum of self-help. . . . I am willing to pledge myself that if the time should ever come that the voluntary agencies of the country, together with the local and State governments, are unable to find resources with which to prevent hunger and suffering in my country, I will ask the aid of every resource of the Federal Government because I would no more see starvation amongst our countrymen than would any Senator or Congressman. I have faith in the American people that such a day will not come."

Such were Hoover's convictions. But to hungry farmers in Arkansas the President who would lend them Federal money to feed their animals, but not to feed their children, seemed callous. Jobless men and women in hard-hit industrial towns were unimpressed by Hoover's tributes to self-reliance.

Even the prosperous conservatives failed him as whole-hearted allies. Business was bad, the President seemed to be doing nothing constructive to help them, and though they did not know themselves what ought to be done or were hopelessly divided in their counsels, they craved a leader and felt they were not being given one. They groused; some of them called Hoover a spineless jellyfish. Meanwhile Charles Michelson, the Democratic party's publicity director, was laying down a diabolically well-aimed barrage of press releases and speeches for Congressional use, taking advantage of every Hoover weakness to strengthen the Democratic opposition; and the President, suffering from his inability to charm and cajole the Washington correspondents, was getting a bad press. The Congressional and State elections of November, 1930, brought Democratic victories, confronting Hoover with the prospect, ere long, of a definitely hostile Congress.

Those elections brought, incidentally, a smashing victory in New York State to Governor Franklin D. Roosevelt, who was re-elected by the unexpectedly large plurality of 725,000. The afternoon following the election, Roosevelt's State chairman, an ex-boxing commissioner named James A. Farley, produced with the aid of Roosevelt's political mentor, Louis McHenry Howe, a statement which he was afraid the Governor might not like. It said: "I do not see how Mr. Roosevelt can escape being the next presidential nominee of his party, even if no one should raise a finger to bring it about." Having issued the statement at the Hotel Biltmore in New York, Farley telephoned the Governor in Albany to confess what he had done. Roosevelt laughed and said, "Whatever you said, Jim, is all right with me." Here too, had Hoover but known it, was another portent for him.

But things were bad enough even without borrowing trouble from the future. In midwinter there was an encouraging upturn in business, but as the spring of 1931 drew on, the retreat began once more. Hoover's convictions were being outrun by events.

§ 6

During all this time, many men were earnestly citing the hardships suffered in the depressions of 1857 and 1875 and 1893 as proofs that nothing ailed America but a downswing in the business cycle. The argument looked very reasonable —but these men were wrong. Something far more profound than that was taking place, and not in America alone.

The nineteenth century and the first few years of the twentieth century had witnessed a remarkable combination of changes which could not continue indefinitely. Among these were:—

1. The rapid progress of the industrial revolution—which brought with it steam power, and then gasoline and electric power and all manner of scientific and inventive miracles; brought factory production on a bigger and bigger scale; drew the population off the farms into bigger and bigger cities; transformed large numbers of people from independent economic agents into jobholders; and made them increasingly dependent upon the successful working of an increasingly complex economy.

2. A huge increase in population. According to Henry Pratt Fairchild, if the population of the world had continued to grow at the rate at which it was growing during the first decade of the present century, at the end of 10,000 years it would have reached a figure beginning with 221,848 and followed by *no less than 45 zeros.*

3. An expansion of the peoples of the Western world into vacant and less civilized parts of the earth, with the British Empire setting the pattern of imperialism, and the United States setting the pattern of domestic pioneering.

4. The opening up and using up of the natural resources of the world—coal, oil, metals, etc.—at an unprecedented rate, not indefinitely continuable.

5. A rapid improvement in communication—which in effect made the world a much smaller place, the various parts of which were far more dependent on one another than before.

6. The rapid development and refinement of capitalism on a bigger and bigger scale, as new corporate and financial devices were invented and put into practice. These new devices (such as, for example, the holding company), coupled with the devices added to mitigate the cruelties of untrammeled capitalism (such as, for example, labor unionism and labor legislation), profoundly altered the working of the national economies, making them more rigid at numerous points and less likely to behave according to the laws of laissez-faire economics.

Which of these phenomena were causes, and which were effects, of the changes in the economic world during the century which preceded 1914, is a matter of opinion. Let us not concern ourselves with which came first, the hen or the egg. The point is that an immense expansion and complication of the world economy had taken place, that it could not have continued indefinitely at such a pace, and that as it reached the point of diminishing returns, all manner of stresses developed. These stresses included both international rivalries over colonies (now that the best ones had been exploited—and were incidentally no longer paying their mother countries so well) and internal social conflicts over the division of the fruits of industry and commerce. The World War of 1914-18, brought about by the international rivalries, had left Europe weakened and embittered, with hitherto strong nations internally divided and staggering under colossal debts.

Presently there were ominous signs that the great age of inevitable expansion was over. The population increase was slowing up. The vacant places of the world were largely preempted. The natural resources were limited and could hardly be exploited much longer so quickly and cheaply. As the economic horizons narrowed, the struggle for monopoly of what was visibly profitable became more intense. Nations sought for national monopoly of world resources; corporate and financial groups sought for private monopoly of national resources and national industries. Meanwhile each national economy became more complex, less flexible, and more subject to the hazards of bankruptcy by reason of unbearable debts.

One way of expansion still remained open. Invention did not stop; the possibilities of increased comfort and security through increasingly efficient mechanical production (and through improvement in the means of communication) remained almost limitless. But the economic apparatus which was at hand, and men's mental habits and outlook, were adjusted to the age of pioneering expansion rather than to reliance on increasing efficiency alone; and what sort of economic apparatus the new age might require no one knew.

During the nineteen-twenties the United States, comparatively unhurt by the war and adept at invention and mechanization, had continued to rush ahead as if the age of pioneering expansion were not over. Still, however, it was a victim of the vices of its pioneering youth—an optimistic readiness to pile up debts and credit obligations against an expanding future, a zest for speculation in real estate and in stocks, a tendency toward financial and corporate monopoly or quasi-monopoly which tended to stiffen a none-too-flexible economy. These vices combined to undo it. As Roy Helton remarks in this connection, when one is grown up one can no longer indulge with impunity in the follies of youth. While the bellows of speculation and credit inflation blew, the fires of prosperity burned brightly; but once the bellows stopped blowing, the fires dimmed. And when they dimmed in the United States, they dimmed all the more rapidly in Europe, where since the war they had burned only feebly.

As the contraction of one national economy after another set in, men became frantic. The traditional economic laws and customs no longer seemed to work; the men of learning were as baffled as anybody else; nobody seemed to know the answer to the economic riddle. Russia offered an alternative set of laws and customs, but enthusiasm for the Marxian way as exemplified in Russia was limited. What else was there for men to fasten their hopes upon? Nobody knew, for this emergency was unprecedented. So it happened that the world entered upon a period of bewilderment, mutual suspicion, and readiness for desperate measures.

Nor was the United States, falling from such a pinnacle of apparent economic success, to escape the confusion and dismay of readjustment.

Chapter Three
DOWN, DOWN, DOWN

§ 1

JUNE, 1931: twenty months after the Panic.

The department-store advertisements were beginning to display Eugenie hats, heralding a fashion enthusiastic but brief; Wiley Post and Harold Gatty were preparing for their flight round the world in the monoplane "Winnie Mae"; and newspaper readers were agog over the finding, on Long Beach near New York, of the dead body of a pretty girl with the singularly lyrical name of Starr Faithfull.

On the New York stage, in June, 1931, Katharine Cornell was languishing on a sofa in "The Barretts of Wimpole Street," de Lawd was walking the earth in "The Green Pastures," and the other reigning successes included "Grand Hotel" and "Once in a Lifetime." At the movie theatres one might see African lions and hear native tom-toms in "Trader Horn," or watch Edward G. Robinson in "Smart Money" or Gloria Swanson in "Indiscreet." As vacationists packed their bags for the holidays, the novel that was most likely to be taken along was Pearl S. Buck's *The Good Earth*, which led the best-seller lists. The sporting heroes of the nineteen-twenties had nearly all passed from the scenes of their triumphs: Bobby Jones had turned professional the preceding fall; Tilden had lost the tennis championship the preceding summer; Dempsey and Tunney had long since relinquished their crowns, and boxing was falling into uncertain repute; Knute Rockne, the Notre Dame football coach, had recently been killed in an airplane crash; and even Babe Ruth was no longer the undisputed Sultan of Swat: Lou Gehrig was now matching him home run for home run.

During that month of June, 1931, there was a foretaste —and a sour one—of many a financial scandal to come, when three officers of the Bank of United States were convicted by a jury in New York, after shocking disclosures of the mismanagement of the bank's funds during the speculative saturnalia of 1928 and 1929. There was the inception of a romance that was to shake an empire to its foundations: on June 10 a young American woman living in London, a Mrs. Ernest Simpson, was presented at Court and met for the first time the Prince of Wales. At Hopewell, New Jersey, the scene was being unwittingly set for the most tragic crime of the decade: Colonel Lindbergh's new house—described in newspaper captions as "A Nest for the Lone Eagle"—was under construction, the scaffolding up, the first floor partly completed.

During that month a young man from St. Louis came on to New York, with arrangements all made, as he supposed, for the transfer to him of a seat on the New York Stock Exchange. But one detail had been neglected: the Exchange was virtually a club, and a candidate for membership must have a proposer and seconder. There was some delay before the young man from St. Louis, whose name was William McC. Martin, Jr., could be proposed and seconded, for he did not know anybody on the Exchange. The gentlemen of Wall Street, having no inkling of the changes in store for them during the next few years, would have been thunderstruck if they had been told that before the decade was out, this unknown youth would be President of an Exchange operating under close governmental supervision. The President in 1931 was Richard Whitney, hero of the bankers' foray against the Panic; on April 24, 1931, Mr. Whitney had made an impressive address before the Philadelphia Chamber of Commerce on "Business Honesty." Prices on the Exchange had been going down badly and brokers were pulling long faces, but there was still a little gravy left for those who knew what the next move would be in Case Threshing or Auburn Auto.

On a Sunday morning in June, 1931, two men spent some busy hours in a small room in a very big house in Hyde Park, New York, poring over maps of the United States and railroad timetables and lists of names. They were the Governor of New York, Franklin D. Roosevelt, who had been so impressively re-elected the preceding November, and the Chairman of his Democratic State Committee, James A. Farley. Mr. Farley had conceived the idea of attending the forthcoming Elks' Convention at Seattle, and he and Governor Roosevelt were planning how he might make the most of the expedition, covering eighteen states in nineteen days and talking with innumerable Democratic leaders, with most of whom he had already been corresponding profusely and cordially. The object of this prophetic journey, needless to say, was to sound out Democratic sentiment in the West and to suggest as disarmingly as possible that the leaders might do well to unite behind Governor Roosevelt in 1932.

And it was during that month of June, 1931, that President Hoover gave up waiting for economic conditions to improve of their own accord and began his real offensive against the Depression—began it with a statesmanlike stroke in international finance which seemed briefly to be victorious, and which failed in the end only because the processes of economic destruction were too powerful and too far developed to be overcome by any weapon in the Hoover armory. On the hot afternoon of Saturday, June 20, Hoover proposed an international moratorium in war reparations and war debts.

§ 2

For a long time past, as business slowed up in Europe, a sort of creeping paralysis had been afflicting European finance. Debts—national and private—which had once seemed bearable burdens had now become intolerably heavy; new financial credits were hardly being extended except to shore up the old ones; prices fell, anxiety spread, and the whole system slowed almost to a standstill. During the spring of 1931 the paralysis had become acute.

It is ironical, in retrospect, to note that what made it acute was an attempt on the part of Germany and Austria to combine for limited economic purposes—to achieve a customs union—and the fierce opposition of the French to any such scheme. Anything which might bring Germany and Austria together and strengthen them was anathema to the French, who little realized then the possible consequences of Central European bankruptcy.

Already the biggest bank in Austria, the Credit Anstalt, had been in a tight fix. When the altercation over the customs union still further increased the general uncertainty, the Credit Anstalt had been obliged to appeal to the none-too-solvent Austrian government for aid. Immediately panic was under way. Quickly it spread to Germany. In May and June, 1931, capital was fleeing both countries, foreign loans were being withdrawn, and a general collapse seemed imminent—a collapse which might cause the downfall of Germany's democratic government. For that cloud on the German horizon which in 1929 had seemed no bigger than a man's hand was now growing fast: Hitler's Brown Shirts were becoming more and more powerful.

On the sixth of May, 1931, when few Americans had the faintest idea of how critical the European financial situa-

TICKER TAPE FOR BOBBY JONES

He disentangles himself from a streamer as he returns to New York on July 2, 1930, after winning two British golf championships. (Note Mrs. Jones's helmet-like hat and the almost perpendicular windshield of the car.)

WANTED

INFORMATION AS TO THE WHEREABOUTS OF

CHAS. A. LINDBERGH, Jr.

OF HOPEWELL, N. J.

SON OF COL. CHAS. A. LINDBERGH

World-Famous Aviator

This child was kidnaped from his home in Hopewell, N. J., between 8 and 10 p. m. on Tuesday, March 1, 1932.

DESCRIPTION:

Age, 20 months　　　　Hair, blond, curly
Weight, 27 to 30 lbs.　Eyes, dark blue
Height, 29 inches　　　Complexion, light
Deep dimple in center of chin
Dressed in one-piece coverall night suit

ADDRESS ALL COMMUNICATIONS TO
COL. H. N. SCHWARZKOPF, TRENTON, N. J., or
COL. CHAS. A. LINDBERGH, HOPEWELL. N. J.

ALL COMMUNICATIONS WILL BE TREATED IN CONFIDENCE

COL. H. NORMAN SCHWARZKOPF
March 11, 1932　　Supt. New Jersey State Police, Trenton, N. J.

LINDBERGH KIDNAPPING POSTER
Sent to police chiefs in 1400 American communities in March, 1932

tion was becoming, the American Ambassador to Germany had dined with President Hoover at the White House; and since then the President, fearing that a collapse in Europe might have grave consequences to the United States, had been turning over in his mind the idea of an international moratorium—of postponing for a year all payments on inter-governmental debts, including the reparations which Germany was then obliged to pay and the war debts owed to the United States by her former European allies. Mr. Hoover had then begun a long period of consultation —with members of his Cabinet, with Federal Reserve officials, with ambassadors, with bankers. Always a terrific worker—at his desk before eight-thirty, taking only fifteen minutes for lunch unless he had White House guests, and often burning the lights in the Lincoln study late into the night—he now concentrated all the more fiercely. Before long he had drafted tentatively a moratorium statement, laboring over it so grimly that he broke pencil point after pencil point in the writing.

Yet he had delayed issuing it. The dangers of the scheme were apparent. Congress might object, and this would be fatal. Other nations, particularly proud and jealous France, might object. The budget-balancing on which he had set his heart might be imperiled by cutting off the debt payments to America. Furthermore such a proposal, by calling attention to the international panic, might accentuate rather than ease it. Meanwhile the storm in Europe spread. Hoover's advisers were pleading with him to act, but still he would not. He waited. In mid-June he was scheduled to go on a speaking trip through the Middle West (which included the somewhat dubious pleasure of speaking at the dedication of a memorial to President Harding); he went off with the proposal yet unmade, while almost hourly the inside news was relayed to him from Washington: the European collapse was accelerating.

By the time he got back to Washington it was clear that he must act at once or it would be much too late. He began telephoning senators and representatives to get their advance approval. Congress was not sitting, and the telephone operators had to catch for him men widely dispersed all over the country, on speaking trips, on motor trips, on golf courses, on fishing trips deep in the woods; one lawmaker, hearing that the White House wanted him, called it from a Canadian drugstore; another was reached just as he was about to rise for an after-dinner speech. Hour after hour the indefatigable Hoover sat at the telephone explaining to man after man what he wanted to do—and fearing that the news would leak before he could act. At last, on that broiling Saturday, June 20, the news was already leaking and he had to give out the announcement—with France still unconsulted.

He called the newspaper men to the White House and read them a long statement which contained both his proposal for an international moratorium and the names of 21 senators and 18 representatives who had already approved it. The newspaper men grabbed their copies and rushed for the telephones.

When the news was flashed over the world a chorus of wild enthusiasm arose. The stock market in New York leaped, stock markets in Europe rallied, bankers praised Hoover, editorial writers cheered; the sedate London *Economist* came out with a panegyric entitled "The Break in the Clouds" which called the proposal "the gesture of a great man"; and millions of Americans who had felt, however vaguely, that the government ought to "do something" and who had blamed Hoover for his inactivity, joined in the applause. Little as they might know about the international financial situation (which had been getting nowhere near as much space in the press as the Starr Faithfull mystery), this was action at last and they liked it. To the worried President's surprise, he had made what seemed to be a ten-strike. It was the high moment of his Presidency.

Only the French demurred. Hoover sent his seventy-seven-year-old Secretary of the Treasury, Andrew Mellon, to reason with them, and exhausted the old man with constant consultations by transatlantic telephone. After a long delay—over two weeks—the French agreed to the plan with modifications, and the day appeared to have been saved.

§ 3

But it was not saved at all.

Presently panic in Germany became intensified; the big Danat Bank was closed. The panic spread to England. The pound sterling was now in danger. A new National Government, headed by the Laborite MacDonald but composed mostly of Tories, took office to save the pound—and presently abandoned it. When England went off the gold standard, every nation still on gold felt the shock, and most of them followed England into the new adventure of a managed currency.

In the United States this new shock of September, 1931, was sharp. The archaic American banking system, which had never been too strong even in more prosperous days, was gravely affected; all over the United States banks were collapsing—banks which had invested heavily in bonds and mortgages and now found the prices of their foreign bonds cascading, the prices of their domestic bonds sliding down in the general rush of liquidation, and their mortgages frozen solid. In the month of September, 1931, a total of 305 American banks closed; in October, a total of 522. Frightened capitalists were hoarding gold now, lest the United States too should go off the gold standard; safe-deposit boxes were being crammed full of coins, and many a mattress was stuffed with gold certificates.

American business was weakening faster than ever. In September the United States Steel Corporation—whose President, James A. Farrell, had hitherto steadfastly refused to cut the wage-rate—announced a ten-per-cent cut; other corporations followed; during that autumn, all over the United States, men were coming home from the office or the factory to tell their wives that the next pay check would be a little smaller, and that they must think up new economies. The ranks of the unemployed received new recruits; by the end of the year their numbers were in the neighborhood of ten millions.

So far, in a few months, had the ripples of panic and renewed depression spread from Vienna.

Again Hoover acted, and again his action was financial. Something must be done to save the American banking system, and the bankers were not doing it; the spirit of the day was *sauve qui peut*. Hoover called fifteen of the overlords of the banking world to a secret evening meeting with him and his financial aides at Secretary Mellon's apartment in Washington, and proposed to them that the strong banks of the country form a credit pool to help the weak ones. When it became clear that this would not suffice—for the strong banks were taking no chances and this pool, the National Credit Corporation, lent almost no money at all— Hoover recommended the formation of a big governmental credit agency, the Reconstruction Finance Corporation, with two billion dollars to lend to banks, railroads, insurance companies.

As the winter of 1931-32 arrived and the run on the country's gold continued, and it seemed as if the United States might presently be forced off the gold standard, Hoover issued a public appeal against hoarding and then proposed an alteration in Federal Reserve requirements which—embodied in the Glass-Steagall Act—eased this situation. Again with the idea of improving credit conditions, he urged, and secured, the creation of a chain of home-loan discount banks, and the provision of additional capital for the Federal Land Banks. Steadily he fought against those measures which seemed to him iniquitous: he appeared before the American Legion and appealed to the members not to ask for the immediate cash payment of the rest of their Bonus money; he vetoed a bill for the distribution of direct Federal relief; and again and again he made clear his opposition to any proposals for inflation or for (in his own words) "squandering ourselves into prosperity."

Still the Depression deepened.

Already the pressure of events had pushed the apostle of rugged individualism much further toward state socialism than any previous president had gone in time of peace. Hoover's Reconstruction Finance Corporation had put the government deeply into business. But it was state socialism of a very limited and special sort. What was happening may perhaps be summed up in this way:—

Hoover had tried to keep hands off the economic machinery of the country, to permit a supposedly flexible system to make its own adjustments of supply and demand. At two points he had intervened, to be sure: he had tried to hold up the prices of wheat and cotton, unsuccessfully, and he had tried to hold up wage-rates, with partial and temporary success; but otherwise he had mainly stood aside to let prices and profits and wages follow their natural course. But no natural adjustment could be reached unless the burdens of debt could also be naturally reduced through bankruptcies. And in America, as in other parts of the world, the economic system had now become so complex and interdependent that the possible consequences of widespread bankruptcy—to the banks, the insurance companies, the great holding-company systems, and the multitudes of people dependent upon them —had become too appalling to contemplate. The theoretically necessary adjustment became a practically unbearable adjustment. Therefore Hoover was driven to the point of intervening to protect the debt structure—first by easing temporarily the pressure of international debts without canceling them, and second by buttressing the banks and big corporations with Federal funds.

Thus a theoretically flexible economic structure became rigid at a vital point. The debt burden remained almost undiminished. Bowing under the weight of debt—and other rigid costs—business thereupon slowed still further. As it slowed, it discharged workers or put them on reduced hours, thereby reducing purchasing power and intensifying the crisis.

It is almost useless to ask whether Hoover was right or wrong. Probably the method he was driven by circumstances to adopt would have brought recovery very slowly, if at all, unless devaluation of the currency had given a fillip to recovery—and devaluation to Hoover was unthinkable. It is also almost useless to ask whether Hoover was acting with a tory heartlessness in permitting financial executives to come to Washington for a corporate dole when men and women on the edge of starvation were denied a personal dole. What is certain is that at a time of such widespread suffering no democratic government could *seem* to be aiding the financiers and *seem* to be simultaneously disregarding the plight of its humbler citizens without losing the confidence of the public. For the days had passed when men who lost their jobs could take their working tools elsewhere and contrive an independent living, or cultivate a garden patch and thus keep body and soul together, or go West and begin again on the frontier. When they lost their jobs they were helpless. Desperately they turned for aid to the only agency responsible to them for righting the wrongs done them by a blindly operating economic society: they turned to the government. How could they endorse a government which gave them—for all they could see—not bread, but a stone?

The capitalist system had become so altered that it could not function in its accustomed ways, and the consequences of its failure to function had become too cruel to be borne by free men. Events were marching, and Herbert Hoover was to be among their victims, along with the traditional economic theories of which he was the obstinate and tragic spokesman.

§ 4

As the second year of the Depression drew to an end and the third one began, a change was taking place in the mood of the American people.

"Depression," as Peter F. Drucker has said, "shows man as a senseless cog in a senselessly whirling machine which is beyond human understanding and has ceased to serve any purpose but its own." The worse the machine behaved, the more were men and women driven to try to understand it. As one by one the supposedly fixed principles of business and economics and government went down in ruins, people who had taken these fixed principles for granted, and had shown little interest in politics except at election time, began to try to educate themselves. For not even the comparatively prosperous could any longer deny that something momentous was happening.

The circulation departments of the public libraries were reporting an increased business, not only in the anodyne of fiction, but also in books of solid fact and discussion. As a business man of "Middletown" later told the Lynds, "Big things were happening that were upsetting us, our businesses, and some of our ideas, and we wanted to try to understand them. I took a lot of books out of the library and sat up nights reading them." Ideas were in flux. There was a sharp upsurge of interest in the Russian experiment. Lecturers on Russia were in demand; Maurice Hindus's *Humanity Uprooted* and *New Russia's Primer* were thumbed and puzzled over; Ray Long, editor of Hearst's usually frivolous *Cosmopolitan* magazine, had gone to Moscow to sign up Soviet writers and gave a big dinner to a Russian novelist at the massively capitalistic Metropolitan Club in New York; gentle liberals who prided themselves on their open-mindedness were assuring one another that "after all we had something to learn from Russia," especially about "planning"; many of the more forthright liberals were tumbling head over heels into communism.

For more orthodox men and women, the consumption of Walter Lippmann's daily analysis of events—written for the New York *Herald Tribune* and syndicated all over the country—was becoming a matutinal rite as inevitable as coffee and orange juice. When the New York *World*—famous for its liberalism and the wit of its columnists—had ceased publication in February, 1931, Lippmann, its editor, had gone over to the *Herald Tribune* and to sudden national fame. Clear, cool, and orderly in his thinking, he seemed to be able to reduce a senseless sequence of events to sense; he brought first aid to men and women groping in the dark for opinions—and also to men and women who foresaw themselves else tongue-tied and helpless when the conversation at the dinner party should turn from the great Lenz-Culbertson bridge match to the Reconstruction Finance Corporation and the gold standard.

The autumn of 1931 brought also an outburst of laughter. When old certainties topple, when old prophets are discredited, one can at least enjoy their downfall. By this time people had reached the point of laughing at *Oh, Yeah,* a small book in which were collected the glib prophecies made by bankers and statesmen at the onset of the Depression; of relishing the gossipy irreverence of *Washington*

Merry-Go-Round, which deflated the reputations of the
dignified statesmen of Washington; of getting belly-laughs
from a new magazine, *Ballyhoo,* whose circulation rocketed
to more than a million as it ridiculed everything in business and politics, even the sacred cow of advertising; and
of applauding wildly the new musical comedy, "Of Thee I
Sing," which made a farce of the political scene, represented
a vice-president of the United States, Alexander Throttle-
bottom, as getting lost in a sight-seeing party in the White
House, represented a presidential candidate as campaigning
with Love as his platform, and garbled the favorite business slogan of 1930 into a slogan for newly-weds: "Pos-
terity is just around the corner."

As Gilbert Seldes has noted, when Rudy Vallee, at the
opening of George White's "Scandals" on September 13,
1931, sang softly

> "Life is just a bowl of cherries.
> Don't make it serious.
> Life's too mysterious. . . ."

he summed up both the disillusionment and bewilderment
of Depression, and the desire to take them, if possible,
lightly.

§ 5

Statistics are bloodless things.

To say that during the year 1932, the cruelest year of
the Depression, the average number of unemployed people
in the country was 12½ million by the estimates of the
National Industrial Conference Board, a little over 13
million by the estimates of the American Federation of
Labor, and by other estimates (differently arrived at, and
defining unemployment in various ways) anywhere from
8½ to 17 million—to say this is to give no living impression

of the jobless men going from office to office or from factory gate to factory gate; of the disheartening inevitability of the phrase, "We'll let you know if anything shows up"; of men thumbing the want ads in cold tenements, spending fruitless hours, day after day and week after week, in the sidewalk crowds before the employment offices; using up the money in the savings bank, borrowing on their life insurance, selling whatever possessions could be sold, borrowing from relatives less and less able to lend, tasting the bitterness of inadequacy, and at last swallowing their pride and going to apply for relief—if there was any to be got. (Relief money was scarce, for charitable organizations were hard beset and cities and towns had either used up their available funds or were on the point of doing so.)

A few statistical facts and estimates are necessary, however, to an understanding of the scope and impact of the Depression. For example:—

Although the amount of money paid out in interest during the year 1932 was only 3.5 per cent less than in 1929, according to the computations of Dr. Simon Kuznets for the National Bureau of Economic Research, on the other hand the amount of money paid out in salaries had dropped 40 per cent, dividends had dropped 56.6 per cent, and wages had dropped 60 per cent. (Thus had the debt structure remained comparatively rigid while other elements in the economy were subjected to fierce deflation.)

Do not imagine, however, that the continuation of interest payments and the partial continuation of dividend payments meant that business as a whole was making money. Business as a whole lost between five and six billion dollars in 1932. (The government figure for all the corporations in the country—451,800 of them—was a net deficit of $5,640,000,000.) To be sure, most of the larger and better-managed companies did much better than that. E. D. Kennedy's figures for the 960 concerns whose earnings were tabulated by Standard Statistics—mostly big ones whose stock was active on the Stock Exchange—show that these 960 leaders had a collective profit of over a third of a billion. Yet one must add that "better managed" is here used in a special sense. Not only had labor-saving devices and speed-ups increased the output per man-hour in manufacturing industries by an estimated 18 per cent since 1929, but employees had been laid off in quantity. Every time one of the giants of industry, to keep its financial head above water, threw off a new group of workers, many little corporations roundabout sank further into the red.

While existing businesses shrank, new ones were not being undertaken. The total of domestic corporate issues —issues of securities floated to provide capital for American corporations—had dropped in 1932 to just about *one twenty-fourth* of the 1929 figure.

But these cold statistics give us little sense of the human realities of the economic paralysis of 1932. Let us try another approach.

Walking through an American city, you might find few signs of the Depression visible—or at least conspicuous—to the casual eye. You might notice that a great many shops were untenanted, with dusty plate-glass windows and signs indicating that they were ready to lease; that few factory chimneys were smoking; that the streets were not so crowded with trucks as in earlier years, that there was no uproar of riveters to assail the ear, that beggars and panhandlers were on the sidewalks in unprecedented numbers (in the Park Avenue district of New York a man might be asked for money four or five times in a ten-block walk). Traveling by railroad, you might notice that the trains were shorter, the Pullman cars fewer—and that fewer freight trains were on the line. Traveling overnight, you might find only two or three other passengers in your sleeping car. (By contrast, there were more filling stations by the motor highways than ever before, and of all the retail businesses in "Middletown" only the filling stations showed no large drop in business during the black years; for although few new automobiles were being bought, those which would still stand up were being used more than ever—to the dismay of the railroads.)

Otherwise things might seem to you to be going on much as usual. The major phenomena of the Depression were mostly negative and did not assail the eye.

But if you knew where to look, some of them would begin to appear. First, the breadlines in the poorer districts. Second, those bleak settlements ironically known as "Hoovervilles" in the outskirts of the cities and on vacant lots—groups of makeshift shacks constructed out of packing boxes, scrap iron, anything that could be picked up free in a diligent combing of the city dumps: shacks in which men and sometimes whole families of evicted people were sleeping on automobile seats carried from auto-graveyards, warming themselves before fires of rubbish in grease drums. Third, the homeless people sleeping in doorways or on park benches, and going the rounds of the restaurants for leftover half-eaten biscuits, piecrusts, anything to keep the fires of life burning. Fourth, the vastly increased number of thumbers on the highways, and particularly of freight-car transients on the railroads: a huge army of drifters ever on the move, searching half-aimlessly for a place where there might be a job. According to Jonathan Norton Leonard, the Missouri Pacific Railroad in 1929 had "taken official cognizance" of 13,745 migrants; by 1931 the figure had already jumped to 186,028. It was estimated that by the beginning of 1933, the country over, there were a million of these transients on the move. Forty-five thousand had passed through El Paso in the space of six months; 1,500 were passing through Kansas City every day. Among them were large numbers of young boys, and girls disguised as boys. According to the Children's Bureau, there were 200,-000 children thus drifting about the United States. So huge was the number of freight-car hoppers in the Southwest that in a number of places the railroad police simply had to give up trying to remove them from the trains: there were far too many of them.

Among the comparatively well-to-do people of the country (those, let us say, whose pre-Depression incomes had been over $5,000 a year) the great majority were living on a reduced scale, for salary cuts had been extensive, especially since 1931, and dividends were dwindling. These people were discharging servants, or cutting servants' wages to a minimum, or in some cases "letting" a servant stay on without other compensation than board and lodging. In many pretty houses, wives who had never before—in the revealing current phrase—"done their own work" were cooking and scrubbing. Husbands were wearing the old suit longer, resigning from the golf club, deciding, perhaps, that this year the family couldn't afford to go to the beach for the summer, paying seventy-five cents for lunch instead of a dollar at the restaurant or thirty-five instead of fifty at the lunch counter. When those who had flown high with the stock market in 1929 looked at the stock-market page of the newspapers nowadays their only consoling thought (if they still had any stock left) was that a judicious sale or two would result in such a capital loss that they need pay no income tax at all this year.

Alongside these men and women of the well-to-do classes whose fortunes had been merely reduced by the Depression were others whose fortunes had been shattered. The crowd of men waiting for the 8:14 train at the prosperous suburb included many who had lost their jobs, and were going to town as usual not merely to look stubbornly and almost hopelessly for other work but also to keep up a bold front of activity. (In this latter effort they usually succeeded:

one would never have guessed, seeing them chatting with their friends as train-time approached, how close to desperation some of them had come.) There were architects and engineers bound for offices to which no clients had come in weeks. There were doctors who thought themselves lucky when a patient paid a bill. Mrs. Jones, who went daily to her stenographic job, was now the economic mainstay of her family, for Mr. Jones was jobless and was doing the cooking and looking after the children (with singular distaste and inefficiency). Next door to the Joneses lived Mrs. Smith, the widow of a successful lawyer: she had always had a comfortable income, she prided herself on her "nice things," she was pathetically unfitted to earn a dollar even if jobs were to be had; her capital had been invested in South American bonds and United Founders stock and other similarly misnamed "securities," and now she was completely dependent upon hand-outs from her relatives, and didn't even have carfare in her imported pocketbook.

The Browns had retreated to their "farmhouse" in the country and were trying to raise crops on its stony acres; they talked warmly about primal simplicities but couldn't help longing sometimes for electric light and running hot water, and couldn't cope with the potato bugs. (Large numbers of city dwellers thus moved to the country, but not enough of them engaged in real farming to do more than partially check the long-term movement from the farms of America to the cities and towns.) It was being whispered about the community that the Robinson family, though they lived in a $40,000 house and had always spent money freely, were in desperate straights: Mr. Robinson had lost his job, the house could not be sold, they had realized on every asset at their command, and now they were actually going hungry—though their house still looked like the abode of affluence.

Further down in the economic scale, particularly in those

industrial communities in which the factories were running at twenty per cent of capacity or had closed down altogether, conditions were infinitely worse. Frederick E. Croxton's figures, taken in Buffalo, show what was happening in such communities: out of 14,909 persons of both sexes willing and able to work, his house-to-house canvassers found in November, 1932, that 46.3 per cent were fully employed, 22.5 per cent were working part time, and as many as 31.2 per cent were unable to find jobs. In every American city, quantities of families were being evicted from their inadequate apartments; moving in with other families till ten or twelve people would be sharing three or four rooms; or shivering through the winter in heatless houses because they could afford no coal, eating meat once a week or not at all. If employers sometimes found that former employees who had been discharged did not seem eager for re-employment ("They won't take a job if you offer them one!"), often the reason was panic: a dreadful fear of inadequacy which was one of the Depression's commonest psycho-pathological results. A woman clerk, offered piecework after being jobless for a year, confessed that she almost had not dared to come to the office, she had been in such terror lest she wouldn't know where to hang her coat, wouldn't know how to find the washroom, wouldn't understand the boss's directions for her job.

For perhaps the worst thing about this Depression was its inexorable continuance year after year. Men who have been sturdy and self-respecting workers can take unemployment without flinching for a few weeks, a few months, even if they have to see their families suffer; but it is different after a year . . . two years . . . three years. . . . Among the miserable creatures curled up on park benches or standing in dreary lines before the soup kitchens in 1932 were men who had been jobless since the end of 1929.

At the very bottom of the economic scale the conditions

may perhaps best be suggested by two brief quotations. The first, from Jonathan Norton Leonard's *Three Years Down*, describes the plight of Pennsylvania miners who had been put out of company villages after a blind and hopeless strike in 1931: "Reporters from the more liberal metropolitan papers found thousands of them huddled on the mountainsides, crowded three or four families together in one-room shacks, living on dandelions and wild weed-roots. Half of them were sick, but no local doctor would care for the evicted strikers. All of them were hungry and many were dying of those providential diseases which enable welfare authorities to claim that no one has starved." The other quotation is from Louise V. Armstrong's *We Too Are the People*, and the scene is Chicago in the late spring of 1932:——

"One vivid, gruesome moment of those dark days we shall never forget. We saw a crowd of some fifty men fighting over a barrel of garbage which had been set outside the back door of a restaurant. American citizens fighting for scraps of food like animals!"

Human behavior under unaccustomed conditions is always various. One thinks of the corporation executive to whom was delegated the job of discharging several hundred men: he insisted on seeing every one of them personally and taking an interest in each man's predicament, and at the end of a few months his hair had turned prematurely gray. . . . The Junior League girl who reported with pride a Depression economy: she had cut a piece out of an old fur coat in the attic and bound it to serve as a bathmat. . . . The banker who had been plunged deeply into debt by the collapse of his bank: he got a $30,000 job with another bank, lived on $3,000 a year, and honorably paid $27,000 a year to his creditors. . . . The wealthy family who lost most of their money but announced bravely that they had "solved their Depression problem" by discharging fifteen

BONUS MARCHERS ON THE CAPITOL STEPS

The siege of the Senate at Washington, July, 1932

THE OLD ORDER CHANGETH
President Hoover and President-elect Roosevelt ride together to
the Inauguration, March 4, 1933

of their twenty servants, and showed no signs of curiosity as to what would happen to these fifteen. . . . The little knot of corporation officials in a magnificent skyscraper office doctoring the books of the company to dodge bankruptcy. . . . The crowd of Chicago Negroes standing tight-packed before a tenement-house door to prevent the landlord's agents from evicting a neighbor family: as they stood there, hour by hour, they sang hymns. . . . The one-time clerk carefully cutting out pieces of cardboard to put inside his shoes before setting out on his endless job-hunting round, and telling his wife the shoes were now better than ever. . . . The man in the little apartment next door who had given up hunting for jobs, given up all interest, all activity, and sat hour by hour in staring apathy. . . .

It was a strange time in which to graduate from school or college. High schools had a larger attendance than ever before, especially in the upper grades, because there were few jobs to tempt any one away. Likewise college graduates who could afford to go on to graduate school were continuing their studies—after a hopeless hunt for jobs—rather than be idle. Look, for example, at a sample page of the first report of the Harvard College Class of 1932, made up in the spring of 1933. At first glance it would seem to testify to a remarkable thirst for further knowledge (I quote it verbatim, omitting only the names):

—— does not give his occupation
—— is studying abroad
—— is a student at the Harvard Law School, 1st year
—— is at the University of North Carolina, Chapel Hill, N. C.
—— is a student in the Harvard Medical School, 1st year
—— has not been heard from
—— is a student in the Harvard Engineering School, 4th year
—— is interested in the Communist movement
—— is a student in the Harvard Law School, 1st year
—— is a student in Harvard College

—— is a student in the Harvard School of Architecture, 1st
    year
—— is with the Cleveland Twist Drill Co.
—— is a student in the Harvard School of Business Adminis-
    tration, 1st year
—— is manufacuring neckwear
—— is a student in the Harvard Graduate School of Arts and
    Sciences, 1st year
—— is a student in the Harvard Law School, 1st year
—— is a student in the Harvard Graduate School of Business
    Administration, 1st year
—— is a student in Manhattan College

The effects of the economic dislocation were ubiquitous.
Not business alone was disturbed, but churches, museums,
theatres, schools, colleges, charitable organizations, clubs,
lodges, sports organizations, and so on clear through the
list of human enterprises; one and all they felt the effects
of dwindling gifts, declining memberships, decreasing box-
office returns, uncollectible bills, revenue insufficient to pay
the interest on the mortgage.

Furthermore, as the tide of business receded, it laid bare
the evidence of many an unsavory incident of the past. The
political scandals which were being investigated in New
York City by Samuel Seabury, for instance, came to light
only partly as a result of a new crusading spirit among the
citizenry, a wave of disgust for machine graft; it was the
Depression, bringing failures and defaults and then the
examination of corporate records, which had begun the
revelations. The same sort of thing was happening in almost
every city and town. As banks went under, as corporations
got into difficulties, the accountants learned what otherwise
might never have been discovered: that the respected family in the big house on the hill had been hand-in-hand with
gangsters; that the benevolent company president had been
living in such style only because he placed company orders

at fat prices with an associated company which he personally controlled; that the corporation lawyer who passed the plate at the Presbyterian church had been falsifying his income-tax returns. And with every such disclosure came a new disillusionment.

§ 6

On the evening of the first of March, 1932, an event took place which instantly thrust everything else, even the grim processes of Depression, into the background of American thought—and which seemed to many observers to epitomize cruelly the demoralization into which the country had fallen. The baby son of Colonel and Mrs. Charles A. Lindbergh was kidnapped—taken out of his bed in a second-story room of the new house at Hopewell, New Jersey, never to be seen again alive.

Since Lindbergh's flight to Paris nearly five years before, he had occupied a unique and unprecedented position in American life. Admired almost to the point of worship by millions of people, he was like a sort of uncrowned prince; and although he fiercely shunned publicity, everything he did was so inevitably news that the harder he tried to dodge the limelight, the more surely it pursued him. Word that he had been seen anywhere was enough to bring a crowd running; he was said to have been driven at times to disguise himself in order to be free of mobbing admirers. He now occupied himself as a consultant in aviation; late the preceding summer he and his wife, the former Anne Morrow, had made a "flight to the Orient" which Mrs. Lindbergh later described in lovely prose; and since his meeting with Dr. Alexis Carrel late in 1930 he had begun experiments in the construction of perfusion pumps which were to bring him a high reputation as a biological technician. His new house at Hopewell, remote and surrounded by woods, had been built largely as a retreat in which the Lindberghs could be at peace from an intrusive world.

And now, suddenly, this peace was shattered. Within a few hours of the discovery that the Lindbergh baby's bed was empty—the blankets still held in place by their safety pins—a swarm of police and newspaper men had reached the house and were trampling about the muddy grounds, obliterating clues. And when the news broke in the next morning's newspapers, the American people went into a long paroxysm of excitement.

More police and reporters arrived; the nearest railroad station was transformed into a newspaper headquarters; news from Hopewell crowded everything else to the back pages of the papers; President Hoover issued a statement, the Governor of New Jersey held police conferences, anti-kidnapping bills were prepared by legislators in several states, the *New York Times* reported the receipt on a single day of 3,331 telephone calls asking for the latest news. Bishop Manning of New York sent his clergy a special prayer for immediate use, declaring, "In a case like this we cannot wait till Sunday." William Green asked members of the American Federation of Labor to aid in the hunt for the criminal. Commander Evangeline Booth urged all commanding officers of the Salvation Army to help, and referred to "the miraculous accomplishments with which God has honored our movement along these very lines through our lost and found bureau." Clergymen of three denominations prayed over the radio for the baby's deliverance. Wild rumors went about. Babies resembling the Lindbergh child were reported seen in automobiles all over the country. The proprietor of a cigar store in Jersey City brought the police on the run by reporting that he had heard a man in a telephone booth say something that sounded like a kidnapper's message. And the Lindberghs received endless letters of advice and suggestion—the total running, in a few weeks, to one hundred thousand.

From day to day the drama of the search went on—the Lindberghs offering immunity to the kidnapper in a signed statement, giving out the pathetic details of the baby's accustomed diet, asking two racketeering bootleggers named Spitale and Bitz to serve as intermediaries with the underworld; and soon the chief actors in the Hopewell drama became as familiar to the American newspaper-reading public as if the whole country had been engaged in reading the same detective story. Mr. and Mrs. Oliver Whateley, the butler and his wife; Betty Gow, the nurse; Arthur Johnson, her sailor friend; Colonel Schwarzkopf of the New Jersey State Police; Violet Sharpe, the maid at the Morrows' house, who committed suicide; and Dr. John F. Condon ("Jafsie"), the old gentleman in the Bronx who made the first personal contact with the kidnapper—these men and women became the subjects of endless conjectures and theorizings. When a stranger asked one, "Have they found the baby?" there was never an instant's doubt as to what baby was meant, whether the question was asked in New Jersey or in Oregon. One would hear a hotel elevator man saying out of the blue, to an ascending guest, "Well, I believe it was an inside job"—to which the guest would reply heatedly, "Nonsense, it was that gang in Detroit." If the American people had needed to have their minds taken off the Depression, the kidnapping had briefly done it.

On March 8, a week after the crime, old Dr. Condon—college lecturer and welfare worker in "the most beautiful borough in the world," as he called the Bronx—conceived the odd idea of putting an advertisement in the Bronx *Home News*, to the effect that he would be glad to serve as an intermediary for the return of the Lindbergh child. The next day he received a letter, misspelled in an odd Germanic way, containing an enclosure addressed to Colonel Lindbergh. He called up the house at Hopewell, was asked to open the enclosure, described some curious markings on it, and at once was asked to come and see Colonel Lindbergh—for those markings were identical with the code symbols on a ransom note which had been left on the window sill of the baby's room! On March 12, Dr. Condon received a note which told him to go to a hot-dog stand at the end of the Jerome Avenue elevated railroad. He found there a note directing him to the entrance of Woodlawn Cemetery. He presently saw a man in the shrubbery of the cemetery, and he went with this man to a bench near by, where they sat and talked. The kidnapper had a German or Scandinavian accent, called himself "John," and said he was only one of a gang.

Further negotiations—which left no doubt that "John" was indeed the kidnapper, or one of the kidnappers—led to the payment of $50,000 in bills to "John" by Dr. Condon (accompanied by Colonel Lindbergh) in St. Raymond's Cemetery in the Bronx on April 2—whereupon "John" handed Dr. Condon a note which said that the baby would be found safe on a "boad" (meaning *boat*) near Gay Head on Martha's Vineyard. The Colonel made two flights there by plane and found no "boad"; clearly the information given was false.

Then on the evening of May 12, 1932, about six weeks after the kidnapping, the newsboys chanted extras in the streets once more: the child's body had been found by chance in a thicket near a road five and a half miles from the Lindbergh place. Whether he had been killed deliberately or accidentally would never be known; in any event, the kidnapper had chosen that spot to half-bury the little body.

"BABY DEAD" announced the tabloid headlines: those two words sufficed.

A great many Americans whose memories of other events

of the decade are vague can recall just where and under what circumstances they first heard that piece of news.

The story seemed to have reached its end, but still the reverberations of horror continued. Soon it was clear, not only that the kidnapper had added the cruelty of Lindbergh's hopeless search by plane to the barbarity of the original crime; not only that Gaston B. Means had wangled $100,000 out of Mrs. McLean of Washington on the criminally false pretense that he could get the child back; but also that John Hughes Curtis of Norfolk, Virginia, who had induced Colonel Lindbergh to go out on a boat in Chesapeake Bay to make contact with the kidnappers, had concocted—for whatever reason—one of the most contemptible hoaxes ever conceived. These revelations, coming on top of the shock of seeing the Lindberghs forced to deal with representatives of the underworld (as if the underworld were quite beyond the law), brought thunders of dismay from preachers, orators, editorial-writers, columnists: there was something very rotten indeed in the State of Denmark. And the tragic sense that things were awry was deepened.

There the Lindbergh case rested in 1932. But we must go ahead of our history to recount the sequel. It came over twenty-eight months later, on September 19, 1934, when the kidnapper was arrested. Ironically, one of the things which facilitated his capture was that in the meantime the New Deal had come in, the United States had gone off the gold standard, and the gold certificates which had been handed over to the kidnapper had become noticeable rarities.

The kidnapper proved to be not a member of the organized underworld but a lone criminal—a fugitive felon from Germany, illegally in the United States—one Bruno Richard Hauptmann. He was arrested in the Bronx, was tried at the beginning of 1935 at the Hunterdon County Court

House at Flemington, New Jersey, was convicted, and—
after an unsuccessful appeal and a delay brought about by
the inexplicable unwillingness of Governor Harold Hoff-
man of New Jersey to believe in his guilt—was electrocuted
on April 3, 1936.

The evidence against Hauptmann was overwhelming.
Leaving aside the possibly debatable identifications of him
and other dubious bits of evidence, consider these items
alone: 1. Hauptmann lived in the Bronx, where Dr. Condon's advertisement had appeared, where Dr. Condon had
met "John" and where "John" had received the ransom
money. 2. The numbers of the ransom bills had been recorded: many of these bills had been passed in parts of
New York City accessible to a resident of the Bronx; it was
the passing of one by Hauptmann in a Bronx garage which
led to his arrest. 3. When arrested, Hauptmann had a $20
ransom bill on his person. 4. No less than $14,600 in ran-
som bills was found secreted in his garage. 5. He was a
German, his tricks of speech corresponded roughly to those
in the ransom letters, he had once used in an account book
the spelling "boad," and he used other misspellings and
foreign locutions like those in the ransom notes. 6. His
handwriting was similar to those in the notes. 7. He had
had no regular means of support after March 1, 1932, but
had nevertheless spent money freely and had had a broker-
age account of some dimensions (with which he was quite
unsuccessful). 8. His story of how he got his money, through
an alleged partnership in a fur business with one Frisch,
and how he kept it in a shoe box on a shelf, was vague and
unconvincing. 9. Furthermore, the kidnapper had left
behind, at Hopewell, a ladder of odd construction. An
expert from the Department of Agriculture, Arthur Koeh-
ler, not only found, from the sort of wood used in the
making of this ladder and from peculiarities in its cutting,
that it had been a part of a shipment to a Bronx firm, but

also that irregularities in the planing of it corresponded to irregularities in a plane in Hauptmann's possession. 10. Finally, one piece of the wood used in the ladder fitted precisely a piece missing from a floor board in Hauptmann's attic, even the old nail holes in it matching to a fraction of an inch!

§7

Down, down, down went business.

Calvin Coolidge, who had been the chief patron saint of the prosperity of the nineteen-twenties, paced in unhappy bewilderment about the lawn at "The Beeches," his Northampton estate. One day he dropped in at his barber's for his monthly haircut. "Mr. Coolidge," said the barber deferentially, "how about this depression? When is it going to end?" "Well, George," said the ex-President, "the big men of the country have got to get together and do something about it. It isn't going to end itself. We all hope it will end, but we don't see it yet."

Andrew Mellon, who had been shunted into the Ambassadorship to the Court of St. James's to give Ogden Mills, a younger and livelier man, a chance to run the Treasury, no longer wore the halo in Wall Street which had once been his; when he left the Treasury the stock market—which in other years would have expressed itself sharply —never wavered; yet Mellon had been one of those "big men" of the country to whom Coolidge presumably referred, a man of vast wealth, financial acumen, financial prestige. What did he have to say? In the spring of 1932 he spoke in London. "None of us has any means of knowing," said he, "when and how we shall emerge from the valley of depression in which the world is traveling. But I do know that, as in the past, the day will come when we shall find ourselves on a more solid economic foundation and the onward march of progress will be resumed." And again, before the International Chamber of Commerce: "I do not believe in any quick or spectacular remedies for the ills from which the world is suffering, nor do I share the belief that there is anything fundamentally wrong with the social system under which we have achieved, in this and other industrialized countries, a degree of economic well-being unprecedented in the history of the world. . . ."

Not much satisfaction there for men and women in trouble!

A few months later another great man of finance spoke in London—Montagu Norman, governor of the Bank of England. Even making allowance for the hopeful passages in his address, and for British self-deprecation, those who read his cabled remarks got a shock from them. Speaking of the world-wide economic crisis, he said: "The difficulties are so vast, the forces so unlimited, so novel, and precedents are so lacking, that I approach this whole subject not only in ignorance but in humility. It is too great for me."

Didn't *he* know either?

Nor did Wall Street seem to have any answer. The men of Wall Street were complaining that the trouble lay in a "lack of confidence" (how often had we all heard, how often were we all to hear those hoary words parroted!); and that this lack of confidence arose from fear of inflation and from the unpredictable and dangerous behavior of Congress, which was all-too-lukewarm about balancing the Federal budget and was full of unsound notions. The defenders of the old order seemed as bewildered as any one else; they didn't know what had hit them. Said a banker noted for his astuteness, in a newsreel talk, "As for the cause of the Depression, or the way out, you know as much as I do." And Charles M. Schwab of Bethlehem Steel, who had once been unfailingly optimistic, was quoted as saying at a luncheon in New York, ". . . . I'm afraid, every man is afraid. I don't know, we don't know, whether the values we have are going to be real next month or not."

The astrologers and fortunetellers were in clover; Evangeline Adams and Dolores were getting letters by the basketful—and from financiers as well as from those of humbler station. When all other prophets failed, why not try the stars?

The spring of 1932 was a bad season for financial reputations. On that very March 12 when "Jafsie" met Hauptmann and talked with him beside Woodlawn Cemetery, a strange thing happened in Paris: one of the supposed miracle workers of international industry and finance, the Swedish match king, Ivar Kreuger, carefully drew the blinds of the bedroom in his apartment in the Avenue Victor Emmanuel III, smoothed the covers of the unmade bed, lay down, and shot himself an inch below the heart. During the following weeks, out trickled the story behind the suicide: that Kreuger's operations had been fraudulent, and that he had readily deceived with false figures and airy lies the honorable members of one of the most esteemed American financial houses. On April 8 Samuel Insull, builder of a lofty pyramid of public-utility holding companies—that same Insull of whom it had been said, only a few years before, that it was worth a million dollars to anybody to be seen talking with him in front of the Continental Bank— went to Owen D. Young's office in New York, confronted there Mr. Young and a group of New York bankers, was told that the jig was up for him, and said sadly, "I wish my time on earth had already come"; Insull's house of cards, too, had gone down. A Senate investigation was beginning to show up the cold-blooded manipulations by which stocks had been pushed up and down in the stock market by corporate insiders of wealth and prominence and supposed responsibility. The president of Hoover's Reconstruction

Finance Corporation, Charles G. Dawes, had to resign and hurry to Chicago in order that the Corporation might authorize the lending of ninety million dollars to save his bank, caught in a Chicago banking panic. Rumors of all sorts of imminent collapses were going about. Of whom and of what could one be sure?

By the middle of 1932 industry was operating at less than half its maximum 1929 volume, according to the Federal Reserve Board's Adjusted Index of Industrial Production: the figure had fallen all the way from 125 to 58. Cotton was selling below 5 cents, wheat below 50 cents, corn at 31 cents; bond prices had taken a headlong tumble; and as for the stock market, once the harbinger of so many economic blessings, it had plumbed such depths as to make the prices reached at the end of the Panic of 1929 look lofty by comparison. Here are a few comparisons in tabular form:—

	High Price on Sept. 3, 1929	Low Price on Nov. 13, 1929 after the Panic	Low Price for 1932
American Telephone...........	304	197¼	70¼
General Electric...............	396¼	168½	34*
General Motors................	72¾	36	7⅝
New York Central.............	256⅜	160	8¾
Radio........................	101	26	2½
U. S. Steel...................	261¾	150	21¼

* Adjusted to take account of a split-up in the meantime. The actual price was 8½.

Thus spoke the stock market, that "sensitive barometer" of the country's economic prospects. Thus had departed the hopes of yesteryear. Was there no savior anywhere in sight?

Chapter Four

A CHANGE OF GOVERNMENT

§ 1

IT BEGAN to look as if the job of saving the United States would fall into the willing hands of Franklin D. Roosevelt.

Early in June, 1932, the Republicans held a dull convention with their Old Guard in full control, wrote a dull and verbose platform, and nominated Herbert Hoover for re-election because they had to. Considering what was going on in the world, the general aspect of the Republican deliberations was ichthyosaurian.

When the Democrats went to Chicago for their convention—to a Chicago still reeling from a local panic in which nearly forty banks had gone under and the Dawes bank had been hard hit—Roosevelt had a long lead for the Democratic nomination. For his aides had been doing hard and effective work. Jim Farley—large, amiable, energetic, shrewd in the politics of friendships and favors—had been rushing about the country with glad hand outstretched and had been using to the utmost his incredible capacity for mass production of personal correspondence. He sometimes called in six stenographers at a time, spent eight consecutive hours signing letters in green ink; at night, when safe from interruption, he could sign at the rate of nearly two thousand letters an hour. While Farley commanded the Roosevelt forces in the field, the Roosevelt chief-of-staff was Louis McHenry Howe, a little wizened invalid with protruding eyes and unkempt clothes who worshipped Roosevelt and lived to further his career. Remaining in a shabby office in Madison Avenue, New York, sitting at a desk littered with newspapers and pamphlets, or lying on an old day bed when his chronic asthma exhausted him, Howe studied the political map and gave Farley sage advice. "Louis would sit in front of me in his favorite pose," writes Farley, "his elbows resting on his knees, and his face cupped in his hands so that practically nothing was visible of his features except his eyes." A masterly strategist of politics, Howe thought out the plan of campaign.

While these men gathered delegates for Roosevelt, others gathered ideas for him. In March, 1932—the month of the Lindbergh kidnapping and the Kreuger suicide—Roosevelt's friend and adviser Samuel I. Rosenman had suggested to him that it might be a good idea to get a group of university professors to help him formulate his program; and, when Roosevelt smilingly agreed that it might, Rosenman had invited Professor Raymond Moley of Columbia to dinner and had thrashed the matter out with him over coffee and cigars. Moley had been working with Roosevelt for months on various New York problems and thus naturally became the recruiting officer and unofficial chairman of a group of advisers which included (in addition to Moley and Rosenman) Rexford Guy Tugwell and Adolph A. Berle, Jr., both of Columbia, and Basil O'Connor, Roosevelt's law partner. Roosevelt at first dubbed the group his "privy council"; in July, James Kieran of the *New York Times* christened it the "brains trust"; the general public took over this name but inevitably changed the awkward plural into a singular and spoke of the "brain trust." Members of the group would go to Albany, dine with Governor Roosevelt, talk with vast excitement for hours, and return to New York to study and report on national problems for the candidate and to draft memoranda and rough out speeches for him.

But at first Roosevelt was very cautious in his use of such

material or in taking a definite position upon anything. He was handsome, friendly, attractive; he had the smiling magnetism, the agreeable voice which Hoover so dismally lacked; he had not only had political and administrative experience as Governor of New York, but knew Washington as a former Assistant Secretary of the Navy. With Farley and Howe to help him, and with delegates flocking to him because of his political "availability," all he apparently needed in order to win the nomination—and the election, for that matter—was to exercise his charm, look just conservative enough to fall heir to the votes of Republicans who were sick of Hoover, look just radical enough to keep the rebellious from turning socialist or communist, and not make enemies. So he spoke kindly of "the forgotten man at the bottom of the economic pyramid" but failed to specify exactly how this man should be remembered; he said that "the country demands bold, persistent experimentation" but engaged, in his speeches, chiefly in the sort of experimentation practiced by the chameleon. So gentle was he with the Tammany graft being disclosed by Samuel Seabury, and so tentative was he in expressing economic ideas, that Walter Lippmann warned those Western Democrats who regarded Roosevelt as a courageous progressive and an "enemy of evil influences" that they did not know their man.

"Franklin D. Roosevelt," wrote Lippmann, "is an amiable man with many philanthropic impulses, but he is not the dangerous enemy of anything. He is too eager to please. . . . Franklin D. Roosevelt is no crusader. He is no tribune of the people. He is no enemy of entrenched privilege. He is a pleasant man who, without any important qualifications for the office, would very much like to be President."

On the first ballot for the nomination, taken in the Chicago Stadium in a sweltering all-night session after interminable nominating speeches, Roosevelt already had a

majority of the delegates. The only obstacles now remaining
were the ancient rule which required a two-thirds vote for
the nomination, and the possibility that the opposition
forces of John Nance Garner of Texas or of Roosevelt's
former friend and mentor, Al Smith, might be unbreak-
able. Two more ballots followed without important change
as night gave way to day, and at 9:15 on the morning of
July 1st the delegates—"stupefied by oratory, brass bands,
bad air, perspiration, sleeplessness, and soft drinks," as Walter Lippmann said—stumbled out of the Stadium into the
sunshine with no decision taken.

Only Huey Long, the Louisiana Kingfish, had seemed un-
wilted during that exhausting night: Heywood Broun saw
him dash down to the aisles to soothe a swaying delegation, pause to greet a blonde stenographer with "How
are you, baby?" and continue energetically on his political
errand. When Farley got back to Louis Howe's room to report, he found Howe lying on the floor in his shirt sleeves,
his head on a pillow, two electric fans blowing on him;
Farley sprawled on the carpet beside him to confer on the
strategy of the hour. The two men decided that Farley
should look for Sam Rayburn of Texas and see if the Texas
delegation could be persuaded to forsake Garner for Roosevelt, in return for aid in getting Garner the vice-presidential nomination. Farley then dragged himself to Pat Harrison's rooms in search of Rayburn; and when he found
that Rayburn had not yet arrived, Farley sat down to wait
and presently was snoring in his chair. Under such conditions do our statesmen make their vital choices.

But soon it was all over. Rayburn arrived at the Harrison suite. He did not commit himself definitely but said,
"We'll see what can be done"; and Farley felt that victory
was on the way. That afternoon Garner telephoned from
Washington to recommend that his leaders should release
their delegations. (What part Hearst, who had been backing

Garner, had in this surrender is uncertain.) When, that night, the delegates assembled once more, the opposition lines had broken. On the first ballot that night—the fourth for the nomination—Roosevelt was chosen. Garner thereupon got the vice-presidential nomination.

Dramatically, Roosevelt refused to wait weeks for a notification ceremony. Throwing aside tradition, he chartered a plane, flew to Chicago, and made an immediate speech of acceptance promising a "new deal." (This was the first public appearance of the phrase. Moley, perhaps thinking of Stuart Chase's book, *A New Deal*, had used it in a memorandum to Roosevelt six weeks before, and Roosevelt had seized upon it.)

The origin of this acceptance speech was a little drama in itself. For weeks Roosevelt and the Brain Trust had been working on a draft of the address. During the plane trip Roosevelt had made a few last-minute revisions. But at the airport at Chicago he was met by Louis Howe, who thrust another manuscript into his hand. Howe, in Chicago, had been shown a copy of the Brain Trust draft by Moley, had disliked it, and had written a revised version: it was this new version which he was now handing to the nominee. As Roosevelt rode to the Stadium through roaring crowds he had no chance to compare the two documents; not until he was on the platform, facing the Convention, could he lay them side by side. During the cheering he glanced them over. Then he began to speak. The beginning of his address was his faithful Howe's first page; the rest was the original Brain Trust draft!

Nothing in the speech was as bold as Roosevelt's flight to make it. "Taking note, apparently, of the charges of straddling that had been flung at him," wrote Elmer Davis, "he promised to make his position clear; and he did—upon the Prohibition plank [demanding Repeal] which the party had adopted by a vote of five to one. For the rest, you could not quarrel with a single one of his generalities; you seldom can. But what they mean (if anything) is known only to Franklin D. Roosevelt and his God."

In the speech there were many passages which foreshadowed the subsequent vigorous measures of his Presidency, but they were vague in phrasing. In only one place, where he suggested that a force of unemployed men be put at conservation work, did he seem to have a really novel plan (this was the germ of the CCC). He endorsed some ideas which he was later to forsake, as when he said that government "costs too much" and that the Federal government should set an example of solvency. And he accepted "one hundred per cent" the new Democratic platform: a short specific document which, though it called for financial reforms such as Roosevelt was later to push through Congress, and called also for "control of crop surpluses," represented in the main an old-fashioned liberalism—a return to the days of small and simple business units and modest and frugal governmental units—and certainly gave no hint of any intention to expand enormously the Federal power.

Events were moving fast in that summer of 1932, ideas were boiling, and counsels were divided. The Democratic candidate was astute: he had less to lose by facing two ways than by standing fast; by talking about candor than by exercising it.

§ 2

Not only were ideas boiling; the country was losing patience with adversity. That instinct of desperate men to rebel which was swelling the radical parties in a dozen Depression-hit countries and was gathering stormily behind Hitler in Germany was working in the United States also. It was anything but unified, it was as yet little organized, and only in scattered places did it assume the customary Euro-

pean shape of communism. It had been slow to develop—
partly because Americans had been used to prosperity and
had expected it to return automatically, partly because when
jobs were vanishing those men who were still employed
were too scared to be rebellious, and simply hung on to
what they had and waited and hoped. (It is not usually
during a collapse that men rebel, but after it.) There had
been riots and hunger-marches here and there but on the
whole the orderliness of the country had been striking, all
things considered. Yet men could not be expected to sit
still forever in the expectation that an economic system
which they did not understand would right itself. The ferment of dissatisfaction was working in many places and
taking many forms, and here and there it was beginning to
break sharply through the orderly surface of society.

In the summer of 1932 the city of Washington was to see
an exciting example of this ferment—and a spectacular
demonstration of how not to deal with it.

All through June thousands of war veterans had been
streaming into Washington, coming from all over the country by boxcar and by truck. These veterans wanted the government to pay them now the "adjusted compensation"
which Congress had already voted to pay them in 1945. They
set up a camp—a shanty-town, a sort of big-scale "Hoover-
ville"—on the Anacostia flats near the city, and they occupied
some vacant land with disused buildings on it on Pennsylvania Avenue just below the Capitol. More and more of
them straggled to Washington until their number had
reached fifteen or twenty thousand.

Among such a great crowd there were inevitably men of
many sorts. The Hoover Administration later charged that
many had had criminal records, or were communists. But
unquestionably the great majority of them were genuine
veterans; though there was one small communist group, it
was regarded with hostility by the rest; in the main this

"Bonus Expeditionary Force" consisted of ordinary Americans out of luck. They were under at least a semblance of military discipline and were on the whole well-behaved. Many brought their wives and children along, and as time went on the Anacostia camp took on an air half military and half domestic, with the family wash hanging on the line outside the miserable shacks, and entertainers getting up impromptu vaudeville shows.

General Pelham D. Glassford, the Washington superintendent of police, sensibly regarded these invaders as citizens who had every right to petition the government for a redress of grievances. He helped them to get equipment for their camp and treated them with unfailing consideration. But to some Washingtonians their presence was ominous. A group of the veterans—under a leader who wore a steel neck-brace and a helmet with straps under the chin, to support a broken back—picketed the Capitol for days while the Bonus bill was being considered; and on the evening when the bill was to come to a vote, the great plaza before the Capitol was packed with veterans. The Senate voted No. What would the men do? There were people looking out the windows of the brightly lighted Senate wing who wondered breathlessly if those thousands of ragged men would try to rush the building. But when their leader announced the news, a band struck up "America" and the men dispersed quietly. So far, so good.

Some of them left Washington during the next few days, but several thousand stayed on, hopelessly, obstinately. (Where had they to go?) Officialdom became more and more uneasy. The White House was put under guard, its gates closed and chained, the streets about it cleared, as if the man there did not dare face the unrest among the least fortunate of the citizenry. It was decided to clear the veterans out of the disused buildings below the Capitol (to make way for the government's building program); and on the morning of July 28, 1932, General Glassford was told that the evacuation must be immediate. He set about his task.

It began peacefully, but at noon somebody threw a brick and there was a scuffle between the veterans and the police, which quickly subsided. Two hours later there was more serious trouble as a policeman at whom the veterans had thrown stones pulled his gun; two veterans were killed before Glassford could get the police to stop shooting. Even this battle subsided. All Glassford wanted was time to complete the evacuation peacefully and without needless affront. But he was not to get it.

Earlier in the day he had told the District Commissioners that if the evacuation was to be carried out speedily, troops would be required. This statement had been needlessly interpreted as a request for military aid, which Glassford did not want at all. President Hoover had ordered the United States Army to the rescue.

Down Pennsylvania Avenue, late that hot afternoon, came an impressive parade—four troops of cavalry, four companies of infantry, a machine-gun squadron, and several tanks. As they approached the disputed area they were met with cheers from the veterans sitting on the curb and from the large crowd which had assembled. Then suddenly there was chaos: cavalrymen were riding into the crowd, infantrymen were throwing tear-gas bombs, women and children were being trampled and were choking from the gas; a crowd of three thousand or more spectators who had gathered in a vacant lot across the way were being pursued by the cavalry and were running wildly, pell-mell, across the uneven ground, screaming as they stumbled and fell.

The troops moved slowly on, scattering before them veterans and homegoing government clerks alike. When they reached the other end of the Anacostia bridge and met a crowd of spectators who booed them and were slow to "move on," they threw more gas bombs. They began burning the shacks of the Anacostia camp—a task which the veterans themselves helped them accomplish. That evening the Washington sky glowed with fire. Even after midnight the troops were still on their way with bayonets and tear-gas bombs, driving people ahead of them into the streets of Anacostia.

The Bonus Expeditionary Force had been dispersed, to merge itself with that greater army of homeless people who were drifting about the country in search of an ever-retreating fortune. The United States Army had completed its operation "successfully" without killing anybody—though the list of injured was long. The incident was over. But it had left a bitter taste in the mouth. Bayonets drawn in Washington to rout the dispossessed—was this the best that American statesmanship could offer hungry citizens?

§ 3

The farmers were rebellious—and no wonder. For the gross income of American agriculture had declined from nearly 12 billion dollars in 1929—when it had already for years been suffering from a decline in export sales—to only 5¼ billions in 1932. While most manufacturing businesses dropped their prices only a little and met slackened demand with slackened production, the farmer could not do this, and the prices he got went right down to the cellar. Men who found themselves utterly unable to meet their costs of production could not all be expected to be philosophical about it.

Angry Iowans, organized by Milo Reno into a Farmers' Holiday Association, were refusing to bring food into Sioux City for thirty days or "until the cost of production had been obtained"; they blockaded the highways with spiked telegraph poles and logs, stopped milk trucks and emptied the milk into roadside ditches. Said an elderly Iowa farmer with

a white mustache to Mary Heaton Vorse, "They say block-
ading the highway's illegal. I says, 'Seems to me there was a
Tea Party in Boston that was illegal too.' "

Elsewhere farmers were taking the obvious direct means
to stop the tidal wave of mortgage foreclosure sales. All
through the prairie country there were quantities of farmers who not only had heavy mortgages on their property but
had gone deeply into debt for the purchase of farm machinery or to meet the emergencies of years of falling prices;
when their corn and wheat brought to even the most industrious of them not enough money to meet their obligations,
they lost patience with the laws of bankruptcy. If a man sees
a neighbor of his, a formerly successful farmer, a substantial,
hard-working citizen with a family, coming out of the office
of the referee in bankruptcy stripped of everything but an
old team of horses, a wagon, a few dogs and hogs, and a few
sticks of furniture, he is likely to see red. Marching to the
scene of the next foreclosure sale, these farmers would drive
off prospective bidders, gather densely about the auctioneer,
bid in horses at 25 cents apiece, cows at 10 cents, fat hogs
at a nickel—and the next morning would return their purchases to the former owner.

In a quiet county seat, handbills would appear: "Farmers and workers! Help protect your neighbors from being
driven off their property. Now is the time to act. For the
past three and a half years we have waited for our masters,
who are responsible for the situation, to find a way out. . . .
On Friday the property of ———— is to be sold at a forced
auction at the courthouse. . . . The Farmers Committee
has called a mass protest meeting to stop the above-men-
tioned sale." And on Friday the trucks would drive up to
the courthouse and men by the hundreds, quiet, grim-faced,
would fill the corridors outside the sheriff's office while their
leaders demanded that the sale be not held.

They threatened judges in bankruptcy cases; in one case

a mob dragged a judge from his courtroom, beat him, hanged him by the neck till he fainted—and all because he was carrying out the law.

These farmers were not revolutionists. On the contrary, most of them were by habit conservative men. They were simply striking back in rage at the impersonal forces which had brought them to their present pass.

All through the summer and autumn of 1932—when the Olympic Games were being held with high pageantry at Los Angeles, when people were gathering in the open fields of Maine and New Hampshire to witness as much of a total eclipse of the sun as drifting clouds would permit, when Mayor Jimmy Walker of New York was being tried before Governor Roosevelt for misconduct in office and was resigning to seek a temporary exile in the south of France, when the report that a nudist camp had been established anywhere was enough to bring the reporters on the dead run, and when Roosevelt was campaigning against Hoover— all through that summer and autumn the ferment of ideas, plans, notions for defeating the Depression increased.

In July and August, barter schemes were going into effect in Dayton and Yellow Springs, Ohio, and soon they were being set up in numerous communities: men and women were organizing the dispossessed to pool their various abilities and make goods for one another—only to discover, after months or even years of heroic effort, that "mutual exchanges" and attempts to set up little systems of production within the existing system could be only makeshifts at best. Towns from which money had almost disappeared were adopting scrip currency—issuing local money good in the local shops. Huey Long, who had arrived in Washington as a Senator in January and had electrified the gentlemen of the press by receiving them in lavender pajamas, had proposed a Share-our-Wealth scheme in March; and although Huey now occupied an ostentatious position on the Roose-

velt band wagon, he had not forgotten his slogan: the time
was ripe for it. Father Coughlin's big radio audience heard
him excoriating both the New York financiers and the
Hoover Administration and calling Morgan, Mellon, Meyer,
and Mills the "Four Horsemen"; the radio priest was getting ready to come out for revaluation of the currency.

Magazine editors were being inundated with manuscripts
explaining how the Depression could be ended—manuscripts
proposing huge bond issues for public works, recommending
inflation, recommending all sorts of other expedients, rational or ridiculous: "hot money" which would decline in
value if unspent; the Douglas credit plan; other complex
improvements in the banking and credit system; schemes
for the general reduction of debts; "work-sharing" schemes
for shorter hours of labor to soak up unemployment; proposals for the seizure and operation of industries by the
government. Communism was notably gaining strength,
both among the unemployed workers and—more rapidly—
among the urban intellectuals: Edmund Wilson, John Dos
Passos, Malcolm Cowley, V. F. Calverton, Theodore Dreiser,
and other able writers were fighting the good fight for Marx,
and young novelists by the dozens were sitting down to
write proletarian fiction.

The yeast was slowly working, and with the advent of
winter it suddenly produced an astonishing and significant
phenomenon: the frenzy of interest in Technocracy.

§ 4

To nobody was this frenzy more bewildering than to
Howard Scott, the father of the Technocratic idea. He was
an eccentric, boastful, haphazard young man who claimed
to have had an important career in engineering and certainly had conducted a small paint and floor-wax business.
For years he had been buttonholing people at The Meeting

Place or Van's Place or other Greenwich Village speak-easies and restaurants to expound his strange economic theories—and had been finding it difficult to get people to listen. But when the Depression routed economic orthodoxy, heterodox notions began to look less crazy; Scott got enough backing to put a squad of unemployed architects to work at Columbia University on an "Energy Survey of North America." Then the *Living Age* came out with an article about Technocracy; and then, abruptly—in December, 1932 —the thing was everywhere: in the newspapers, in the magazines, in sermons, in radio-actors' gags, in street-corner conversation. The amazed Scott, who a little while before had been jubilant when a newspaper gave a few lines to Technocracy, was now pursued by interviewers ready to hang upon his lightest word.

Scott's theory—developed partly from the writings of Veblen and Soddy—had a basis of good hard sense. He argued that it was not necessary for our economic system to falter and slow down; our enormous scientific and technical progress and the vast potentialities of machine power offered a basis for unparalleled prosperity—if only our money and credit arrangements could be prevented from jamming the works. The trouble with the system, argued Scott, was that discoveries and improvements which should cause us to be able to enjoy the affluence of plenty did not do so, but added to the debt burden and stalled the economic machinery.

At this point the argument became more difficult. What was wrong, insisted Scott, was the price system. What we needed was a price system based on energy—in units like ergs and joules. And the people who could put such a system into effect and operate it were the technologists—the scientists and engineers.

To try to put into effect a new price system seemed a sufficiently hazardous proceeding—considering the vast number of changes it would necessitate in everyday transactions— even if Scott and his disciples had been able to explain how this very difficult change was to be brought about. (No adequate explanation was forthcoming.) Practical men boggled at such a proposal. Practical men also smiled at putting the vital decisions in a society into the hands of scientific specialists. They remembered that politicians are always needed in the making of social decisions, because they know how to take account of human nature. Other critics of Technocracy pointed out that Scott's statements about the great potentialities of new engineering devices like the electric eye were optimistic at best. Still others were irritated by the abstruse language and the complicated mathematical formulae in which the Technocrats expressed themselves: when Scott himself wrote for publication he said of Technocracy that "its methods are the result of a synthetic integration of the physical sciences that pertain to the determination of all functional sequences of social phenomena," and he defined science as "the methodology of the determination of the most probable."

But the Technocratic idea fitted precisely the American mood of the moment. It offered an answer to the pervasive riddle of the times. This answer was new; it did not—as did communism—run head on into ingrained prejudices and emotional conflicts. It seemed to be scientific, and thus commended itself to a people who venerated science as the source of progress. As a new fad, it was as much fun as a round-the-world flight or Amos 'n' Andy. The very fact that it was abstruse, that it broke clean away from the world of practical problems and intelligible statements, gave it a mystical irresistibility to a nation searching for a magic key to recovery, for something which would both bring prosperity and serve as a religion. Technocracy was hopeful, too, looking forward as it did to an era of possible plenty; this fact helped to make it palatable to a public of habitual optimists. And its vogue came at the moment when millions of Americans had decided that they were sick of the old order and were ready for a new one—they didn't know what.

During the last month of 1932 and the first month of 1933 America took up the idea with a whoop. The columns of newspapers and magazines were full of it; bankers and taxi drivers alike argued its merits and fallacies; *The ABC of Technocracy* leaped into the best-seller lists, half-forgotten volumes by Soddy and Veblen suddenly met a lively demand, and several new books on Technocracy were hurriedly announced. When ship-news reporters boarded an incoming liner, the first question they asked a returning banker or movie star was "What do you think of Technocracy?" Howard Scott was invited by the largest apartment house in New York to act as Santa Claus at its Christmas tree celebration, quite as if he were a Channel swimmer or a nonstop flyer. A rift between Scott and his Columbia associates became a front-page news sensation.

Then the interest almost as quickly waned. Technocracy was too far removed from the practical issues of the day to remain in the forefront of attention. By the time the New Deal arrived, it was already *vieux jeu* to most Americans—like a memory of a half-forgotten folly.

Yet in the meantime it had offered an object-lesson in the readiness of the American people for a new messiah and a new credo. In a lesser degree they were exhibiting the same emotional willingness to get up and go, they knew not where, that was being exhibited in Germany by multitudes of men and women who were not convinced by Hitler but followed him because he was marching and seemed sure of his destination, and because they could face a hopeless future no longer.

§ 5

Poor Hoover!

In June he had made a bold disarmament proposal in the hope of ending a long European deadlock over arms limitations, a deadlock which was deepening the bitterness in Germany—but French and British opposition brought it to nought, and the move had come too late anyhow. He labored with a recalcitrant Congress in the fervent hope of balancing the budget—and won only a partial victory. Anxiety sat heavy upon him. As he hurried from his desk to a quick luncheon and back again, he hardly spoke to members of the White House staff in the corridors, but passed them half-unseeing, a frown upon his face. Democrats like Garner who gave him scant co-operation he regarded with wrath; the White House correspondents found him suspicious, unwilling to hold press conferences, resentful of attacks upon him in the press. No man in the White House had ever struggled harder and seen his efforts so scantily rewarded.

In August things seemed to be looking better. The Bonus Army—that hateful reminder of a bitterness and distress of which he was already painfully conscious—had been driven from the city. Better still, the business index had turned upward. A conference in Lausanne, which had ended German reparations, appeared to have eased the financial tension in Europe. Gold was no longer leaving the United States; indeed, by the end of August over a third of the gold that had been frightened away in the latter months of 1931 and the early months of 1932 had returned. The RFC had slowed up the rate of bank failures. And once again the stock market was showing healthy plus signs. Perhaps at last the corner to prosperity had been turned, and even if Hoover lost the election he might go down in history as the man who had seen the United States through the crisis.

Already, however, the campaign was upon him, and to the terrific burdens of the Presidential office he had to add the burden of drafting long speeches in self-defense—dictating them in the Lincoln study to relays of stenographers, correcting the typewritten copy, rushing it to the printer, and then laboriously going over the proofs sentence by sentence with his advisers. Every statistical evidence of improvement in the economic situation must be used to the utmost; every Hoover move against the Depression must be dramatized as a battle in a winning war; he must defend even the Smoot-Hawley tariff and warn his audience that if a Democratic tariff were put into effect "the grass will grow in the streets of a hundred cities" and "weeds will overrun the fields of millions of farms."

Sometimes, on his speech-making tours, he was heartened by roars of vigorous applause—but again there would be evidences of hostility, as when a group of jeering demonstrators gathered opposite a station when his train stopped and threw into a group of his aides a 150-watt electric-light bulb which exploded with a startlingly bomblike sound. So near was Hoover to complete exhaustion that on one of the last nights of the campaign, when he was on his way across the country to vote at Palo Alto, he lost his place repeatedly in his address at St. Paul, and throughout the address a man sat behind him gripping the arms of a chair and ready to push it under the President if he should collapse.

More debonair was Roosevelt as he went about the country preaching his New Deal. The Democratic candidate was less vague, now, than he had been. For his Brain Trust, now much enlarged and established in a suite in the Roosevelt Hotel in New York, was strenuously rounding out a program for him—or rather, a series of programs which sometimes conflicted with the plans of his more conservative advisers, if not with one another.

Roosevelt was explicit in his promise of financial reforms such as the regulation of securities and commodity exchanges, the regulation of holding companies, the separation of commercial and investment banking, the protection of investors through demands for full publicity about issues of securities. He was explicit about the need for a "competitive tariff" and for reciprocal tariff negotiations. He demanded that the Federal government develop power projects on the Columbia and Tennessee Rivers, and elsewhere, and use them as "yardsticks" with which to measure the service given by private utilities. Calling for control of crop surpluses, he defined the objectives of what was later to be the AAA, and he promised that the Federal government would lighten the load of farm mortgages. He insisted that it owed its citizens the positive duty of stepping into the breach when the states were unable to meet the burdens of relief. He came out for old-age insurance and unemployment insurance. At the Commonwealth Club in San Francisco he gave a real indication of the attitude he was to take during his Presidency when he insisted that "private economic power is . . . a public trust," and that "continued enjoyment of that power by any individual or group must depend upon the fulfillment of that trust." Yet at the instance of his more conservative advisers he came out also for a "definite balancing of the budget," berated the Hoover Administration for its extravagance, and promised drastic Federal economies. Furthermore, he said definitely, when questioned, that he was for "sound money"—which was generally taken to mean the gold standard; he said that "no responsible government would have sold to the country securities payable in gold if it knew that the promise—yes, the covenant—embodied in these securities was . . . dubious. . . ." Needless to say, he was explicit about repeal of the Prohibition Amendment; on this point opinion had so clearly swung his way that there was next to no danger in being positive.

Those critics who had earlier been uneasy at Roosevelt's light-footedness were still uneasy. There were still ambiguities and contradictions in the program: how, for example, could a Federal government assume so many duties and obligations and simultaneously reduce expenses? And just what did "sound money" mean? It was difficult to judge the

real significance of a program which contained so many
potential contradictions. But Roosevelt's confidence was
infectious, his smile was winning, and the times were on his
side. The business upturn which had so encouraged Hoover
in the late summer was flattening out, the stock market was
definitely turning down after its sally, and with every month
of continued hard times the general desire for change became
more intense.

Election Day came—and that night the rejoicing was not
in Palo Alto but at the Democratic headquarters at the Biltmore Hotel in New York, where Roosevelt and Farley and
one or two others heard the good news in a secluded room
while happy crowds of Democrats milled about outside. For
Roosevelt had won 472 electoral votes to Hoover's 59—had
carried every state but Connecticut, Delaware, Maine, New
Hampshire, Pennsylvania, and Vermont.

So Franklin D. Roosevelt was to be President. But what
sort of President? That depended upon events to come as well
as upon himself—upon circumstances which neither he nor
anybody else could foresee.

§ 6

There followed a strange interregnum. Business recovery
was stalled again (from fears of what Roosevelt might do,
claimed the Republicans). Congress, meeting in December,
was more definitely insurgent than ever, and turned a deaf
ear to the defeated President. Nor was the President-elect
co-operative. Hoover wished to make preparations for a
world economic conference, and also to set up a debt-funding
commission to deal with European requests for revision of
the war debts, and he felt that he could not fairly do either
of these things without the approval of Governor Roosevelt
as the incoming President. He invited Roosevelt to a conference; Roosevelt politely came to the White House, where

he and Hoover sparred conversationally, each man being attended by a second as if for a verbal battle. But nothing came of the conference, nor of a second one, nor of other Hoover suggestions for joint action in "restoring confidence." Hoover suggested that Roosevelt issue a statement assuring the country that "there will be no tampering or inflation of the currency," and Roosevelt—after a long delay —replied that he doubted if a mere statement would do much good. The President-elect wouldn't play ball.

To Hoover it seemed perfectly clear that a recovery which he had helped to start was being dissipated through Roosevelt's refusal to co-operate. And his anger was all the more vehement because he believed that the bank panic which was developing was due to Roosevelt's silence (now that the campaign was over) about inflation of the currency, and to a general fear of what the wild men of the Democracy might do after March 4. There were explicit stories going about to the effect that Roosevelt had said he favored inflation. Hoover was told that Professor Tugwell had spoken jauntily of the danger of a general bank closing and had said, "We should worry about anything except rehabilitating the country after March 4," adding that one of the first Roosevelt moves might be "reflation if necessary." ("Reflation" was a current euphemism for inflation.) This was too much: Hoover wrote furiously to his informant that Tugwell "breathes with infamous politics devoid of every atom of patriotism." The unhappy President believed that Roosevelt was irresponsibly ready to see the country go to pot in order to get the credit for rescuing it.

On the other hand, Roosevelt felt that as a private citizen until March 4, he himself must not join in Presidential action; and also that it was unreasonable to expect him to tie himself to the policies of an unsympathetic and already discredited administration—especially when the situation was changing fast and his own plans, different from Hoover's at many points, were still in flux. Both positions were natural under the circumstances; one need only add that the real villain of the piece was the antiquated political arrangement by which an administration had to remain in nominal power for nearly four months after it had been rejected at the polls.

Slowly and uncertainly the drama of Presidential frustration proceeded—and then suddenly, about the middle of February, 1933, when Hoover's term of office had less than three weeks to run, it went into double-quick time. The banking system gave way.

Again and again during the preceding year or two there had been local bank panics; the Federal Reserve had come to the rescue, RFC money had been poured in, and a total collapse had been averted. Now a new panic was beginning, and it was beyond the power of these agencies to stop. Perhaps the newspaper publication of the facts about RFC loans was a factor in bringing about this panic—though to say this is to beg the question whether a banking system dependent upon secret loans from a democratic government is not already in an indefensible position. Probably the banks would have collapsed anyhow, so widely had their funds been invested in questionable bonds and mortgages, so widely had they been mismanaged through holding companies and through affiliation with investment companies, so lax were the standards imposed upon them in many states, and so great was the strain upon the national economy of sustaining the weight of obligations which rested in their hands. At any rate, here at the heart of the national debt-and-credit structure a great rift appeared—and quickly widened.

On the 14th of February the condition of some of the banks in and about Detroit had become so critical that Governor Comstock of Michigan ordered an eight-day bank holiday for the State. All over the country there began a whispering, barely audible at first, then louder and louder:

"Trouble's coming. They say there's a run on the trust company down the street. Better get your money out of the bank." The murmur ran among the bankers: "Trouble's coming. Better sell some bonds and get cash before it's too late. Better withdraw your balances on deposit in New York." It ran among the men of wealth: "Better put everything into cash. Get gold if you can." It spread to Europe: "Better get gold out of the United States. Better sell the dollar." The financial machinery of the country began to freeze into rigidity, the industrial and commercial machinery to slow down. Nor was there anything that Hoover could do to stop the panic. Laboring ceaselessly, sleeping no more than five hours a night, he saw all the ground he had gained since June being lost.

§ 7

Faster moved the clock of history.

On the 15th of February—the day after the Michigan bank closing—the whole course of events in America was nearly altered by an assassin. In Miami a man named Zangara fired several shots at Roosevelt in a crowd, missed him, fatally wounded Mayor Cermak of Chicago.

The next day—the 16th—the Senate voted to repeal the Prohibition Amendment. Four days later—on the 20th— the House followed, and the issue of repeal went to the States for their action, which by the following December was to make the country legally wet again. (This change in the Constitution required not only a two-thirds vote in both Senate and House—which had been secured—but the approval of conventions in three-quarters of the states.) The supposedly impossible was happening, with consequences to be felt in every American community; another landmark was being quickly swept away by the tide of change.

During all these days there were continuous and feverish

attempts to set the Michigan banking situation straight. In
Detroit the bankers and motor manufacturers labored over
rescue plans; the wires between Detroit and New York and
Washington hummed with anxious talk between the President, the RFC officials, the Federal Reserve officials, Ford
and Chrysler and Sloan, Senator Couzens, and the Michigan
bankers and officials—and no solution was found. Meanwhile armored trucks were running by night from city to
city, carrying cash for beleaguered banks. The Federal Reserve figures were showing sharp increases in hoarding,
sharp losses of gold by the United States, as the panic became
intensified.

On Tuesday, February 21, Roosevelt announced that
his Secretary of State would be Cordell Hull of Tennessee
and his Secretary of the Treasury would be the smiling little
manufacturer, William H. Woodin of New York. (Roosevelt had wanted Carter Glass for the Treasury, but Glass
had realized that Roosevelt was ready if necessary to leave
the gold standard and inflate the currency, and would not
accept; Woodin, a comparatively unknown man, was a
second choice.)

On the same day began the disclosure, by witnesses before
a Senate committee, of some of the most disturbing facts
yet revealed about the behavior of the lords of American
finance during the preceding years. Charles E. Mitchell,
chairman of the big National City Bank in New York, admitted under the questioning of Ferdinand Pecora that he
had received bonuses totaling over three million dollars
from his bank and its affiliates during 1927, 1928, and 1929
—and yet, by selling some bank stock to a member of his family at a loss, he had avoided paying any income tax in 1929,
even though he later repurchased the stock. The next day
it was learned that after the Panic of 1929 the bank had
protected its high officials who had been trading in its own
stock, but that underlings in the bank's employ had had to

pay in full, in installments, for stock which had meanwhile lost most of its value. Though there was nothing criminal about these operations—there were worse things brought out by Pecora later—they were peculiarly infuriating to the sense of democratic fair play. The effect of such disclosures as these, at such a time, upon the attitude of the country toward the big bankers was profound; it was as if a smouldering fire of distrust and disapproval had burst suddenly into flame.

On Friday, the 24th, there were runs on Baltimore banks and Governor Ritchie declared a Maryland bank holiday. On Saturday and Sunday the panic became serious in three Ohio cities. On Monday, the 27th, Mitchell resigned from the chairmanship of the National City Bank; the champion of bull market banking had abdicated before a rising public opinion. The panic was now spreading through Ohio and Indiana into Kentucky and Pennsylvania.

Nor were the only dramatic changes in America. On the evening of the 27th the Nazis burned the German Reichstag, attributing the fire to the Communists; in that conflagration German democracy was effectively destroyed. The new Chancellor, Adolf Hitler, was now swiftly on his way to supreme dictatorship. At the other side of the world, the Japanese government, which had invaded Manchuria in 1931 when the Western world was distracted with financial panic, was marching on into Jehol in complete defiance of the disapproval of the League of Nations. Internationally as well as within the United States, an old order was giving place to new.

Faster, faster.

On Wednesday, the first of March, two more states declared state bank holidays; that evening another four were added to the list. On March 2, ten more fell in line. In numerous cities outside the bank-holiday states, banks were by this time remaining open only on a restricted basis. That same day Roosevelt went by special train from New York to Washington—and spent most of the journey talking with Farley about men's need of religion in the crises of their lives. Jaunty and carefree as he seemed, he knew that he was riding into a hurricane which would presently confront him with the responsibility, not only for making instant and unprecedented decisions, but also for directing in America that insurgency which, the world over, was following upon economic collapse. The unrest which was spreading among the farmers and the unemployed; the anger which was rising against the financial overlords; the longing for a magic formula, manifested in the excitement over Technocracy—these resentments and hopes were his to satisfy. If he could not satisfy them . . .

By March 3—the eve of inauguration—the financial storm was battering at Chicago and New York, the financial strongholds of the country. The tie-up was almost complete. Hoover was making desperate last-minute efforts to work out a solution, but they were unavailing. And at 4:30 in the morning of March 4, the strongholds surrendered: Governor Lehman of New York proclaimed a state bank holiday, and almost simultaneously Governor Horner proclaimed one in Illinois. At 6 o'clock a worn and haggard Hoover got up to perform the last routine tasks of his Presidency. He was told that on his last morning of office the banking system of the United States had stopped functioning.

"We are at the end of our string," said he. "There is nothing more we can do."

The stage manager of history had been too cruelly precise. For all Hoover's asperities, his awkwardness, his political ineptitudes, he had been a resourceful and resolute soldier of a doomed order, and deserved no such personal humiliation. But now the curtain was coming down and he could do no more.

Chapter Five

NEW DEAL HONEYMOON

§ 1

SATURDAY, March 4, 1933.

Turn on the radio. It's time for the inauguration.

There is a tension in the air today—a sense of momentousness and of expectation. When you went downtown this morning you found the banks shut; if you lived in New York State or in Illinois this may have been your first inkling of the general bank closing, since the closing orders in those states had come too late for the early editions of the morning papers of March 4. On the door of each bank was pasted a little typewritten notice that it had been closed at the Governor's order; people by twos and threes went up and read the sign and walked away. Your first thought, perhaps, was that you had only a little money in the house—five dollars, was it? ten dollars?—and you wondered how you would manage when this was used up, and what would happen next. Then you began to realize the significance of this financial stoppage.

Well, it's come at last, you thought. Here is that day of doom that people have been dreading. Just now it isn't so bad; there is a tingle of excitement, the sort of thrill you get from a three-alarm fire. But what next? This may be only the beginning of the crack-up. The one thing you want to hear, that everybody wants to hear, is the inaugural address. All over the country people are huddled round their radios, wondering what Roosevelt's answer to disaster will be.

Here's the voice of a radio reporter describing the prepara-

tions for the inauguration ceremony at the east front of the
Capitol in Washington—the notables coming to their places
on the platform, the dense crowds flooding the Capitol
square below under a chill, cloudy sky. The reporter is talking with all the synthetic good cheer of his kind—bearing
down hard on the note of optimism, in fact, for he knows
that worried and frightened people are listening to him. He
describes Hoover coming alone, gravely, to his place on the
platform; then Roosevelt coming up a ramp on the arm of
his son James. The ceremony begins. You hear Chief Justice
Hughes administer the oath of office; you hear Roosevelt's
reply, phrase by phrase, uttered clearly and firmly. Then
comes the inaugural.

The new President's voice is resolute. It comes into your
living room sharply.

"President Hoover, Mr. Chief Justice, my friends," the
voice begins. "This is a day of national consecration, and I
am certain that my fellow Americans expect that on my
induction into the Presidency I will address them with a
candor and a decision which the present situation of the
nation impels. This is pre-eminently the time to speak the
truth, frankly and boldly. Nor need we shrink from hon-
estly facing conditions in our country today. This great
nation will endure as it has endured, will revive and will
prosper. So, first of all, let me assert my firm belief that the
only thing we have to fear is fear itself—nameless, unreason-
ing, unjustified terror which paralyzes needed efforts to
convert retreat into advance."

This doesn't sound like "prosperity is just around the
corner" talk. It sounds like real confidence.

The voice goes on to blame "the rulers of the exchange of
mankind's goods" for the troubles of the country. "True,
they have tried, but their efforts have been cast in the pattern of an outworn tradition. . . . The money changers
have fled from their high seats in the temple of our civiliza-

tion." Through the radio comes a burst of applause: after the bank smash-ups and scandals, this condemnation of the big financiers expresses the mood of millions of Americans.

The voice speaks of the primary need of putting people to work; of the need for "making income balance outgo"; of the need for an "adequate but sound currency" (sharp applause for that!); promises a "good neighbor" policy in foreign affairs, but says domestic affairs must come first. Most striking of all, however, is the constant emphasis upon the need for action. Again and again comes the word "action." And after the new President has said he believes that the sort of action which is needed may be taken under the Constitution, the loudest applause of all comes for his declaration that if the occasion warrants he will not hesitate to ask for "broad executive power to wage a war against the emergency, as great as the power that would be given to me if we were in fact invaded by a foreign foe."

A ten-strike, this declaration. For the people have been sick of watching an Executive devote his strongest energies to opposing action, however questionable: they want a positive policy.

"We do not distrust the future of essential democracy," the President continues. "The people of the United States have not failed. In their need they have registered a mandate that they want direct, vigorous action. They have asked for discipline and direction under leadership. They have made me the present instrument of their wishes. In the spirit of the gift I take it."

You can turn off the radio now. You have heard what you wanted to hear. This man sounds no longer cautious, evasive. For he has seen that a tortured and bewildered people want to throw overboard the old and welcome something new; that they are sick of waiting, they want somebody who will *fight* this Depression for them and with them; they want leadership, the thrill of bold decision. And not only in his words but in the challenge of the very accents of his voice he has promised them what they want.

If only the performance measures up to the promise!

§ 2

Action there was, in abundance; and it came fast.

On Sunday, March 5, the day after the inauguration, the new President not only called Congress to meet in special session on Thursday, but also issued a proclamation putting the bank holiday on a national basis and prohibiting the export of gold and all dealings in foreign exchange. (Thus the country went at least part way off the gold standard—on a temporary basis.)

On Thursday Congress met and passed with a whoop a law validating everything that the executive had done to date and tightening still further its control over banking operations, gold, silver, currency, and foreign exchange.

On Friday the President asked Congress for immediate action to cut Federal expenses to the bone—and Congress rushed at the task, despite the political distastefulness of slashing the veterans' allowances.

On Saturday—after a week of furious activity at the Treasury, during which regulations were devised and altered, plans for the issue of clearing-house certificates were made and abandoned, plans for the issue of new currency were promulgated, and a rough classification of banks into more and less sound was made with the aid of advice from Federal Reserve Banks and chief national bank examiners—the President announced that most of the banks of the country would open the following Monday, Tuesday, and Wednesday.

On Sunday night the President, in his first "fireside chat," explained to the people of the country with admirable simplicity, clarity, and persuasiveness just how the re-opening of the banks would be managed and how his hearers could help to make the process orderly.

On Monday, the 13th of March, the banks began to open. And on the same day the President asked Congress to legalize beer—thus closing his tremendous first ten days of office on a note of festivity.

Such were the bare facts of those ten days. But the mere catalogue of them gives little idea of their overtones of significance, or of what those ten days were like to the American people.

The predicament of the incoming Administration was staggering. A new President and new Cabinet, unaccustomed even to the ordinary routine of their positions, largely unacquainted with their staffs, and forced to rely heavily upon the services of Hoover officials who stayed on to help them, had to deal with an unprecedented emergency which confronted them with unforeseen problems. Everything had to be done at top speed. Nobody could tell what might be the future cost of mistakes made under such pressure. Nobody could be sure, for that matter, that this was not just the first of a progressive series of emergencies which would bring conditions infinitely worse. Never did a green Administration seem to be walking into such a potential hornet's nest of difficulties.

But other circumstances aided them. In the first place, the accident of fate which had been so cruel to Hoover gave the country an Administration which could start from scratch in its race against panic, unhandicapped by memories of previous failures. It is traditional for the American people to feel kindly toward a new administration and support its first moves; in this case the friendly feeling was not only ready-made but intense. An enormous majority of the population desperately wanted the New Deal to succeed. Even the Wall Street bankers were ready to give Roosevelt full powers and wish him well, wince though they might at being called money changers who had "fled from their high seats in the temple." They were badly frightened, their institutions were demoralized, their collective reputation was besmirched anyhow, their only hope lay in Roosevelt's success. The newspapers, too, were loud now with enthusiasm. For weeks they had been burying bank-panic news in the back pages; now they could let go—and out gushed, on the news pages and in the editorials, all that zest for whooping it up, for boosting, for delivering optimistic fight talks, that was innate and habitual in the American temperament. Congress, usually divided in opinion and intractable, became almost as unanimous and enthusiastic as a cheering section—because public opinion told them to. The Congressmen's mail was heavy, and the burden of it was "Support the President." It was as if a people rent by discords suddenly found themselves marching in step.

There was another favorable circumstance. In *The Folklore of Capitalism*, Thurman W. Arnold tells of a conversation he had, before the bank panic, with a group of bankers, lawyers, and economists. They were one and all aghast at the possibility of a general bank closing. "My mind," said one of them, "fails to function when I think of the extent of the catastrophe that will follow when the Chase National Bank closes its doors." Mr. Arnold told his friend Professor Edward S. Robinson about this conversation, and found him unaccountably cheerful. "Do you think," asked Professor Robinson, "that when the banks all close people will climb trees and throw coconuts at each other?" Mr. Arnold replied that this seemed to him a little unlikely but that a bank crash of such magnitude suggested to him rioting and perhaps revolution. Whereupon Professor Robinson said, "I will venture a prediction. . . . When the banks close, everyone will feel relieved. It will be a sort of national holiday. There will be general excitement and a feeling of great interest. Travel will not stop; hotels will not close; everyone will have a lot of fun, though they will not admit that it's fun at the time."

Despite the fact that indirectly the bank holiday brought new distress, through new curtailments of business and new layoffs, and intensified the suffering of many people who were already hard hit, Professor Robinson was essentially right. The majority of Americans felt a sense of relief at having the lid of secrecy blown off. Now everything was out in the open. They felt that this trouble was temporary. They felt no shame now in being short of money—everybody seemed to be. They were all in the same boat. And they responded to one another's difficulties good-naturedly.

The grocer lent credit (what else could he do?), most hotels were glad to honor checks, shops were cordial about charge accounts. The diminished advertising columns of the newspapers contained such cheerful announcements as "IN PAYMENT FOR PASSAGE WE WILL ACCEPT CHECKS OR PROPERLY AUTHORIZED SCRIP" (this was in the early days of the bank holiday, when the issue of clearing-house scrip appeared likely); "RADIO CITY HAS CONFIDENCE IN AMERICA AND ITS PEOPLE—until scrip becomes available our box offices will accept checks"; "WE WILL TAKE YOUR CHECK DATED THREE MONTHS AHEAD for a three months' supply of Pepsodent for yourself and your family."

True, the shopping districts were half deserted; on the upper floors of department stores, clerks were standing about with no customers at all; there was a Saturday air about the business offices, trains were sparsely filled, stock exchanges and commodity exchanges were closed. But in the talk that buzzed everywhere there was less of foreboding than of eager and friendly excitement. "Are they going to put out scrip?—and how do we use it?" "What's a 'conservator'—is that a new word?" "You say you had thirty dollars on you when the banks closed? Well, you're in luck. I had only three-fifty—I'd planned to go to the bank that morning." "They say the Smiths stocked their cellar with canned goods last week—three months' supply; they thought there was going to be a revolution!" "Did you see those pictures of the gold hoarders bringing bags full of gold back to the Federal Reserve Bank? Those birds are getting off easy, if you ask me." "Mrs. Dodge beat the bank holiday all right— overdrew her account last Friday. No, not intentionally. Just a mistake, she says. Shot with luck, I call it." "Stop me if you've heard this banker story: it seems that a banker died and when he got to the gates, St. Peter said. . . ."

To this public mood President Roosevelt's first fireside chat was perfectly attuned. Quiet, uncondescending, clear, and confident, it was an incredibly skillful performance. (According to Raymond Moley's *After Seven Years*, the first draft of this chat was written by Charles Michelson of the Democratic publicity staff; Arthur Ballantine, Under Secretary of the Treasury for Hoover, completely rewrote it; Roosevelt revised it.) The banks opened without any such renewed panic as had been feared. They might not have done so had people realized that it was impossible, in a few days, to separate the sound banks from the unsound with any certainty, and that errors were bound to be made. The story goes that one bank had been in such bad shape that its directors decided not even to put in an application to re-open; through a clerical slip this bank was put on the wrong list, received a clean bill of health, and opened with flying colors! In some places, to be sure, there were bank runs even after the opening—runs which had to be met unquestioningly with Federal funds, lest the whole trouble begin over again. And so many banks had to be kept shut anyhow that ten per cent or more of the deposits of the country were still tied up after March 15, and the national economic machinery thus remained partially crippled. On the whole, however, the opening was an immense success. Confidence had come back with a rush; for the people had been captivated and persuaded by a President who seemed to believe in them and was giving them action, action, action.

The New Deal had made a brilliant beginning.

§ 3

The next few months in Washington provided a spectacle unprecedented in American history. The pace at which the New Deal had started its career slackened hardly at all. The administrative hopper produced bill after bill, the President passed the bills on to Congress with terse recommendations for passage, and Congress—almost as if mesmerized—passed them, often with scant debate, sometimes without an opportunity for all the members to read them, much less comprehend their full significance. Never before except in wartime had the Executive been so dominant over Congress. Never before, even in wartime, had a legislative program been pushed through with such terrific speed and daring.

The very air of Washington crackled. Suddenly this city had become unquestionably the economic as well as the political capital of the country, the focus of public attention. The press associations had to double their staffs to fill the demand for explanatory dispatches about the New Deal bills. And into Washington descended a multitude of men and women from all over the country.

First there were bankers by the thousands, thronging the corridors of the Treasury, buttonholing their Senators to explain just why their banks should be permitted to re-open, and converging upon an emergency office set up in the Washington Building by the Acting Comptroller of the Currency—an office in which four men found themselves the bottleneck of communication between the banking system and the government. Amid the hammering of workmen putting up partitions, these men were trying simultaneously to hire stenographers and clerks, to draft regulations and letters, to interview importunate bankers, and to deal with incoming telephone calls which were backed up two and three days by the congestion of appeals from all over the country. Every banker had his own story to tell— his own account of how his mortgages had been undervalued by the bank examiners, or an entire community was dependent upon his institution. Some of them brought their directors along. Who could deal with these men? So terrific was the strain of those first days that on at least two nights the Acting Comptroller of the Currency went home only to take a shower, change his clothes, and go back to work; when he did snatch a few hours' sleep, his wife had to sit by a constantly ringing telephone and explain that he might not be disturbed. Another high official would lie down on a couch in the office of the Secretary of the Treasury, go to sleep, be awakened by a question, answer it, and drop off to sleep again.

In that GHQ at the Treasury during the bank holiday there was an almost continuous executive conference, day and night. Woodin and Moley, Democrats; Mills, Ballantine, and Awalt, Republicans, were the nucleus of a group which labored without thought of party. Even in their brief intervals of rest the problems remained with them; at breakfast on the Tuesday morning after the Inauguration little Woodin reported to Moley how he had solved the knotty question of whether and how to issue scrip: "I played my guitar a little while and then read a while and then slept a little while and then awakened and then thought about this scrip thing and then played some more and read some more and slept some more and thought some more. And, by gum, if I didn't hit on the answer that way! . . . We don't have to issue scrip!" The ordeal of twenty-hour days was too much for Secretary Woodin; his health had not been good, and there are those who think that it was the labor and responsibility of those weeks in March which killed him; he died the following year.

Droves of Democratic office-seekers, too, were descending upon Washington: so many of them that Postmaster-General Farley, whom they knew to be the chief patronage dispenser of the Administration, found them haunting the corridors of his hotel; he "virtually had to slip back and forth to his office like a man dodging a sheriff's writ," and he found that the only way to get rid of the hordes that packed his reception room at the Old Post Office Building was to make the rounds of the room five or six times a day with his secretary, taking down the name of each individual and a brief description of the sort of job he sought.

Experts and specialists of all sorts were coming into town to help in the framing of new laws and regulations and in the setting up of new government agencies. Financiers and their lawyers and brief-case-toting assistants were coming to take the witness stand in Ferdinand Pecora's intermittently sensational investigation of the scandals of the banking world. Special emissaries from Great Britain, Canada, France, Italy, Argentina, Germany, Mexico, China, Brazil, Japan, and Chile arrived in quick succession, each with his entourage, to consult with the President and his advisers on economic and diplomatic problems; from Great Britain came Ramsay MacDonald, the Prime Minister; from France came Edouard Herriot, the Premier; there were receptions, conferences, dinners, long discussions between groups of experts, in endless and fatiguing succession.

To Washington as by a magnet were drawn, too, innumerable idealists, enthusiasts, radical national-planners, worldsavers of all degrees of hard- and soft-headedness, each with his infallible prescription for ending the Depression.

Meanwhile into the White House poured thousands of plans for recovery, for the great American public wanted to help. They ranged, these plans, from semi-literate scrawls on ruled paper to 175-page mimeographed booklets with graphs and statistical tables, and they displayed a touching confidence that the President himself would carefully consider their suggestions. (All these plans were read, considered, and politely acknowledged—but not by him.) "In the present national emergency," began a characteristic letter, "surely I will be pardoned if it is presumptuous to bring views to your attention. If the ideas are in the least beneficial then the end will justify the beginning." And another: "Being one of those Americans who love their country and having a sort of an idea which may have some merit, I am taking the presumptuous liberty of passing it along to you in this letter." Business men, bankers, students, housewives, unemployed laborers, they had ideas and threw them into the hopper.

Furious work was being done in Washington in that spring of 1933. The lights burned late in government offices as the architects of the New Deal, official and unofficial, drafted bills and regulations and memoranda, tore their drafts to pieces and began all over again, and then rushed off to consult other groups and revise and revise again. In the vast new office buildings along the Mall there was sublime confusion as new jobholders arrived and began searching for their offices, for desks, for people who could tell them what they were supposed to do. Government departments were overflowing into office buildings everywhere; and the streets were full of apartment-hunters, while the real-estate men of Washington rubbed their hands at the sudden boom in the housing market.

§ 4

Out of all this pandemonium emerged in short order an extraordinary array of new legislative measures. To summarize the chief ones very briefly:—

1. Devaluation.

After the banks opened there was a prompt improvement in business, but during the first few weeks it was only moderate. The President became impatient; and Congress, likewise impatient, became so enamoured of the idea of inflating the currency that a bill sponsored by Senator Wheeler of Montana, providing for the free coinage of silver on the old Bryan basis of 16 to 1, almost passed the Senate despite Roosevelt's opposition. Under these circumstances Roosevelt took the plunge off the gold standard. Half convinced that some sort of inflation was necessary anyhow as a shot in the arm for the American economy; unwilling to let Congress take the initiative away from him and force the country into some ill-devised inflation scheme; and convinced that if it were done when 'tis done, then 'twere well it were done quickly, Roosevelt on April 19th placed an embargo on gold —thus serving notice that the gold standard had been definitely abandoned. Then he laid before Congress a bill— which was passed—giving him permissive authority to inflate in any one of five ways if he saw the need to do so.

Shortly afterward there followed a law which forbade the issue of bonds, governmental or corporate, payable in gold, and which abrogated all existing contractual obligations to pay bonds in gold. Still later, when the World Economic Conference, assembling in London, turned to the international stabilization of currencies as its first important task, Roosevelt heaved a bombshell into it—with distressing damage to the prestige of his own delegation—by refusing to let the United States be a party to even a vague and general stabilization agreement at that juncture. And from time to time, while these moves were going on, he declared his intention to raise American prices "to such an extent that those who have borrowed money will, on the average, be able to repay that money in the same kind of dollar which they borrowed." (It was not until later in 1933 that he devalued the American dollar progressively to 59.06 cents, in terms of its former gold value, through the amazing—and none too successful—scheme of progressively raising the price which the United States would bid for gold.)

The result of these various orders, laws, and statements in the spring of 1933 was to bring about a quick jump in prices, a burst of upward activity on the stock exchanges and commodity exchanges, a hurried buying of supplies by business men for their inventories in expectation of further rises in prices, and a much sharper recovery of business than had previously seemed likely. It is difficult to disentangle causes and effects when a government is doing everything at once, but the evidence would seem to show that the shot in the arm administered in the spring of 1933 had a definitely stimulating effect. (In fact, there would seem to be room for the somewhat cynical comment that of all the economic medicines applied to the United States as a whole during the nineteen-thirties, only two have been of proved general effectiveness, and both of these have a habit-forming tendency and may be lethal if too often repeated: these two medicines are devaluation and spending.)

2. *Crop Control.*

The New Deal came to the rescue of the farm population with a bill which aimed to raise the prices of the major American farm crops by offering payments to farmers to leave part of their acreage unplanted. The money for the payments was to be raised by a processing tax, which in effect was a light sales tax on the consumption of these crops—penalizing everybody a little in order to help the hard-hit farm population. (With cotton the method was different: the crop having already been planted, rewards were offered for plowing up part of it.) The complicated business of administering this Act was entrusted to an Agricultural Adjustment Administration—AAA for short.

The promise of the AAA program, along with the promise

of inflation, lifted farm prices sharply in the spring of 1933, and thus brought early and substantial relief to the farmers; the effect of the AAA after it went into full operation in 1934 was more debatable, and was obscured anyhow by subsequent droughts.

3. Stimulating Employment.

Roosevelt's pet scheme for putting a quarter of a million young men into the woods for conservation work was quickly approved by Congress, and presently the young men of the CCC were off to army camps and then to the forests. There was also passed a bill providing $3,300,000,000 for public works—a staggering sum by Hoover standards. (Roosevelt's heart was not in the public-works program, it was difficult to spend any large amount of money quickly and yet wisely on dams, bridges, and other major works, and therefore slow progress was made; a good deal of the $3,300,000,000 was diverted into relief and national defense.)

4. Federal Relief.

To aid the unemployed—whose condition was desperate— the Federal government went for the first time on a large scale into the distribution of relief funds. These, in the early months of the New Deal, were mostly dispensed through state and local machinery; but the new assumption of responsibility was nevertheless significant.

5. The Tennessee Valley Experiment.

Not only did a bill passed in May, 1933, provide for the Federal operation of that subject of long previous argument, the dam at Muscle Shoals; it provided also for an ambitious development of the whole Tennessee Valley through the building of other Federal dams, through the sale of power from them at low prices, and through Federal subsidizing of conservation measures in the Valley. This bill—which went considerably beyond Roosevelt's campaign proposals—was perhaps the most revolutionary measure of the early New Deal in its long-term significance, for it put the government directly into industry and into a dominating position in developing a whole section of the country.

6. Lightening the Debt Burden.

Federal agencies were set up to refinance farm and home mortgages, lowering the interest rate on them and putting a Federal guarantee behind them, thus easing the back-breaking pressure of debt on farmers and other householders —and, incidentally, further freezing the debt-structure of the country.

7. Financial Reforms.

A Securities Act was passed which provided that those who issued securities must provide the government with full—in fact voluminous—information about the enterprises to be financed. And a banking act was passed which, though it did not grapple with the knotty problem of unifying the banking system of the country, struck at certain conspicuous abuses: it provided that no banking house might both accept deposits and issue securities, and it forbade commercial banks to have securities affiliates. (These reforms were the forerunners of others to come.)

Last in our list, but far from least, there was set up

8. The NRA.

The genesis and motivation of the NRA provide a beautiful example of the wild confusion of those honeymoon days of the New Deal, and deserve special mention. The NRA's paternity was multiple, to say the least.

Soon after the bank holiday Senator Hugo Black (of subsequent Supreme Court fame) pushed through the Senate a bill decreeing a thirty-hour week in all businesses engaged in interstate commerce; and although the measure was held up by a motion to reconsider, the size of the Senate vote and the fact that the House was giving a favorable reception to a similar measure (the Connery Bill), showed that Congress meant business. (Here was NRA idea No. 1: spread employment by shortening hours of labor.) Thereupon Secretary of Labor Frances Perkins insisted any such bill must contain a minimum-wage provision. (Here was idea No. 2: "put a floor under wages.") By this time the President and various members of his Administration had become worried over the possibility that wholesale and inflexible legislation on hours and wages might prove a Pandora's box of troubles, and had begun to wrestle with ideas for a more flexible and comprehensive Administration measure, which could be substituted somewhat as the discretionary inflation bill had been substituted for the Wheeler Bill.

A number of business men also swung into action. For a long time the Chamber of Commerce of the United States had been opposing what it called "cut-throat competition" and had wanted the Sherman Anti-Trust Act modified so that trade associations might set wages and adopt "codes of practice" with governmental permission. Hoover had flatly opposed any such scheme as monopolistic—as allowing established companies to combine to prevent, not only "cut-throat competition," but all real competition of any sort. Roosevelt seemed to have no such fears—and the business men saw their opportunity. (Thus arose idea No. 3: "self-government for business," with the trade associations doing the governing under government auspices.)

Meanwhile there was also much enthusiasm among the young liberals in Washington for the idea of "national planning" for industry. Impressed by the Russian Five-Year Plan, they wanted the government to regulate the functioning of the helter-skelter American business system. (Here was idea No. 4.) There was a widespread hope, too, chiefly among these same liberals, that purchasing power might be expanded by a concerted raising of wages—on the theory that if the raising were general no business would suffer and all would benefit. (Idea No. 5.)

Each of these ideas was represented in the framing of the National Industrial Recovery Act.

After numerous conferences of various groups of men of diverse economic philosophies, there emerged as the principal artificer of the project a man whose own central interest was in the Chamber of Commerce idea: a former Army officer, former plow manufacturer, and protégé of Bernard Baruch named General Hugh S. Johnson, who had worked in the Brain Trust group during the campaign and now had a desk in the office of Raymond Moley, the new Assistant Secretary of State. And there emerged a bill which provided that each industry, through its trade association, would write for itself a "code" prescribing maximum hours and minimum wages and rules of fair competition for that industry, subject to the approval of the government. What was thus prescribed and approved might be done regardless of the Sherman Act, and in fact might not be transgressed under penalty of the law. Since the men who were thus to be allowed to organize and write their own codes were the employers, the Department of Labor insisted that their employees should also be permitted to organize; and so was written into the National Industrial Recovery Act the famous Section 7a, which stated that "employees shall have the right to organize and bargain collectively through representatives of their own choosing, and shall be free from the interference, coercion, or restraint of employers of labor or their agents." For further protection for labor and for consumers there were elaborate provisions for setting up Labor Advisory Boards and Consumers' Advisory Boards, to make sure that every interest was consulted.

On June 16, 1933, the National Industrial Recovery Act was signed amid much fanfare. Said President Roosevelt, "History probably will record the National Industrial Recovery Act as the most important and far-reaching legislation ever enacted by the American Congress." On that same day General Johnson was named Administrator of the NRA. And it became obvious that this unprecedented organization was to be the focal point of the whole New Deal program of 1933.

Having produced the NRA, Congress adjourned, bringing to an end what was indeed an extraordinary session.

§ 5

The contrasts between this 1933 New Deal program and the Hoover program were sharp. It was not a program of defense but of multiple and headlong attack. In most of the laws and certainly in the intent behind them there was a new emphasis on the welfare of the common man; a new attempt, as was often said, to build prosperity from the bottom up rather than from the top down. There was a new willingness to expand the scope of government operations; for a long time past these had been expanding out of sheer political and economic necessity, as the inevitable long-term tendency toward centralization took effect upon government as well as upon business, but now the brakes were removed and the expansion was abrupt. Also in contrast was the visible distrust by Roosevelt of the bankers and corporate insiders of Wall Street; Hoover had leaned upon them for advice and assistance (which was not always forthcoming), Roosevelt disregarded them. He preferred the assistance of supposedly impartial (if impractical) professors to that of supposedly practical (if partial) business men. There was a new encouragement of labor unions, a new hospitality to liberal and radical ideas which would reduce the power of the owning class. The governmental center of gravity had moved to the left.

At the same time the program represented a strange jumble of theories. For example, the Economy Act—and to a certain extent the financial reform measures—had a deflationary effect; whereas devaluation—and to a certain extent the public-works plan and the Federal relief plan—had an inflationary effect. The AAA bill tried to bring recovery by inducing scarcity—as did much of the NRA as it later developed; whereas the public-works and TVA plans operated on the abundance theory. The conferences with foreign emissaries and the plans for international economic cooperation ran head on into the devaluation policy—with a resounding explosion in London. The financial reform measures sought to discourage concentrations of economic power; the NRA—in practice—tended to encourage them.

In addition to these conflicts of theory, there were numerous collisions between governmental organizations trying to do the same thing, between organizations trying to do opposite things, between old policies being pursued as a matter of habit and new ones being introduced.

Some of these conflicts were due, of course, to the sheer impossibility of achieving legislative and administrative perfection at a hand gallop. Some were due to the fact that Washington was full of able and eager men with contrasting ideas: in a multitude of counselors there is confusion. Some were due to the political necessity of devising measures which could win the support of diverse interests. And some were due to the fact that the New Deal program of those first few months was like a geological formation built up in several layers. At the bottom were the old-fashioned liberal measures, the economy and reform measures, of the 1932 platform. On top of these were the more ambitious programs adumbrated by the Brain Trust during the campaign and after, and other measures hustled into action when the bank panic produced a much graver crisis than had been foreseen in early 1932. Then there were the measures which grew, perforce, out of the bank panic itself—including, if you wish, devaluation. On top were the bright ideas that bloomed in the fertile spring of 1933; chief among these was the NRA, which was a whole plum pudding of contrasting elements in itself. Yet even if one took account of all these reasons for inconsistency, there remained something in Roosevelt's try-everything attitude which reminded one of the man who, feeling unwell, took in quick succession all the tonics on the shelf.

But if the President preferred bold action to careful deliberation, so too did the country. The sickness of the economic system was infinitely complicated and little understood. Now a physician had come along who had a lot of medicines in his bag, who had an air of authority and an agreeable bedside manner; and the American people hailed him with delight. His medicines were better than most which were currently suggested, and certainly the patient's morale was improved by having a friendly physician who was willing to do something and not just wait for nature to effect a cure. In the spring and summer of 1933 the American economic system took its new medicines cheerfully, sat up in bed, and said, "I feel better already."

§ 6

What a flood tide of returning hope was running in those first six months of the New Deal!

That was the season when the Chicago Fair opened—that Fair whose intention to chronicle "A Century of Progress" had seemed only a few months before so unmitigatedly ironical. What did Chicagoans care if Sally Rand stole the show with her fan dance? She too had been a victim of the Depression, earning a precarious living dancing in small-time cabarets in Western cities, and her fortunes had sunk low in 1932; in her own reported words, she had "never made any money until she took off her pants"; but now the crowds surged to see her come down the velvet-covered steps with her waving fans (and apparently nothing else) before her, and Chicago profited. General Balbo's armada of Italian airplanes flew to the fair; and in that same summer of 1933 Charles and Anne Lindbergh, leaving behind them for a time the scenes of their tragedy, flew to Greenland, to proceed thence to Europe and Africa and—*Listen! The Wind*—to South America.

That was the season when the Senate Banking Committee drew from the Morgan partners the story of the "preferred lists" of subscribers to the stock of their corporations; and when the orderly processes of financial exemplification were interrupted, to everybody's dismay, by a circus promoter who placed a midget in J. P. Morgan's lap. It was the season when the country first became wonderingly aware of the extent to which the amiable First Lady of the land embodied the law of perpetual motion; and when her husband, after putting his name to the National Industrial Recovery Act, climbed aboard the little *Amberjack II*, put on his oilskins, and went sailing up the New England coast to Campobello.

That was the season when Max Baer knocked out Schmeling in the tenth, and the massive Primo Carnera knocked out champion Jack Sharkey in the sixth, and an unidentified man almost knocked out Huey Long in the Sands Point washroom, and Glenn Cunningham began breaking the running records for the mile, and *Anthony Adverse* began breaking records for fiction sales as it enthralled lovers of vicarious adventure on thousands of summer porches.

Once more the business men of the country began to know hope. The Federal Reserve Board's adjusted index figure for Industrial Production in the bank-holiday month of March, 1933, had been 59 (as against 58 for the preceding July, the month of the Bonus March). In April it jumped from 59 to 66; in May it jumped to 78; in June, to 91; in July, to 100 (as against a 1929 high of 125). There was no such proportionate gain in employment, to be sure; for as the pace of business increased, there was much slack to be taken up simply by working factories full time that had been working part time, by working office clerks overtime, by keeping shopgirls on the run. Still there remained millions of unemployed men, whose poverty was as yet unrelieved by any Federal expenditures for their aid. So greatly had the Depression stimulated working efficiency and the installation of labor-saving devices that a far sharper increase in production than this would be needed to give jobs to those men. Nor were the men who went back to work any too tractable. They had suffered, they had become embittered, and as hope returned, anger rose with it: strikes began to increase in number. The mood of the farm population was still rebellious, for until their crops were harvested the rise in farm prices would do them little good; the speculators would get the money. There were still riots and disorders in the farm belt. But the prospects were promising. "Give us just a few months more of this improvement . . ." men said to themselves.

The speculators leaped into action. As the stock market spurted, out of the highways and byways came the little stock gamblers. For three and a half years they had been telling themselves—if they had any money left—that speculation was no more for them. During the past few months they had been in the grip, most of them, of a mounting distrust of Wall Street bankers in particular and all bankers in general, and had been telling and re-telling derisive anecdotes in which bankers figured. But when they began to see the plus signs among the stock quotations, back to the brokers' offices they thronged, ready to stake their last savings on Commercial Solvents and Standard Brands and the alcohol stocks; and meanwhile as cold-blooded a lot of pool operators as had ever been seen in the unregenerate days of 1929 manipulated and unloaded, manipulated and unloaded. The Securities Act had been signed, reform was the order of the New Deal day, one might have expected these gentry to be newly cautious; but all such considerations apparently meant nothing to them. So violently did the stock market boil, so frequently were there five- and six-million-share days, that the total volume of trading in the month of June, 1933, and again in the month of July, 1933, was greater than it had been in any single month in the Big Bull Market of 1929—with the sole exception of the Panic month of October. Meanwhile the grain market and the other commodity markets boiled too. Who could lose? argued the little speculators. "If we don't have prosperity we'll at least have inflation." (In 1932 the thought of inflation had prompted selling, now it prompted buying: the mood had changed.)

Late in July the stock and commodity markets broke badly, and day after day the speculators' favorites tumbled; one of these favorites, American Commercial Alcohol, actually collapsed from 89⅞ to 29⅛ in four days. But at that very moment the President was having distributed to business men all over the country the blanket NRA code that would "start the wheels turning." It was difficult to find a daily paper which did not contain somebody's glowing tribute to the NRA. It had "abolished child labor," it was introducing "a new era of co-operation between industry and government," it was "an attempt to substitute constructive co-operation for destructive competition," it would cause "management and labor to join hands," it would "end the flat-wallet era," and it held out "the promise of a new day." The break in the markets checked confidence a bit; but was it not predicted that millions of men would go back to work "before the snow flies"?

In Washington the excitement was still feverish. Congress had adjourned, but now the business men were there by the bewildered thousands to draw up NRA codes. Up and down the interminable corridors of the Commerce Building they tramped, buttonholing any hatless man to ask their way, under the impression that he must be a high official.

They wanted their own codes, industry by industry, and cach of them had his own idea of what ought to go into his code to stop the particular kind of "cut-throat competition" that his company hated. But first these men had to find out what industry they belonged to. Was candlewick-bedspread-making a part of the cotton-textile industry, or should it have a code of its own? Shouldn't the dog-food industry insist on special treatment? And where should the academic costume men go to solve their code problems? And the fly-swatter manufacturers? Where was General Johnson's office? And who was this "Robbie" whose ear it was considered so valuable to get? And might it not be better to go back to the Mayflower and confer there, even though the hotel telephone service was so jammed that you couldn't get a connection?

In the center of this wild confusion—as Jonathan Mitchell wrote—General Johnson "sat at ease, coat off, blue shirt open at the neck, red-faced, and looking uncannily like Captain Stagg in Stallings and Anderson's 'What Price Glory.' Like captured peasants, squads of sweating business men . . . were led in before him." Part cavalry officer, part veteran business man, part economic seer, part government administrator (he could assume any of these roles at will, said Mitchell), the General coaxed or prophesied or wisecracked or thundered as the occasion seemed to warrant, and the business men would go forth obediently—or so they felt at the moment—to do his bidding. So completely did the General captivate the Washington newspaper men that they began to regard the NRA as the center of the government exhibit and the White House as a side show. His vehement oratory, his references to "cracking down on the chiselers" and to the "dead cats" of criticism, his torrential enthusiasm, held the country spellbound. General Johnson had become the personification of Recovery.

When you went to the movies to see "Cavalcade" (that

life-preserver with TITANIC on it!), or "Mädchen in Uniform," or "Reunion in Vienna," you would see also a short
picture, accompanied by a voice thrilling with patriotism,
telling how America was marching on to prosperity under
the slogan "We do our part." The Blue Eagle appeared in
shop windows, in advertisements. There were splendid
NRA parades, with thousands marching and airplanes dron-
ing overhead. Grover Whalen organized a New York compliance campaign enlivened by the appearance of Miss
Nira (short for National Industrial Recovery Act) and Miss
Liberty; 150 women from the Bronx marched to NRA
headquarters bearing 250,000 pledges and accompanied by
a brass band; it was estimated that a quarter of a million
people marched in New York and a million and a half
looked on, and it cost $4,980.70 to clean up the streets
afterwards.

Yes, America was on its way. Though the stock market
looked ragged as the summer came to an end, and the
business indices had slipped back from the pinnacle of July,
and doubts and disagreements were beginning to cloud the
brightness of the economic and political skies, still the prevailing mood of the general public was aptly reflected in the
song of the three little pigs in Disney's new picture, then
going the rounds of the movie houses: America had learned
to sing "Who's Afraid of the Big Bad Wolf?"

Chapter Six

A CHANGE OF CLIMATE

§ 1

THE processes of social change are continuous and endlessly complex. To contrast the manners and morals and customs of one historical "period" with those of another is surely to over-simplify and almost surely to exaggerate. Yet the social climate does alter, just as the seasons do change—even though the shifts in temperature from day to day may be highly spasmodic and Detroit may be enjoying its "first day of spring" while Philadelphia is being swept by a blizzard. Looking back, one notices various contrasts between the social climate of the nineteen-twenties and that of the nineteen-thirties; and one notices, too, that most of these changes did not become clearly marked until about the year 1933, when the New Deal came in and the Eighteenth Amendment was repealed. It is almost as if the people of the United States had walked backward into the Depression, holding for dear life to the customs and ideals and assumptions of the time that was gone, even while these were one by one slipping out of reach; and then, in 1933, had given up their vain effort, turned about, and walked face-forward into the new world of the nineteen-thirties.

The post-war decade had brought to America a sharp revolution in manners and morals—a revolution the shock troops of which were a younger generation addicted to knee-length skirts, hip flasks, mixed drinking in the speakeasy, petting in the parked car, uninhibited language, a second-hand knowledge of Freudian complexes, and a disposition to defy their more puritanical parents and ridicule the whole Puritan tradition. Already by the end of the nineteen-twenties the revolution was playing itself out, at least in the centers of population where Puritanism had been most readily undermined. The older generation were gradually becoming accustomed to the outlandish ways of their progeny and relaxing somewhat their own codes of conduct, and the younger generation were getting older and learning the practical advantages of moderation. By the time of the Panic, the "Flaming Mamie" of the coeducational campus, though she still won admirers, was a little less likely to be regarded as a portent of the future than as a relic of the past. As the nineteen-thirties got under way, the change in the climate became clearly discernible.

Not that there was any measurable increase in abstinence, continence, or modesty; indeed there were some areas— some Middle-Western towns, many country villages—where the proprieties of an earlier day had been only slowly broken down and the sound of breakage was still loud; where the behavior of the "young married set" at the Saturday night rout at the local country club was more abandoned than ever, and where parents were comparing horrified notes about that appalling "new" phenomenon, the tendency of girls of fifteen and sixteen to come back from high-school parties smelling of gin and disturbingly rumpled. Said the Lynds of their findings in "Middletown," ". . . one got in 1935 a sense of sharp, free behavior between the sexes (patterned on the movies), and of less disguise among the young. A high-school graduate of eight years ago, now in close touch professionally with the young people of the city, was emphatic as regards the change: 'They've been getting more and more knowing and bold. The fellows regard necking as a taken-for-granted part of a date. We fellows used occasionally to get slapped for doing things, but the girls don't do that much any more.' "

Yet in the country at large there was a change of mood, a change of emphasis. The revolution was being consolidated. The shock troops were digging in in the positions they had won.

A neat measure of this change was offered in Hornell Hart's study of social attitudes in *Recent Social Trends*, which appeared at the beginning of 1933. Mr. Hart set forth the results of a careful statistical study of the beliefs and points of view reflected in the magazines of the country at various times. This study showed that the rebellion against the traditional code of sex morals—or, to put it another way, the rush of sentiment in favor of sex freedom—had reached its peak in the years 1923-1927; and although the magazines contained more discussions of family and sex problems during 1930 and 1931 than at any time during the preceding years, the tone was on the whole more conservative. In the year 1930 the magazines expressed more approval of marriage and family life, more approval of "comradeship, understanding, affection, sympathy, facilitation, accommodation, integration, co-operation" than in 1920.

If the change of mood became more striking as the years rolled by and the Depression deepened, one may ascribe this to a number of causes: the fact that any idea palls after a time, any bright new revolution begets doubts and questionings; the fact that young Mr. X, whose alcoholic and amorous verve had seemed so brilliantly daring in 1925, was now beginning to show not altogether attractive signs of wear and tear; the fact that Mrs. Y, who had so stoutly believed in her right to sleep where she pleased and had been sure that she didn't care with whom Mr. Y slept, had found she couldn't take it after all and had marched off to Reno; the fact that the Z children were having nightmares which the school psychiatrist attributed to the broken home from which they came; and the fact that the younger brothers and sisters of the X's and Y's and Z's were tired of seeing their elders carom against the furniture and make passes at one another, and concluded that these old people were a messy lot. But the most important reason for the change was probably the Depression.

Hundreds of thousands of young people who wanted to get married could not afford to. The song "I Can't Give You Anything But Love, Baby" dated from 1928, but it might well have been the theme-song of the nineteen-thirties. The marriage rate per thousand population fell from 10.14 in 1929 to 7.87 in 1932. (Likewise the birth rate per thousand population also fell, from 18.9 in 1929 to 17.4 in 1932 and 16.5 in 1933—the 1933 figure reflecting, of course, largely the economic conditions of 1932.) When it was so difficult to marry, an increase in pre-marital sex relations was almost inevitable. "A confidential check-up of one group of more than two dozen young business-class persons in their twenties," reported the Lynds, "showed seven out of every ten of them, evenly balanced as to sex, to have had sexual relations prior to marriage." The huge sales of con-traceptives—totaling, annually, according to various author-ities, from an eighth to a quarter of a billion dollars, and transacted not only in drugstores but in filling stations, tobacco stores, and all sorts of other establishments—were certainly not made only to the married.

Yet the new state of affairs was hardly conducive to a frivolous or cynical attitude toward marriage and the fam-ily; and it pushed into the forefront of attention a relatively new problem: what was to be the future of the jobless young man and his girl, who loved each other deeply and really wanted to marry? Were they to postpone marriage and live resolutely apart? Or prevail upon their families to support them, perhaps letting them live in the spare room or the attic or some other corner of a parental home?

Often the elders could ill afford to feed another mouth;

and many a father who had slaved and scrimped for years, dreaming of retirement, and who now wondered how long his own job would last, blazed with anger to hear that young Harry had brought home a bride to consume the family savings. There were other elders who could well afford to shelter a young couple but who had been brought up to believe that no self-respecting young man married until he could support a wife, and who would cling to this idea, talk about a spoiled generation, tell how *they* hadn't *thought* of marrying till they were making forty dollars a week, and refuse to countenance any such nonsense. As a result, many young couples accepted as an alternative to immediate marriage an occasional night in a cheap hotel room or an auto-tourist cabin (many of these tourist cabins accepted, knowingly or innocently, a large proportion of local traffic). Hating the furtiveness of such meetings, hating the conventions which made them furtive, these young couples nevertheless felt their behavior was right—a response to necessity.

To many others, even less fortunate, the jobless children of jobless parents, the wandering nomads of the Depression, hitch-hiking through the country, riding the freight cars, sex became something that you took when you could; marriage was too remote to think about. Yet even here there was something new about the mood. There was little sense of a change in the moral code being willfully made, little sense that stolen love was "modern" adventure. The dilemma was practical. One managed as best one could, was continent or incontinent according to one's individual need and one's individual code, whether of morals or aesthetics or prudence or convenience. If the conventions were in abeyance, it was simply because the times were out of joint and no longer made sense; but that did not mean that one might not long for wedded security.

Among the hatless and waistcoatless young men of the college campuses, with their tweed coats and flannel slacks, and among the college girls in their sweaters and tweed skirts and ankle socks, there was little of the rebellious talk about sex and marriage that had characterized the nineteen-twenties, little of the buzz of excitement that had accompanied the discussion of Freud and Havelock Ellis and Dora Russell. Whether there was less actual promiscuity is doubtful: a study of 1364 juniors and seniors in 46 colleges and universities of all types from coast to coast—made by Dorothy Dunbar Bromley and Florence Haxton Britten—showed that half the young men and a quarter of the girls had had pre-marital sex intercourse. The striking thing was that there was less to-do about sex. One's personal affairs were one's personal affair. As the editors of *Fortune* said in their account of the college youth of 1936: "As for sex, it is, of course, still with us. But the campus takes it more casually than it did ten years ago. Sex is no longer news. And the fact that it is no longer news is news."

The Depression also cut the divorce rate sharply: it dropped from 1.66 per thousand population in 1929 to only 1.28 per thousand population in 1932. Divorces cost money; and besides, in times of stress the fancy is likely to be less free. There was a good deal of pious talk about the way in which couples were re-united in love by hardship, but it is likely that in most cases what the hardship did was to subordinate everything to the stark necessity for getting along, love or no love. After the worst years the divorce rate rose again; no great reform had been effected; people who couldn't get on still separated when they must and could. Yet here again there was a change in emphasis: a more wide-spread sense of the damage inevitably done by a wrecked marriage to the children and to the separated partners themselves. It was perhaps significant that a public-opinion poll taken by *Fortune* in 1937 showed a majority against easy divorce. A similar poll in 1936 showed 63 per cent in favor of the teaching and practice of birth control, and in

1937 as many as 22.3 per cent approved of pre-marital experience *for both men and women*: there was no return to the old Puritan code. Yet there was a strong disposition to protect going marriages.

In short, although there was considerable public acceptance of pre-marital sex relations as inevitable and not sinful, and a tendency to approve of what one observer had called "a single standard, and that a low one," nevertheless marriage seemed to have become more highly prized as an institution than in the nineteen-twenties. The family seemed to have become more highly prized as an institution. "Sixty per cent of the college girls and fifty per cent of the men would like to get married within a year or two of graduation, and fifty per cent of each sex would like to have children soon after marriage," reported the editors of *Fortune* in their 1936 survey. The fact that the college girls of the nineteen-thirties were more eager for early marriage than those of the nineteen-twenties was noted by many college administrators. These same undergraduates and their contemporaries were on the whole less scornful of their parents and of parental ideas, less likely to feel that family life was a mockery, than the young people of ten years before.

Not only had the Depression made them more respectful of a meal ticket and of security; they had become preoccupied with other things besides intimate personal relationships, as we shall presently see.

§ 2

The vagaries of fashion are so haphazard and are influenced by so many business expediencies that one cannot ascribe them wholly to changes in the social climate. Yet in their main outlines they at least provide suggestions worth correlating with other evidences of the social trend.

If, for example, the women's fashions of the nineteen-twenties called for short skirts, a great reduction in the weight and cumbersomeness of clothes, a long-waisted, flat-fronted figure, and short hair cut in a Dutch bob or shingled almost like a boy's, surely here was a hint that women had become tired of the restrictions and responsibilities of conventional maturity and wanted a freedom and gaiety that they associated with immaturity: not the freedom of an old-fashioned little girl, sheltered and innocently pretty, but of an aggressively "modern" one—hard-boiled, "sophisticated" (to use a favorite complimentary term of that day), and ready to carry on with the boys. If the mannikins in the shop-windows and the sketches in the department-store advertisements gave the well-dressed woman a hard, blank, world-weary expression, here again was a hint as to the feminine ideal of the nineteen-twenties: she was a girl who, even before her figure had ripened, had become old in experience, had passed beyond the possibility of shock or enduring enthusiasm. And if, during the early years of that decade, the tail coat was a rarity among men and the dinner jacket was the standard wear even for the most formal occasions, here was a hint that the men, as well as the women, were in revolt against dignity and formality. In the nineteen-twenties, Americans wanted to be boys and girls together, equipped for a wild party but refusing to let it be thought that even the wildest party would arouse in them more than a fleeting excitement.

Now notice what happened later. Already before the end of the nineteen-twenties the tail coat was coming in again, with all the dignity that it conveyed. By 1929 the women's evening dresses were tentatively reaching for the floor—and for an effect of graciousness impossible to achieve with a knee-length gown. By 1930 they definitely were long—to remain thus, actually or virtually sweeping the floor, for the rest of the decade. And the women's daytime dresses gradually lengthened too until by 1933 they reached to within a foot or even nine inches of the ground. The severe helmet hat of 1929, pulled down on the back of the head, gave way to a variety of styles all of which sought at prettiness, pertness, a gentler or more whimsical effect than had been aimed at in the 'twenties. Women's hair, too, became less severe, was curled at the back of the head more gaily. Ruffles came in, bows, furbelows, with nostalgic hints of the prettiments of long-dead days. Gone was the little-girl long-waisted effect; the waist returned where it belonged.

As for the flat figure, that was abandoned too. Said *Vogue* in April, 1932, "Spring styles say 'CURVES'!" By 1933, when the amply contoured Mae West was packing the motion-picture theatres in "She Done Him Wrong," Lily of France was advertising "the new boneless Duo-Sette," saying, "It beautifully emphasizes the uplift bust," and Formfit, illustrating a new creation with pictures of young women whose breasts were separately and sharply conspicuous, was calling attention to "the youthful, pointed, uplifted lines it will give you." The flat-breasted little girl of the nineteen-twenties had attained maturity and was proud of it; indeed so striking was the change between the ideal figure of 1929 and that of 1933 that one might almost have thought a new anatomical species had come into being.

There was a subtle change, too, in the approved type of femininity as represented in the department-store advertisements and the shop-window mannikins. The new type of the early nineteen-thirties was alert-looking rather than bored-looking. She had a pert, uptilted nose and an agreeably intelligent expression; she appeared alive to what was going on about her, ready to make an effort to give the company a good time. She conveyed a sense of competence. This was the sort of girl who might be able to go out and get a job, help shoulder the family responsibilities when her father's or husband's income stopped; who would remind them, in her hours of ease, of the good old days before there were all-determining booms and depressions, the sentimental old days which Repeal itself reminded them of; and who would look, not hard, demanding, difficult to move deeply, but piquantly pretty, gentle, amenable, thus restoring their shaken masculine pride.

Nothing stands still, and as the years went on new changes took place. So many more women of the upper and middle classes were working now than had worked in the pre-Depression years that in their daytime costumes simplicity and practicality were in demand. The prevailing style of hairdress for younger women (a shoulder-length or almost shoulder-length page-boy or curled bob) was likewise simple—and incidentally very lovely: in years to come it may be that one of the most charming recollections of the nineteen-thirties will be of hatless girls striding along like young blond goddesses, their hair tossing behind them. (One recalls the complaint of a young man that almost every girl appeared good-looking from behind: it was only when he overtook her that disillusionment came.) When in the fall of 1938 an attempt was made to get women to put their short hair up, it only half-succeeded: it was too hard to manage.

Yet the impulse toward old-fashioned decoration, frivolity, and impractical eccentricity was all the time at work. There were attempts to re-introduce, in evening dresses, such ancient encumbrances as the bustle and the hoop skirt. Ruffled and pleated shirtwaists—with jabots—reappeared. The sandal idea, winning a rational approval for evening wear, was carried over irrationally into daytime wear, so that during the latter years of the decade half the younger women in the country were equipped with shoes with a small hole in front, which presented a stockinged toe to the eye and offered easy entrance to dust, gravel, and snow. As for the hats of those same latter years, here the modern principle of standardized functional utility surrendered utterly to the modern principle of surrealist oddity.

There were huge hats, tiny hats, hats with vast brims and microscopic crowns, hats which were not hats at all but wreaths about the hair; high fezzes perched atop the head; flat hats, dinner-plate size, which apparently had been thrown at the wearer from somewhere out in front and had been lashed where they landed with a sort of halter about the back of the head; straw birds' nests full of spring flowers, hats with a single long feather pointing anywhere—but why continue the interminable catalogue of variations? It was characteristic of the times that a woman lunching at a New York tearoom in 1938 took the bread-basket off the table, inverted it on her head, and attracted no attention whatever.

Maturity, too, began to pall. Gradually the skirts became shorter and shorter (except in the evening); by 1939 they had retreated almost to the knees. "Little-girl" costumes, "girlish ginghams," "swing" outfits "adapted from skating skirts" were bidding for attention, and the massive president of the woman's club was wondering whether she should try to insert herself into a bolero suit and put one of those bows in her hair. Apparently the old-fashioned little girl was becoming the standard type of the new day—unless the fashion makers should succeed in their attempt, late in 1939, to make her a grown-up old-fashioned woman (at least after nightfall), with a bustle, a wasp waist, and a boned corset startlingly like that in which her grandmother had suffered. Whether the new fashions would last or not, and just what they signified, it was still too early to predict.

§ 3

At thirty-two and a half minutes past three (Mountain Time) in the afternoon of the 5th of December, 1933, the roll call in the ratification convention in Utah was completed, and Utah became the 36th State to ratify the Twenty-first Amendment to the Constitution, repealing the Prohibition Amendment. A telegram went off to Washington, and presently the Acting Secretary of State and the President declared that Prohibition was at an end, after a reign of nearly fourteen years.

Crowds of men and women thronged the hotels and restaurants waiting for the word to come through that the lid was off, and when at last it did, drank happily to the new era of legal liquor. They thronged, too, to those urban speakeasies which had succeeded in getting licenses, and remarked how readily the front door swung open wide at the touch of the doorbell. But the celebration of the coming of Repeal was no riot, if only because in most places the supply of liquor was speedily exhausted: it took time for the processes of distribution to get into motion. And as for the processes of legal manufacture—which for distilled liquors are supposed to include a long period of aging—these were so unready that an anomalous situation developed. The available liquor was mostly in the hands of bootleggers; even the legal liquor was mostly immature. Among the people who, during the first days and months of repeal, rejoiced in at last being able to take a respectable drink of "good liquor" instead of depending upon "this bootleg stuff," thousands were consuming whisky which consisted simply of alcohol acceptably tinted and flavored. To a public whose taste had been conditioned for years by bootleg liquor, good bush needed no wine.

Drinking, to be sure, did not become legal everywhere. Eight States remained dry—all of them Southern except North Dakota, Kansas, and Oklahoma. (These states received—at least in the years immediately following repeal —very little assistance from the Federal government in protecting their aridity.) Fifteen States made the selling of liquor a State monopoly—though seven of these permitted private sale under varying regulations, most of which, in a determined effort to prevent "the return of the saloon," forbade perpendicular drinking and insisted—at least for a time—that drinkers be seated at restaurant tables.

Despite these qualifications, the change in the American *mores* which began in 1933 was tremendous.

Hotels and restaurants blossomed with cocktail lounges and taprooms and bars, replete with chromium fittings, mirrors, bright-colored modern furniture, Venetian blinds, bartenders taken over from the speakeasies, and bartenders who for years had been serving at the oyster bar or waiting on table, and now, restored to their youthful occupation, persuaded the management to put on the wine list such half-forgotten triumphs of their ancient skill as Bronx and Jack Rose cocktails. So little building had been going on during the Depression that the architects and decorators had had almost no chance for years to try out the new principles of functional design and bright color and simplified furniture; now at last they had it, in the designing of cocktail lounges—with the odd result that throughout the nineteen-thirties most Americans instinctively associated modernist decoration with eating and drinking.

Hotels in cities which in days gone by would have frowned upon the very notion of a night club now somewhat hesitantly opened night clubs with floor shows—and found they were a howling success. Neat new liquor stores opened —in some States operated by government authority, in others under private ownership. It took some time for customers to realize that it was no longer necessary for a man carrying home a package of rum to act the part of a man carrying home a shoe box; and in some towns where the dry sentiment was still strong, there were men who continued to patronize bootleggers rather than subject themselves to the embarrassment of walking into the State liquor shop.

Restaurants which in pre-prohibition days would never have dreamed of selling liquor installed bars and made prodigious sales; the tearoom proprietor wrestled with her conscience and applied for a license; and even the Childs' restaurants, unmindful of their traditional consecration to dairy products, pancakes, and calories, opened up slick circular bars and sold Manhattans and old-fashioneds. And if most of the metropolitan speakeasies withered and died, if the speakeasy tickets grew dog-eared in the pocketbook of the man-about-town and at last were thrown away, if the hip flask became a rarity, if the making of bathtub gin became a lost art in metropolitan apartment houses, and the business executive no longer sallied forth to the trade convention with two bottles of Scotch in his golf bag, so many bright new bars appeared along the city streets that drinking seemed to have become not only respectable but ubiquitous.

For a time there was a wishful thought among those of gentle tastes that when good wines became more accessible a good many Americans would acquire fastidious palates. G. Selmer Fougner, Julian Street, Frank Schoonmaker, and other experts in the detection and savoring of rare vintages preached their gospel of deference to the right wine of the right year, and for a time ladies and gentlemen felt themselves to be nothing better than boors if they did not warm inwardly to the story of how somebody found a little French inn where the Château Latour 1929 was incomparable. But the crass American nature triumphed; pretty soon it was clear that even in the politest circles whisky was going to be the drink in greatest demand.

Whether there was more drinking after repeal than before cannot be determined statistically, owing to the obvious fact that the illicit sale of liquor was not measured. The consensus of opinion would seem to be that drinking pretty surely increased during the first year or two, and probably increased in quantity thereafter, but that on the whole it decreased in stridency.

"Less flamboyant drinking is the present-day rule," said the *Fortune* survey of youth in college in 1936; "there is no prohibition law to defy, hence one can drink in peace." There were signs here and there of a reaction against drinking among the boys and girls of college age; observers reported some of them, at least, to be less interested in alcohol than their elders, and were amazed at the volume of their consumption of Coca-Cola and milk (Coca-Cola, long the standard soft drink of the South, had followed its invasion of the campuses of the Middle West by extending its popularity among the young people in the Northeast as well). The American Institute of Public Opinion, taking a poll in 1936 as to whether conditions were "better" or "worse" since repeal, or showed no significant change, arrived at a singularly inconclusive result: 36 per cent of the voters thought things were better, 33 per cent thought they were worse, 31 per cent saw no significant change: not only was the division almost even, but there was no way of knowing what each voter may have meant in his heart by "conditions" being "better."

One change was manifest: there was now more mixed drinking than ever, just as there was more smoking by both sexes. (In the six years from 1930 to 1936 the production of cigarettes went up from 123 billion to 158 billion, while the production of cigars decreased a little and that of smoking tobacco increased a little.) In fact, a phenomenon which had been conspicuous during the nineteen-twenties, when women smokers invaded the club cars of trains and women drinkers invaded the speakeasies, appeared to be continuing: there were fewer and fewer bars, restaurants, smoking cars, and other haunts set apart for men only: on the whole men and women were spending more of their time in one another's company and less of their time segregated

from one another. Perhaps it was not an altogether unrelated fact that most men's clubs were still somewhat anx-
iously seeking members throughout the nineteen-thirties
and that many of the lodges were in dire straits. Was it
not possible to infer that the male sex, for one, was enjoying
mixed company too well to want very urgently to get away
from it? Possibly the cause of feminism was triumphing
in a way which the earnest suffragists of a generation before
would never have expected—and at which they might have
been dismayed.

And what became of the bootleggers? Some of them went
into the legitimate liquor business or other legitimate occupations, some of them went into business rackets and
gambling rackets, some joined the ranks of the unemployed—and a large number of them went right on bootlegging. For one of the most curious facts about the post-
Repeal situation was that the manufacture and smuggling
and wholesaling of illicit liquor continued in great volume.
The Federal government and the States, in their zeal to
acquire revenue from the sale of liquor, had clapped upon
it such high taxes that the inducement to dodge them was
great. Year after year the Internal Revenue agents continued to seize and destroy stills at the rate of something like
15,000 a year, and straightway new ones sprang up. In
his report for the fiscal year ending June 30, 1938, the
Commissioner of Internal Revenue, reporting that only
11,407 stills had been seized, noted, "This is the first year
since the enactment of the Twenty-first Amendment that
there has been a decline in illicit distillery seizures." Likewise rumrunning—or, to be more accurate, the smuggling
of alcohol—continued to provide a headache for the customs
officers and the Coast Guard; in February, 1935, more than
a year after Repeal, the Coast Guard found twenty-two
foreign vessels lying at sea *at one time* beyond our customs
waters, waiting for a chance to sneak in.

HE CAPTURED THE HEADLINES

General Hugh S. Johnson, head of the NRA, who during the latter part of 1933 was
(with the possible exception of the President) the most publicized citizen of America

THE BIG APPLE
Taken at Glen Island Casino, New Rochelle, N. Y., 1938

So easy was it to operate illicit stills, to store bottles and counterfeit labels and counterfeit revenue stamps and alcohol cans in separate places, bottle the illicit liquor, transport it in trucks or automobiles equipped with traps, and offer a liquor store or saloonkeeper a consignment of spurious liquor at a bargain, that a year or two after repeal the best expert opinion was that anywhere from fifteen to sixty per cent of the liquor consumed in the United States was bootleg.

Were the American people glad that they had ended Prohibition? Apparently they were. A *Fortune* Quarterly Survey made late in 1937 showed that only 15.1 per cent of the men of the country and 29.7 per cent of the women wanted complete Prohibition back again. Even combining with this dry group those who were in favor of prohibition of hard liquors but would permit the sale of wine and beer, there was still approximately a two-thirds majority in favor of a wet regime. Americans might or might not think "conditions" were "better," but they did not—most of them—want to reopen the question.

Here and there a new wave of dry sentiment appeared to be forming. In Virginia, for instance, a scholarly book on the effects of alcohol, which was to have been distributed to the schools as a public document, came to the shocked attention of the WCTU at the end of 1937. Because the book contained such statements as, "It has been proved that we cannot abolish drinking by legislation nor frighten a person into sobriety" and "small quantities [of alcohol] may favor digestive activities," the WCTU exerted pressure on the legislature and the whole edition was solemnly burned in the Capitol furnace. In most communities, however, what had been a lively issue till 1933 had dropped almost completely out of the focus of general public attention, as if settled once and for all.

Could it really have been true, the men and women of

1939 asked themselves, that in 1929 Prohibition had been the topic of hottest debate in American public life?

§ 4

We come now to a series of changes in everyday American life during the nineteen-thirties which might seem at first glance to have been unrelated, but which combine, perhaps, into a sort of pattern—a pattern of relaxation.

1. *The five-day week.* During 1931 and 1932, when factories and business offices were short of work, there were very general reductions in hours—intended partly to "spread the work" and partly to appease workers whose pay must be reduced. When the NRA codes came into being in 1933 and 1934 these reductions were continued or extended. After the NRA was abolished most of them—though not all—were continued. The result was that millions of people, rich and poor, found themselves with Saturdays free during part of the year if not all of it. A study made by the National Industrial Conference Board in 1937 showed the extent of the five-day week: out of 2,452 companies (mostly manufacturing companies) reporting, 57.3 per cent had a five-day week for their wage earners, 45.3 per cent had a five-day week for their clerical workers, and 7.5 per cent reported a five-day week but did not specify what types of workers were included. "While five years ago the five-day week was exceptional," summarized the report, "it has now become quite general." Business offices followed a similar pattern in the larger cities (especially New York); and although few shops were closed on Saturdays, there was an increasing tendency among them to stagger the hours of their employees.

Perhaps no change that took place during the decade more sharply altered the weekly routine of millions of men and women. It altered the pattern of automobile and train traffic too, increasing the Friday rush out of the cities, decreasing the Saturday rush. I recall a certain train which until the Depression used to leave New York for Westchester County in two crowded sections every Saturday noon; by 1933 it was running in one modest section, so thin was the Saturday traffic—and presently a second section was added to one of the Friday evening trains. The two-day week end was supplanting the day-and-a-half week end. On Saturday mornings, especially in summer, the business districts of the larger cities were coming to wear a Sunday aspect. Quantities of people had gained new leisure—quite apart from those millions upon whom an unwelcome idleness had been thrust. The long slow trend toward shorter work periods and longer play periods, a trend which had been under way in America for as long as any living man could remember, had been sharply accelerated.

2. *A democratization of sport.* To the aid of men and women who had more leisure and less money came the relief and public-works agencies, putting millions of unemployed men to work building motor parkways, public bathing beaches, playgrounds, and other conveniences for people who were looking for sport. According to the 1935 *Year Book of National Recreation* the number of public bathing beaches, public golf courses, ice-skating areas, and swimming pools in 2,204 communities had already *doubled* since 1925. Some of these new facilities were built on a modest scale, but others were huge: Jones Beach on Long Island, for example, as magnificent an example of enlightened public planning as the decade produced, could and did comfortably accommodate one hundred thousand people or more on a sunny Sunday in midsummer.

Consider what happened to the game of golf. The Depression hit the private golf clubs hard. As many as 1,155 clubs had belonged to the United States Golf Association in 1930; by 1936 the number had been reduced to 763—

and this despite frantic drives for new members, special summer-membership schemes, and other rescue devices. The golf clubs of the country were said to have lost something like a million members since 1929. But the number of municipal golf courses grew from 184 in 1925 to 576 in 1935, and there were over a thousand courses—most of them probably private-club courses which had gone bankrupt—now operating on a daily-fee basis. In short, expensive golf had lost ground; inexpensive golf had gained.

In general the simpler and less pretentious sports made the best headway. Although school and college basketball, professional baseball, and college football were still pre-eminent as sports to watch, nevertheless in the older colleges and schools they attracted a somewhat less devout interest than in earlier years. Let the editors of *Fortune* (writing in 1936) summarize one element in the change: "The football star, the crew captain, the 'muscular Christian' from the college Y.M.C.A., the smoothie from the big prep school who becomes track manager, the socially graceful prom leader—these still have honor and respect. But the intellectually curious person, who used to be considered queer or 'wet' unless he had extra-intellectual characteristics to recommend him, is climbing past the conventional big man. Englishmen, long accustomed to spotting future undersecretaries of the Foreign Office . . . on visits to Cambridge and Oxford, have remarked on this mutation in American campus leadership, and are inclined to set 1932 as the date at which the mutation became apparent." Meanwhile there was a significant increase, in many colleges and schools, in the interest taken in *playing* games such as soccer, lacrosse, rugby, squash racquets, and tennis, which existed without benefit of massive stadia.

In the country at large, the game which made the biggest gain in popularity was softball—that small-scale version of baseball which had once been known chiefly as "indoor

baseball." Coming into its own at about the beginning of
the decade, it grew so fast that by 1939 there were said to
be half a million teams and more than five million players
of all ages; there were numerous semi-professional teams,
there were world's series matches, and among the semi-
professionals were girls' teams, the members of which delighted the crowds by wearing very abbreviated shorts but
occasionally sliding to bases nonetheless. The Depression
also brought minor booms in such sports as bicycling and
roller skating. The bicycling boom began as a fad in the
Hollywood area in the winter of 1932-33 (when it gave
California girls a fine excuse for putting on "trousers like
Dietrich's") and spread widely during the next two or three
years, chiefly, perhaps, because it was inexpensive.

The simultaneous skiing craze was a more complex phenomenon. For country dwellers who lived where the terrain and winter temperature were suitable it was inexpensive; for city dwellers who had to carry their equipment
long distances, it was not. Perhaps one secret of its rise was
the increasing vogue of winter holidaying, which itself had
a complex ancestry (the discovery of the delights of winter
holidaying in the warmth of Florida or California, the
rising popularity of winter-cruising and of motoring outside
the country to escape from Prohibition, the shortening of
the work week, the secularization of Sunday and the rise of
the week-end habit, etc.). At any rate the skiing craze grew
rapidly during the Depression, stimulated in 1932 by the
holding at Lake Placid, New York, of the winter Olympics.
The Boston & Maine Railroad had made such a success of
the experiment of running Sunday "snow trains" into the
comparatively wide open spaces north of Boston that by
1937 snow trains or snow busses were running out of New
York, Pittsburgh, Chicago, Portland, San Francisco, and
Los Angeles; department stores were importing Norwegian
specialists and building ski-slides; the Grand Central Station

in New York was posting prominently in its concourse the daily temperature and snow data for a dozen skiing centers in New England and New York, and rural hotelkeepers in icy latitudes were advertising their unequaled skiing facilities and praying nightly throughout the winter for the snowfall upon which their fortunes depended.

The skiing craze was beyond the means of the urban poor and was geographically limited; nevertheless it confirmed in one respect the general trend. More Americans were getting out into the sun and air; learning to play themselves instead of simply paying to see others play.

Women were purchasing strange new play garments, ranging from shorts to beach pajamas, overalls, slacks, and "play suits." More and more men were going hatless in summer, to the anguish of the hatters. For that matter, more and more men were going waistcoatless and soft-collared and garterless and undershirtless; it is said that when Clark Gable, in the undressing scene in "It Happened One Night" (1935), disclosed that he wore no undershirt, the knitwear manufacturers reeled from the shock to their sales. The bathing suit top had been generally discarded. Men at play were even beginning to break out into bright-colored playshirts, slacks, and shorts. By 1939 one saw men of conservative taste strolling unabashed through summer-resort villages in costumes whose greens and blues and reds would have drawn stares of amazement in 1929.

In short, so far as the tension of the times would permit, Americans were apparently learning to relax.

3. *An increase in bridge playing.* If one superimposes upon a graph of business conditions during the decade a graph showing the taxes collected on playing cards, one notices an odd variation. While the business index was plunging into the depths from 1929 to 1932, the index of playing cards manufactured, after dropping between 1929 and 1930, actually *rose* between 1930 and 1931, only to sag

thereafter and never recover to its 1931 point. The year 1931, it will be recalled, was the year when Mr. and Mrs. Ely Culbertson played contract against Sidney S. Lenz and Oswald Jacoby in a green-and-rose drawing-room at the Hotel Chatham in New York, with favored spectators peeking at them through a screen, star reporters clustering in a neighboring room to study the play-by-play bulletins, and direct news wires flashing to an eager public the narrative of some rather indifferent play. Throughout the following year Culbertson's books on bridge ranked high among the best sellers.

For a long time bridge had been a standard after-dinner sport among the adult prosperous; but now its vogue was spreading. The Lynds reported that in "Middletown" there was much more bridge played in 1935 than in 1925; there was more playing for money; the game had reached down through the high school to children in the sixth grade; and it was invading the working class, "spreading there first through the women's groups and then more slowly to a more resistant group of men, who prefer their pinochle and poker."

4. *An increase in gambling.* Allied, perhaps, to the increase in bridge playing was a notable increase in the number of gambling devices made accessible to the American people. Most of these were devices for wagering a small amount of money in the hope of a big return, and their rise may have been due largely to Depression desperation—the wild hope of winning in a gamble what the ordinary processes of the economic system stubbornly withheld. But they bore witness also to that weakening of the Puritan traditions which helped bring Repeal, the week end of motoring or sport, and the bridge vogue.

According to Samuel Lubell, the business of manufacturing and operating slot machines, punchboards, pinball games, jar deals, and other similar contrivances for separating the public from its nickels grew during the Depression to giant proportions, and in 1939 "its annual take was somewhere between one half and three quarters of a billion dollars—between ten and fifteen billion nickels"—as much money as was spent annually in the shoe stores. There was nothing new in principle about the slot machine, the improved model of which looked like a cash register and was known as a "one-armed bandit": the founder of the leading company engaged in manufacturing them had begun business in 1889 and had died in 1929, a millionaire. Slot machines had had a bad reputation, having been widely in the control of gangs and dependent for operation upon political "fix," yet they continued to flourish widely, sometimes one jump ahead of the police, sometimes with police connivance. And in 1932 a new game, pinball, was introduced which could be played simply for fun, at a nickel a turn, as well as with gambling intent, and it swept the country: pinball boards were to be found in unmolested operation in drugstores, tobacco stores, hotel corridors, cafés, and all sorts of other places. It was based upon the old game of bagatelle: the player shot marbles out of a chute and watched them run down a slope into holes partially protected by pins. The punchboard and jar games—the latter invented in 1933—also prospered; between 1933 and 1939 some two million jar games were sold.

A quite different kind of gamble was represented in the tremendous American participation in the Irish Sweepstakes, a lottery inaugurated in 1930 on behalf of a group of Irish hospitals, and conducted with such honesty and efficiency that within five years it had become the most successful lottery in the world. Although a Federal statute made lottery information unmailable in the United States and this at first prevented newspapers from printing accounts of the Sweeps in their mail editions, the ban on news publication was later relaxed, every Sweeps drawing became a front-page story, and Americans grew used to reading of janitors and unemployed chefs into whose astonished hands a hundred and fifty thousand dollars had dropped. Many of the tickets sold in the United States never reached Ireland; but if, in the drawing for the 1933 Derby, over six and a half million tickets were in the drum (as was estimated) and 214 of the 2,404 winners (or more than one in fifteen) were American, one may reasonably guess that there may have been over four hundred thousand Americans whose tickets actually got into that particular draw.

Nor should we forget, in any survey of the trend, the relaxation in many States of the laws against race-track betting; the "Bank Night" device of drawing for cash prizes in the movie theatres—a device introduced by Charles Urban Yeager in the Egyptian Theatre at Delta, Colorado, and the Oriental Theatre at Montrose, Colorado, in the winter of 1932-33, and subsequently copyrighted by him as it spread to thousands of other theatres, which by 1937 were paying Yeager's firm a total of $30,000 to $65,000 a week; the game of bingo (or beano, or keno), which became immensely popular as a money-making entertainment for churches, and in various forms was widely played in movie theatres and elsewhere, till in 1938 some people were referring to it as the most popular money game in the country; and possibly the pathetic epidemic of chain-letter writing which spread from Denver all over the United States in 1934-35 ("Scratch out the top name and send a dime"). Nor has this brief survey taken account of various older gambling devices which persisted, sometimes in new guises and under new sponsorship—as did the numbers racket when Dutch Schultz, the liquor racketeer, took over its management in the Harlem section of New York and systematized it during the last days of Prohibition.

In 1938 a Gallup poll revealed that during the preceding year an estimated 29 per cent of the American people—

meaning, one supposes, adults—had taken part in church lotteries (presumably including bingo parties), 26 per cent had played punch boards, 23 per cent had played slot machines, 21 per cent had played cards for money, 19 per cent had bet on elections, 13 per cent had taken sweepstakes tickets, 10 per cent had bet on horse races, and 9 per cent had indulged in numbers games. There were no Gallup polls in the preceding decade, but one wonders if any score even approaching that would have been made in the nineteen-twenties—unless, perhaps, playing the stock market and buying Florida real estate had been included in the gambles.

§ 5

Yet despite all these manifestations of gaiety, relaxation, and sport there was a new tension, a disquiet. For the Depression had wrecked so many of the assumptions upon which the American people had depended that millions of them were inwardly shaken.

Let us look for a moment at the pile of wreckage. In it we find the assumption that well-favored young men and women, coming out of school or college, could presently get jobs as a matter of course; the assumption that ambition, hard work, loyalty to the firm, and the knack of salesmanship would bring personal success; the assumption that poverty (outside of the farm belt and a few distressed communities) was pretty surely the result of incompetence, ignorance, or very special misfortune, and should be attended to chiefly by local charities; the assumption that one could invest one's savings in "good bonds" and be assured of a stable income thereafter, or invest them in the "blue-chip" stocks of "our leading American corporations" with a dizzying chance of appreciation; the assumption that the big men of Wall Street were economic seers, business forecasters could forecast, and business cycles followed nice orderly rhythms; and the assumption that the American economic system was sure of a great and inspiring growth.

Not everybody, of course, had believed all of these things. Yet so many people had based upon one or more of them their personal conceptions of their status and function in society that the shock of seeing them go to smash was terrific. Consider what happened to the pride of the business executive who had instinctively valued himself, as a person, by his salary and position—only to see both of them go; to the banker who found that the advice he had been giving for years was made ridiculous by the turn of events, and that the code of conduct he had lived by was now under attack as crooked; to the clerk or laborer who had given his deepest loyalty to "the company"—only to be thrown out on the street; to the family who had saved their pennies, decade after decade, against a "rainy day"—only to see a torrent of rain sweep every penny away; to the housewife whose ideal picture of herself had been of a person who "had nice things" and was giving her children "advantages," economic and social—and who now saw this picture smashed beyond recognition; and to the men and women of all stations in life who had believed that if you were virtuous and industrious you would of course be rewarded with plenty—and who now were driven to the wall. On what could they now rely? In what could they now believe?

One might have expected that in such a crisis great numbers of these people would have turned to the consolations and inspirations of religion. Yet this did not happen—at least in the sense in which the clergy, in innumerable sermons, had predicted it. The long slow retreat of the churches into less and less significance in the life of the country, and even in the lives of the majority of their members, continued almost unabated.

The membership rolls of most of the larger denominations, to be sure, showed increases. Between 1929 and 1937-38, for example, the Roman Catholic population increased from 20,203,702 to 21,322,608—a modest gain. The Methodist, Baptist, and Lutheran churches also grew in numbers. Yet membership figures are a notoriously uncertain measure of religious vitality. As regards the large Protestant—or nominally Protestant—population of the country, the observations of the Lynds, returning to "Middletown" in 1935 and contrasting the religious life of the city then with what it had been in 1925, offer probably a fairer measure.

The Lynds found some imposing new churches in "Middletown"—products of the hopeful days of the Big Bull Market—but inside the churches they saw little visible change. "Here, scattered through the pews," they reported, "is the same serious and numerically sparse Gideon's band— two-thirds or more of them women, and few of them under thirty—with the same stark ring of empty pews 'down front.'" The congregations seemed to the Lynds to be older than in 1925, the sermon topics interchangeable. Consulting the ministers, they gathered such comments as these:—

"The Depression has brought a resurgence of earnest religious fundamentalism among the weak working-class sects . . . but the uptown churches have seen little similar revival of interest."

"There has been some turning to religion during the Depression, but it has been very slight and not permanent."

From a local editor they gleaned the possibly revealing comment that "All the churches in town, save a few denominations like the Seventh Day Adventists, are more liberal today than in 1925. Any of them will take you no matter what you believe doctrinally." They quoted as typical of the attitude of the "Middletown" young people toward formal religion the comment of a college boy on Christianity: "I believe these things but they don't take a large place in my life." Their analysis concluded with the judgment that religion, in "Middletown," appeared to be "an emotionally stabilizing agent, relinquishing to other agencies leadership in the defining of values."

The preponderance of evidence from other parts of the country would seem to sustain this judgment. Put on one side of the balance such phenomena as the upsurge of intense interest, here and there, in the refined evangelism of the Oxford Groups led by Dr. Frank Buchman, and their "Moral Rearmament" campaign in 1938-39; put on the other side the intensified hostility of radicals who regarded the churches as institutions run for the comfort of the rich and the appeasement of the poor; recall how briefly the stream of Sunday-pleasuring automobiles was halted by the men and women straggling at noontime out of the church on Main Street; compare the number of people to whom Sunday evening was the hour of vespers with the number of people to whom it was the evening when Charlie McCarthy was on the air—and one can hardly deny that the shock of the Depression did not find the churches, by and large, able to give what people thought they needed.

§ 6

Yet in the broader sense of the word religion—meaning the values by which people live, the loyalties which stir them most deeply, the aspirations which seem to them central to their beings—no such shock could have failed to have a religious effect. One thinks of the remark of a young man during the dark days of 1932: "If someone came along with a line of stuff in which I could really believe, I'd follow him pretty nearly anywhere." That remark was made, as it happens, in a speakeasy, and the young man was not thinking in terms of puritan morality or even of Christian piety, but in terms of economic and political and social policy. For such as he the times produced new creeds, new devotions.

But these were secular.

Their common denominator was social-mindedness; by which I mean that they were movements toward economic or social salvation—whether conceived in terms of prosperity or of justice or of mercy—not so much for individuals as such but for groups of people or for the whole nation, and also that they sought this salvation through organized action.

In political complexion these secular religionists ranged all the way from the communists at one end of the spectrum to the more fervent members of the Liberty League at the other. They included the ardent devotees of technocracy, Upton Sinclair's "Epic," Huey Long's "Share-Our-Wealth," Father Coughlin's economic program, the Townsend Plan, the CIO, and, of course, the New Deal. Of the way in which the battles between them raged—and the whole battlefield gradually moved to the left, so to speak—we shall hear more in chapters to come. At this point it need only be remarked that most of the new religions of social salvation did not gather their maximum momentum until after the New Deal Honeymoon was over; or perhaps it is more accurate to say that the New Deal, during its Honeymoon, gathered up or overshadowed nearly all of them. It was during the next two or three years that the fires of zeal burned most intensely: that one man in three at a literary party in New York would be a communist sympathizer, passionately ready to join hands, in proletarian comradeship, with the factory hand or sharecropper whom a few years before he had scorned as a member of Mencken's "booboisie"; that daughters of patrician families were defiantly marching to the aid of striking garment workers, or raising money for the defense of Haywood Patterson in the long-drawn-out Scottsboro case; that college intellectuals were nibbling at

Marx, picketing Hearst newsreels, and—with a flash of humor—forming the "Veterans of Future Wars."

How completely the focus of public attention had become political, economic, and social, and how fully the rebelliousness of the rebellious had turned into these channels, may be suggested by the fact that H. L. Mencken, whose *American Mercury* magazine had been the darling of the young intellectuals of the 'twenties, lost ground as it became evident that Mr. Mencken, though liberal in matters of literature and morals, was a tory in matters of politics and economics—until by 1933, when he resigned his editorship, the new highbrows were dismissing him airily as a back number. Nor did the intellectuals rise in furious defense of freedom of expression when the Catholic Legion of Decency imposed a censorship upon the movies in 1934-35. They were tired of all that, and their protests were faint. They had turned to fresh woods and pastures new.

§ 7

Underneath the tumult and the shouting of argument, underneath the ardor for this cause or that, there remained, however, gnawing doubts. The problems were so bewildering, so huge. The unsettlement of ideas had been so shaking. Things changed so frightfully fast. This plan, this social creed, looked all right today—but would it hold tomorrow? To many Americans, if not most, the complexity of the problems, the hopelessness of arriving at sure solutions, were so great that no social ardor could really move them. While the social salvationists marched in earnest procession toward their various goals of revolution or reforms, these others stood silent and bewildered by the roadside. Something had gone wrong with the country but they didn't know what, couldn't figure it out, wondered if anybody could figure it out.

Toward the end of the decade, when Archibald MacLeish published his *Land of the Free*, through the poem he introduced the recurring words, "We don't know—we can't say —we're wondering. . . ." and observers who had talked with numbers of the drought refugees said that these very words were constantly on the refugees' lips. So it was with innumerable others whose lives had been overturned by the Depression, and with still others who had suffered no bitter hurt themselves but realized that something queer and incomprehensible was happening to the community. They didn't know; and they were likely to fall back into apathy or fatalism, into a longing for a safe refuge from the storm of events.

To quote the editors of *Fortune* once more (speaking of the majority of college students, not the intellectual minority): "The present-day college generation is fatalistic . . . the investigator is struck by the dominant and pervasive color of a generation that will not stick its neck out. It keeps its shirt on, its pants buttoned, its chin up, and its mouth shut. If we take the mean average to be the truth, it is a cautious, subdued, unadventurous generation, unwilling to storm heaven, afraid to make a fool of itself, unable to dramatize its predicament. . . . Security is the summum bonum of the present college generation." This sort of caution was not confined to the campuses. One saw it in business men: "We used to feel pretty sure about what would happen. Now we don't know what will happen." One felt it in the constant iteration, in economic discussions, of the word "confidence"—which enters the vocabulary only when confidence is lacking. One detected it in the strength of the movements for old people's pensions, in the push for social security. The sons and daughters of the pioneers might hazard their small change on bingo or the one-armed bandit, but they did not want life to be a gamble.

Except during the hopeful interval of the New Deal

J. P. MORGAN AT THE WITNESS TABLE
This picture was taken at the Senate Munitions Committee hearing in
1936. Left, Frank Vanderlip. Right (behind Morgan), George Whitney
of J. P. Morgan & Co.

BLACK BLIZZARD COMING!
Looking along a western Oklahoma highway in December, 1935,
as a cloud black with powdered topsoil rolls up

Honeymoon, when hope suddenly and briefly rode high, through the shifting moods of the American people ran an undercurrent of fear. They wanted to feel certainty and security firm as a rock under their feet—and they did not, and were afraid.

Chapter Seven

REFORM—AND RECOVERY?

§ 1

THE New Deal Honeymoon ended in the latter months of 1933—not abruptly but (like many a marital infatuation) in a series of annoyances and disappointments and discords.

The upsurge of business, which in the spring of 1933 had carried the Federal Reserve Board's Adjusted Index of Industrial Production all the way from 59 in March up to 100 in July, was followed by a bad setback—the result of over-speculation and over-purchasing for inventories. In August the index receded from 100 to 91; in September it slipped to 84, in October to 76; by November it had reached 72. Two-thirds of the ground which had been gained during that wonderful springtime rise had now been lost— and during the very months when the NRA, vehicle of so many high hopes, was accumulating momentum! No wonder people began to ask themselves whether this New Deal recovery had been just a flash in the pan; to note how the hurriedly devised New Deal machinery was creaking; to turn a more skeptical ear to the President's optimistic assurances and to General Johnson's mighty tub-thumping.

Already the NRA was producing friction and evasion. Henry Ford was refusing to sign the automobile code. William Randolph Hearst, in full-page newspaper advertisements, was attacking the Recovery Act as "a measure of absolute state socialism" and "a menace to political rights and constitutional liberties," and was proclaiming that the letters NRA stood for "No Recovery Allowed." As the various industrial codes were at last worked out and approved, after endless arguments and confusions, some employers were planning to comply with their provisions fairly and honorably; others were welcoming the chance given them to gather round a table and quietly fix prices, but were resolving to evade the wage and hour clauses and to make a dead letter of Section 7a of the Recovery Act, which guaranteed collective bargaining. These companies were piously introducing company unions which looked like the real thing but weren't, or were deciding to have no truck with unions at all and to trust to the courts to uphold them in their defense of their "liberties." Simultaneously the large-waisted officials of the American Federation of Labor were being stirred to unwonted activity, chartering new unions by the hundreds, and workmen who took Section 7a at its face value were striking fiercely for their government-guaranteed rights. From industrial centers came reports of bloody fighting along the picket lines, of tear gas drenching angry crowds, of National Guardsmen marching to action.

Late in the autumn of 1933, George R. Leighton, investigating for *Harper's Magazine* the facts behind the Blue Eagle ballyhoo in four Eastern states, came back with the report that "the spirit and intent of the National Industrial Recovery Act and the codes are being frustrated, openly or in secret." He found that the government's aim to raise wages was being defeated, either by the sheer refusal of employers to obey the minimum-wage provisions of the blanket code, or by their raising some wages up to the minimum and lowering others down to it. He found employees too scared to peep about what was happening. "For God's sake," cried one workman, "don't tell anybody that you've been here. . . . There are men in cement plants near here who have complained and now they're out in the cold." Compliance boards—which were supposed to enforce the codes—were sometimes, Mr. Leighton found, packed with men who saw eye to eye with hard-boiled employers and had no notion of protecting labor or the consumers. He found local NRA officials timid in dealing with powerful industrialists; one official spoke of a big factory owner in his town in revealing words: "It is so hard to get an audience with him."

The evidence was fast accumulating: the Administration's great experiment in "business self-rule" had come into full collision with the ingrained determination of business executives to hold down their costs of doing business, to push up prices if they could, and in general to run their companies as they pleased, come hell, high water, or General Johnson. Where they could turn the machinery of the NRA to their own ends, they did so—and it was they, not labor or the consumers, who held the initiative in framing the codes. Where they could not turn this machinery to their own ends, some of them complied, others fought the law or nullified it. Certain benefits accrued from the NRA experiment: a virtual ending of child labor; some increases in wages, reductions of over-long hours, and elimination of demoralizing practices, especially in the more enlightened industries; some stabilizing of business. But there seemed to be no increase in employment beyond what sprang directly from the shortening of hours, and prices to the ultimate consumer tended to rise along with wages—in some cases faster than wages. Meanwhile as business lagged and strike threats multiplied, the business community in general was becoming more and more antagonistic toward the new dispensation.

Roosevelt himself was deeply concerned by the loss of business momentum and by the downward drift of farm prices. He who had once referred to himself as the quarterback of the offensive against the Depression now saw the game going against him and decided to try a forward pass. He had been listening to the advice of Professor George

F. Warren of Cornell, who had persuaded Farm Credit Administrator Henry Morgenthau that if the government deliberately raised the price at which it could buy gold, the dollar might be cheapened not only in terms of gold, but in terms of other goods as well: in short, that prices should rise. William H. Woodin, the Secretary of the Treasury, was gravely ill, and Dean G. Acheson, who as Under Secretary was in active charge of the Treasury Department, had no use for the Warren gold-buying scheme; but the President, full of his new idea, went ahead regardless, and on October 22, 1933, announced that the Reconstruction Finance Corporation was going to buy gold for the government.

So it happened that at nine o'clock each morning during the late autumn of 1933, two or three men gathered in the President's bedroom at the White House: usually Professor Warren, Henry Morgenthau, and Jesse Jones of the Reconstruction Finance Corporation. While the President breakfasted in bed, they decided what the day's price for gold would be. The President would scribble a couple of "chits"—one for Jones, authorizing the day's gold price; the other for Acheson, breaking the news to the Treasury Department. Presently Acheson left his untenable position at the Treasury and Morgenthau took his place (to succeed to the Secretaryship upon Woodin's resignation); Professor O. M. W. Sprague, financial adviser to the government, also left the Treasury in indignation at such monetary high-jinks; Al Smith was heaping ridicule upon the President's "baloney dollar"; and Wall Street resounded with angry cries: the United States was on its way to the sort of uncontrolled inflation which had run wild in Germany in 1923; over-spending and "rubber-dollar" experimentation would soon result in ruining the government's credit.

Not until the end of January, 1934, did the gold-buying episode come to an end. By that time the dollar had been devalued (in terms of gold) to 59.06 cents. Prices had risen somewhat, but nowhere near proportionately. The great experiment was a failure. Moreover the financial community—which had long since quite recovered from its sheer panic of the preceding spring, and now felt, with rising indignation, that it was being made the scapegoat of the Depression—had become an almost solid anti-Roosevelt phalanx.

(Footnote upon the prophecies of the wise men of Wall Street: Within the following five and a half years there took place no uncontrolled inflation, no collapse of the credit of the government. What did take place was an embarrassingly huge accumulation of gold in the underground vaults of Fort Knox in Kentucky: over fourteen billion dollars' worth of it, at the $35-an-ounce price which the United States was willing to pay and others did not care to pay because most of the nations of the world had gone off the gold standard.)

As the winter of 1933-34 set in, the New Deal's once-solid support was falling into fragments. Most of the radicals had become impatient with Roosevelt: he was moving too slowly, they charged, he was proposing mere palliatives instead of revolutionary remedies. Thousands of farmers were angry at the failure of the AAA thus far to bring them high prices for their crops, and disorder still flared along the highways of the corn belt and the wheat belt. Laboring men, though they credited the government with an intention to let them organize and to be generous with unemployment relief, resented its inability to enforce Section 7a and the capture of the NRA machinery by the employers. Business men who had imagined that Roosevelt, after putting through his rapid-fire program of reforms and recovery measures in the spring of 1933, would rest on his oars, were discovering to their dismay that he had no such intention; what wild scheme, they asked one another, would this man hatch next?

Already he had set up the Civil Works Administration, a vast and unwieldy—and expensive—system of Federal work relief for the unemployed. In his budget message to Congress at the beginning of 1934, he calmly stated that during the fiscal year 1933-34 the excess of government expenditures over government receipts would be over seven billion dollars and that during the fiscal year 1934-35 it would probably be two billion dollars. "This excess of expenditures over revenues, amounting to over nine billion dollars during two fiscal years," announced the President, "'has been rendered necessary to bring the country back to a sound condition after the unexampled crisis which we encountered last spring. It is a large amount, but the immeasurable benefits justify the cost." The words were confident, but what economy-minded business man struggling with his year-end accounts could fail to ask himself just how "immeasurable" the benefits *to him* had turned out to be, or whether this man who contemplated so coolly a nine-billion-dollar increase in the Federal deficit could be the same Franklin Roosevelt who in 1932 had berated the Republicans for gross extravagance and in March, 1933, had introduced the Economy Bill?

The truth was that a major deflation, if it should occur, would be even more damaging to Franklin Roosevelt than it would have been to Herbert Hoover. Under the existing debt structure Roosevelt had now placed, at many new points, the credit of the government itself. He had committed himself to recovery through rising prices and large-scale business expansion, rather than through falling prices and the writing-off of debts. He must keep his foot pressed down on the accelerator, not on the brake. Dark though the road might look ahead, he must drive on. A costly course to take? Perhaps. But it was too late to turn back now.

§ 2

Intermittently throughout the year 1933 the Senate Committee on Banking and Currency, with the aid of its inexorable counsel, Ferdinand Pecora, had been putting on one of the most extraordinary shows ever produced in a Washington committee room: a sort of protracted coroner's inquest upon American finance. One by one, a long line of financial overlords—commercial bankers, investment bankers, railroad and public-utility holding-company promoters, stockbrokers, and big speculators—had filed up to the witness table; and from these unwilling gentlemen, and from their office files, had been extracted a sorry story of public irresponsibility and private greed. Day by day this story had been spread upon the front pages of the newspapers.

The investigation showed how pool operators in Wall Street had manipulated the prices of stocks on the Exchange, with the assistance of men inside the companies with whose securities they toyed. It showed how they had made huge profits (which represented the exercise of no socially useful function) at the expense of the little speculators and of investors generally, and had fostered a speculative mania which had racked the whole economic system of the country —and this not only in 1928 and 1929, but as recently as the spring of 1933, when Roosevelt was in the White House and Wall Street had supposedly been wearing the sackcloth and ashes of repentance. The investigation showed, too, how powerful bankers had unloaded stocks and bonds upon the unwary through high-pressure salesmanship and had made millions trading in the securities of their own banks, at the expense of stockholders whose interests they claimed to be serving. It showed how the issuing of new securities had been so organized as to yield rich fruits to those on the inside, and how opportunities to taste these fruits had been offered to gentlemen of political influence. It showed how that modern engine of financial power, the holding company, had been misused by promoters: how some of these promoters had piled company upon company till their structures of corporate influence were seven or eight stories high; how these structures had become so complex that they were readily looted by unscrupulous men, and so unstable that many of them came crashing down during the Depression. It showed how grave could be the results when the holding-company technic was applied to banking. It showed how men of wealth had used devices like the personal holding company and tricks like the sale of stock (at a loss) to members of their families to dodge the tax collector—at the very moment when men of humbler station had been paying the taxes which supported the government. Again and again it showed how men occupying fiduciary positions in the financial world had been false to their trust.

Naturally the composite picture blocked out by these revelations was not fair to the financiers generally. The worst scandals got the biggest headlines. Yet the amount of black in the picture was shocking even to the most judicial observer, and the way in which the severity of the Depression had been intensified by greedy and shortsighted financial practices seemed blindingly plain. So high did the public anger mount that the New Deal was sure of strong support as it drove on to new measures of reform.

The first move was into Wall Street. The Securities Act of 1933 was followed by the Securities and Exchange Act of 1934, which put the stock exchanges of the country under Federal regulation, lest the next boom (if it ever came) end in another speculative crash. This Act gave the Federal Reserve Board the authority to limit speculative margins; required all directors, officers, and principal stockholders of big corporations to report all their transactions in the securities of their companies; and created a Securities and Exchange Commission—to be known familiarly as the SEC —which was intended to act as chaperon and policeman of the stock exchanges and the investment market generally, and by slow degrees subdue them to the useful and the good.

The next year the New Deal moved against the misuse of the holding company in the area where its performances had been most egregious—in the public utilities. The Public Utility Holding Company Act provided that holding-company structures must not be more than two stories high, that they must be simplified, and that they must limit themselves to the management of economically integrated groups of operating companies.

Turning to the banking system of the country, the New Deal made no attempt to unify it (bringing the national banks and the forty-eight groups of state banks into one system) but in 1935 increased the supervisory power of the Federal Reserve Board over the various Federal Reserve Banks, centering a more effective authority in Washington, and incidentally made permanent the insurance by the government of small bank deposits, as temporarily arranged in 1933.

Other new powers of regulation and compulsion were assumed by the Federal government. For example, the power of the Interstate Commerce Commission was extended to cover not only railroads, as of yore, but interstate bus and truck traffic as well; and for the old Radio Commission was substituted a new Communications Commission which was not only to police the air waves but also to supervise the telegraph and telephone systems. Not until September 2, 1935, did the President announce—in a letter to Roy W. Howard of the Scripps-Howard newspapers—that the New

Deal's legislative program had "reached substantial completion" and that business might expect a "breathing spell."

Throughout a large part of the years 1934 and 1935 the hue and cry over these reform measures of the New Deal reverberated across the country.

No longer, to be sure, did the news from Washington still make the front pages of the newspapers as automatically as it had in the first wild days of the new Administration. Other events, important and unimportant, now claimed a fresher attention. During the winter of 1933-34—a piercingly cold winter in the North, when the Atlantic Ocean was blocked with ice all the way from Nantucket Island to the mainland, and Army fliers, hastily ordered to carry the air mails after Roosevelt's mistakenly sudden termination of the air-mail contracts, were flying to their deaths in ice and fog—there was foreign news to contest for front-page space with General Johnson's latest admonitions and expletives and with Roosevelt's monetary experiments and reform proposals. There were riots in Paris which seemed for a time to presage civil war in France. Foreign excitements continued during the summer of 1934: there came Hitler's blood purge and the assassination of little Chancellor Dollfuss of Austria, which threatened a general European war (with Italy opposed to Germany!). That spring there took place in a humble Canadian home an event which for sheer human interest was the feature-editor's answer to prayer: on May 28, Mrs. Oliva Dionne gave birth to five little girls—and incidentally to a major Canadian industry, the exploitation of the Quintuplets as five modern wonders of the world.

As the summer of 1934 drew to its close the country supped on horror: the Ward Liner *Morro Castle* was burned, with a loss of 137 lives, off the coast of New Jersey. Men and women who were hardly aware what the letters SEC stood for could have told you in detail how the *Morro*

Castle fire was first discovered in a locker off the port-side writing room; how Chief Officer William F. Warms had found himself in precarious command of the vessel owing to the death of the captain from indigestion a few hours previously; how the fire could not be stopped and the passengers took to the boats—or to the open Atlantic; and how the red-hot hulk of the ship was later beached right beside the convention hall at Asbury Park, where it boomed briefly a grim sight-seeing trade.

While the visitors to Asbury Park were still staring at the *Morro Castle*, the most exciting detective-and-trial-scene story of the decade began to unfold itself, as Bruno Richard Hauptmann was captured in the Bronx and was put on trial for the kidnapping of the Lindbergh baby. The furiously ballyhooed trial at Flemington brought once again to everybody's lips the names of Dr. Condon and the Whateleys and Betty Gow, and lifted into brief public prominence new names such as those of Attorney General Wilentz of New Jersey, Justice Trenchard, counsel Reilly for the defense, and the mysterious German of Hauptmann's incredible testimony, Isidor Fisch.

It was during the following summer—the summer of 1935—that public attention was diverted from the debate over the Holding-Company Bill and other Administrative measures by Jim Braddock's capture of the heavyweight boxing championship from Max Baer; by the deaths of Will Rogers and Wiley Post in an airplane crash in Alaska; and by the slow gathering of war clouds over unhappy Ethiopia. All through 1934 and 1935, furthermore, an event of major importance to America—of which we shall hear more in the next chapter of this book—was taking place on the Great Plains: the farms of the Dust Bowl were blowing away.

Yet never quite inaudible, during all the time when these events were taking place, was the rumble of battle over the

New Deal financial reforms. The outcry of protest from Wall Street—which was echoed generally in the conservative press—was terrific. The Securities and Exchange Bill, if passed, would end the liquidity of the investment markets and bring general economic ruin! Roosevelt was taking the high road to communism! Had not Dr. William A. Wirt of Gary, Indiana, told of being at a "brain trust" dinner party where, he insisted, government employees had spoken of Roosevelt as merely the Kerensky of a new American revolution? Did not Rexford Tugwell, the Assistant Secretary of Agriculture, appear to be practically a communist—especially to those newspaper proprietors who feared that his proposed bill to regulate food and drug advertising might cut into their revenues? The government was out to ruin all investors in public utilities: it was enlarging the TVA's sphere of competition with Southern private utilities, it was subsidizing municipalities which wanted to have municipal power and light systems and take their power from the TVA, it was building new dams at Grand Coulee and Bonneville in the West, which would enlarge the area served by public power—and now it was proposing, through the Holding-Company Bill, to apply a "death-sentence" to a lot of helpless holding companies! The issue was clear, shouted the conservatives: it was economic dictatorship versus democracy.

Back from the New Dealers came the reply: Wall Street's record of mismanagement had been spread upon the books of the Senate Committee. "The people of the United States will not restore that ancient order." The New Deal intended to protect the average man against "the selfish interests of Wall Street."

Thus the thunder of battle rolled—while Franklin Roosevelt, still overwhelmingly in command of Congress, pushed the reforms through to enactment.

§ 3

Not only did the New Deal try to restore prosperity through the NRA, the AAA, currency changes, and other measures, and to prevent the recurrence of economic disaster through its reform measures; it also tried to protect individual citizens against the hardships of economic adversity, past, present, and future. It set up so many agencies to lend money to organizations and individuals that the mere listing of them would be wearisome. Through an enactment of major importance in 1935, the Social Security Act, it set up a vast system of unemployment insurance and of old-age assistance for the greater part of the working population of the country—taxing pay rolls to set up a colossal fund out of which might be paid old-age benefits in the long future. Year after year it struggled, too, with the problem of unemployment relief.

The attack upon this desperate problem threw into sharp outline the essential strength of the New Deal, its essential weakness, and the dilemma of the national economy as a whole.

When in the spring of 1933 the Federal government had assumed the responsibility for seeing that men and women and children did not go hungry or shelterless in the United States, it had set aside half a billion dollars out of the public-works fund to aid the states in carrying the burden of unemployment relief; and President Roosevelt had appointed as Federal Emergency Relief Administrator a thin, narrow-faced, alert-looking young Iowan named Harry Hopkins, who had been a zealous and idealistic social worker and had served as relief administrator in New York during Roosevelt's governorship. The distribution of this fund appeared to be simply a temporary expedient, for in those hopeful days recovery was seemingly on its way at the double-quick.

Then came the downturn of the fall of 1933, and the prospect of another dreadful winter. Most of the cities and states of the country were on the verge of bankruptcy and quite unable to bear the relief burden unaided—and unemployment during the winter of 1933-34 was pretty surely going to be almost as severe as during that of 1932-33! Another "temporary" plan was needed, and on no niggardly scale.

So the Civil Works Administration was set up and Harry Hopkins found himself in command of a huge and hasty organization of mercy; and Roosevelt, as we have seen, asked Congress for billions to meet this new need. Surely things would be better next year. In the spring of 1934 the Civil Works Administration—which was proving terrifically expensive—was abandoned, and the organization of relief was altered again.

But things did not prove much better the next year. And so once more the President called for billions of dollars and once more the organization was overhauled: early in 1935 the Works Progress Administration—the WPA—came into being.

Although the WPA was destined to remain throughout the rest of the decade, it was destined also to be subject to constant reorganization and revision. In essence, the history of those first years was to be repeated again and again. Year after year the Administration found the number of unemployed men unexpectedly large, found its funds running out, confronted the new crisis with a new appeal to Congress for more billions, and hastily improvised new and glowing plans. The prevailing pattern was one of administrative makeshift.

The principle upon which Federal relief operated was magnificent. The government said in effect: "These millions of men who are out of work are not to be considered paupers. They are not to be subjected to any humiliation which we can spare them. They are to be regarded as citizens and friends who are the temporary victims of an unfortunate economic situation for which the nation as a whole is responsible. Not only is it far too late in the day, now, to follow the Hoover principle that the acceptance of Federal money undermines men's self-respect; it is even too late in the day to be content with giving handouts. These men want to *work* for the money they receive. Very well, we shall put them to work—as many of them as we possibly can. We shall put them at useful work which will not compete with private business. They shall become government employees, able to hold up their heads again. If putting them to work costs more than a cash dole, the benefits in morale restored will outweigh the expense."

But these things were easier said than done, on the scale on which the government had to operate. Stop for a minute to feel the impact of these figures: The CWA at its peak employed *over four million workers*—enough to man some twenty General Motors Corporations. The WPA began operations with the aim of employing *three and a half million.* (The total number of people dependent upon Federal, state, or local relief—including the families of those to whom payments were made—was variously estimated at various times at from *twenty to twenty-five million.*) How to put this vast horde to work?

First of all, there was the difficulty of finding work that had value, and would not compete with private business, and was fitted to the endlessly varied abilities and experience of millions of individuals. It was decided that the reliefers were not to work on private property, engage in manufacturing, or set up rival merchandising systems. The money went at first mostly into such projects as the repair and building of roads (especially farm-to-market roads), repairs on public buildings and schools, the construction of parks and playgrounds; and—for the professional and clerical workers, the white-collar class—into research projects for the government and for universities, and into engaging reliefers who had some special skill or knowledge to teach it to others who did not have it. Some of the jobs were trivial, or too many men were assigned to them, or these men were conspicuously inexpert; hence the criticisms one constantly heard of "leaf-raking" and of men idling on the job.

During an aldermanic inquiry into New York City relief early in 1935—in which it was discovered that money was being spent for the teaching of tap dancing and the manipulation of shadow puppets, and for such academic enterprises as "a study of the predominating non-professional interests of teachers in nursery schools, kindergarten, and first grade" and "a study of the relative effectiveness of a supervised correspondence course in elementary Latin"—one Robert Marshall testified that he was a "training specialist" who taught the reliefers "boon doggles," explaining that this was an old pioneer term for useful everyday tricks of handicraft such as making belts by weaving ropes. The strange term entranced newspaper-readers, and presently the conservative press everywhere was referring to relief projects of questionable value as "boondoggling."

Another great difficulty was that of enrolling and investigating and assigning workers. Should a job go to the person who could do it best, or to the person in the direst need? If need was to be the criterion, how could any standards of work be maintained? The determination of wage scales offered another series of headaches. Presumably the wages should be lower than those for private business—but what if local wages were on the starvation level? These were only a few of the practical questions for which there seemed to be no possible answer which did not produce either injustice or inefficiency.

Again, there was the grave difficulty of setting up a proper organization, of keeping the control of relief out of the hands of grafters and political hacks, of resolving the endless conflicts between Federal and local agencies. Though the division of authority between Federal and state and local governments varied bewilderingly in different places and at different times, the whip hand was held in the main by the Hopkins organization in Washington, which was vigilant against graft and—at least in the early years—pretty independent of politics. As time went on, the taint of politics became somewhat more noticeable: the relief system was all too valuable to the Democratic party, relief expenditures had a way of rising to a maximum as Election Day approached, and there was ugly evidence here and there of the gross misuse of funds, as in Pennsylvania; but on the whole the record was astonishingly clean considering the vastness of the funds disbursed and the generally low level of political ethics in American local government.

Beyond all these difficulties was the final, inescapable one. Try as Hopkins and his aides might to make the work vital and prideworthy, the fact remained that it was made work, ill-paid, uncertain, undemanding of real quality of workmanship; and that the reliefers became perforce, by degrees, a sort of pariah class, unwelcomed by private industry, dwelling in an economic twilight.

That is a generalization. Against it should be set some high triumphs, including notably those of the Federal Theatre, Music, and Arts projects. Who would have believed, during the Hoover period, that within a few years, under the WPA, orchestras would be getting relief aid for playing to enthusiastic audiences, government-subsidized theatre groups would be packing the playhouses with excellent shows, and able painters who had not sold a picture for months or even years would be getting government assignments to paint post-office murals?

Of all the forms which Federal relief took there is not space here to speak. Yet a word at least should be said of the Transient Camps which offered shelter to those hundreds of thousands of Americans who were traveling about in search of work and could not qualify for regular relief after they left their home towns (who wants to support a non-resident?); of the National Youth Administration, which helped to pay for the education and training of young people who would otherwise have gone without; and of the WPA's purchase of surplus commodities—especially farm products—and their distribution to the needy. (Nor should it be forgotten that the great enterprises—bridges, dams, public buildings, etc.—constructed by the Public Works Administration, and the forest-conservation work of the Civilian Conservation Corps, while not administratively a part of Federal relief, supplemented the relief system.)

Two more generalizations must be made, however, before we leave this twilight zone. The first is that, despite all the inefficiencies of the relief system, its frequent upheavals of organization, its confusion, and its occasional political subversion, it commended itself to the bulk of the American people because of its essential friendliness, of the human decency of its prevailing attitude toward those whom the Depression had thrust into want. Possibly those privileged people who denounced the system as a coddling and spoiling of the unfit may have owed their security from civil revolution during the nineteen-thirties to the fact that the government in power treated the reliefers as citizens worthy of respect.

The second generalization is that the terrific cost of such a relief system bore down upon the working and income-receiving past of the population, even while the expenditures were helping to keep trade going; and that that part of the cost which was not met by current taxes remained, in the form of Federal debt, to bear down upon the job-holding and income-receiving Americans for long years to come. Human decency came very high.

Here was the essential dilemma of the New Deal. Just as it wanted, reasonably enough, to apply the lessons of the 1929-33 débâcle and reform the financial system, but apparently could not do this without setting up a Federal supervisory bureaucracy, without inflicting upon the financial world endless rules and regulations, endless tasks of questionnaire-answering, report-writing, and prospectus-writing, and filling Wall Street with paralyzing fears, rational and irrational, thus delaying recovery; so also it apparently could not deal humanely with the unemployed men and women of the country without imposing heavy taxes, incurring heavy deficits, raising very natural qualms as to its ability to carry on indefinitely with a mounting debt, and thus once again delaying recovery. It had to march toward its goal under a veritable Christian's pack—the burden of the very inadequacies which it was trying to resolve.

§ 4

Early in the evening of July 22, 1934, a group of agents of the Department of Justice, armed with pistols, gathered unobtrusively about a movie theatre on Lincoln Avenue, Chicago. The leader of the group, Melvin H. Purvis, parked his car near the theatre door and carefully scanned the faces of the men and women who entered. At length Purvis recognized the man he wanted—though this man had dyed his hair, had had his face lifted, had grown a mustache, and had put on gold-rimmed glasses.

For two hours Purvis waited in his car, until the man came out of the theatre. Then Purvis signaled to his aides by thrusting an arm out of the car, dropping his hand, and closing it. The aides closed in on the movie-goer, and when he started to draw an automatic they shot him down. The next morning the headlines shouted that John Dillinger, Public Enemy No. 1, had been destroyed.

Another offensive of the reform spirit against things-as-they-had-been was well under way.

During the early years of the decade, as we have seen, there had been immense indignation at the prevalence of crime in America and the inability of the police to cope with it. This indignation had been sharpened by the Lindbergh kidnapping early in 1932. From that time on, every kidnapping case leaped into such prominence in the newspaper dispatches that most Americans imagined that a wave of kidnapping was sweeping the country. The public indignation took an ugly form at San Jose, California, late in 1933, when two men who had kidnapped young Brooke Hart, and had shot him, weighted his body, and thrown it into San Francisco Bay, were taken out of the San Jose jail by an angry mob and hanged on trees near by—whereupon the Governor of California, who had a curious notion of law and order, commented that the lynchers had done "a good job."

Proceeding upon the theory that the states could not be sure of catching criminals (any more than they could be sure of stopping undesirable business practices) without Federal aid, Congress had passed laws giving the Federal authorities a limited jurisdiction over crimes which had hitherto been wholly under state jurisdiction. J. Edgar Hoover, the resourceful head of the Bureau of Investigation of the Department of Justice, saw his chance. When John Dillinger, a bank robber and hold-up man of the Middle West, proved to have a remarkable ability to shoot his way out of difficulty, Hoover sent his Federal men on the trail—though Dillinger's only Federal offense up to that time was said to have been the interstate transportation of a stolen car. Dillinger was labeled "Public Enemy No. 1" (now that Al Capone was in prison), and the public began to take notice.

The Federal agents caught up to Dillinger at St. Paul but

he escaped, wounded. A few days later he appeared in a surgeon's office, leveled a gun, compelled the surgeon to give him treatment for his wound, and got away safely. Again he was found, at a summer resort in Northern Wisconsin; but although agents surrounded the building where he was staying, he escaped after a battle in which two men were killed and two were wounded. At last Purvis caught him in Chicago, as we have seen, and the story of John Dillinger came to an end.

But not the story of J. Edgar Hoover and his Federal agents. For these Federal sleuths now proceeded to capture, dead or alive, "Pretty Boy" Floyd, "Baby Face" Nelson, and so many other public enemies, one after another, that after Alvin Karpis was taken alive in 1936 the public quite lost track of the promotions in the Public Enemy class.

Hoover and his men became heroes of the day. The movies took them up, taught people to call them G-men, and presented James Cagney in the rôle of a bounding young G-man, trained in the law, in scientific detection, in target practice, and incidentally in wrestling. Presently mothers who had been noting with alarm that their small sons liked to play gangster on the street corner were relieved to observe that the favored part in these juvenile dramas was now that of the intrepid G-man, whose machine gun mowed down kidnappers and bank robbers by the score. The real G-men—with the not-quite-so-heavily-advertised aid of state and local police—continued to follow up their triumphs until by the end of 1936 they could claim that every kidnapping case in the country since the passage of the Lindbergh law in 1932 had been closed.

But kidnapping and bank robbery, sensational as they were, were hardly the most menacing of crimes. The depredations of professional gangster-racketeers were more far-reaching and infinitely more difficult to combat. During the nineteen-twenties various gangster mobs, the most notorious of which was Al Capone's in Chicago, had built up larger, better organized, and more profitable systems of business-by-intimidation than the country had ever seen before. The foundation of these rackets was usually beer-running, but a successful beer-runner could readily handle most of the bootlegging trade in whisky and gin as a sideline, branch out to take over the gambling and prostitution rackets, and also develop systems of terrorization in otherwise legitimate businesses, by using what purported to be an employer's association or a labor union but was really a scheme for extortion backed by threats to destroy the members' business—or kill them—if they did not pay. The pattern was different in every city and usually there were many rival gangs at work, muscling in on one another's territory from time to time to the accompaniment of machine-gun battles.

During the early nineteen-thirties the racketeers—like legitimate business men—found business bad. The coming of Repeal, by breaking the back of the illicit liquor business, deprived these gentry of a vital source of revenue. But the technique of politically protected intimidation had been so well learned that racketeering went right on in many cities. Even in New York—a city which had never been so racket-ridden as Chicago and had elected in 1933 an honest and effective mayor, Fiorello LaGuardia—dozens of businesses were in the grip of rackets and their victims were too terrified to testify to what was going on.

But New York was to provide a classic demonstration of what the new reform spirit, properly directed, could do.

The story of the demonstration really began on November 21, 1933—when Roosevelt was engaged in his breakfast-in-bed gold-buying plan, and General Johnson was approving NRA codes, and Mae West was appearing on the screen in "I'm No Angel," and Katharine Hepburn in "Little Women," and copies of *Anthony Adverse* were everywhere, and the first bad dust storm had just raged in the Dust Bowl, and the Century of Progress Fair at Chicago had just ended its first year, and the CWA had just been organized, and the United States had just recognized Soviet Russia. On that day the New York papers had carried on their inside pages an item of local news: the appointment as local Federal Attorney of one Thomas E. Dewey, who was only thirty-one years old. During the next year and a half young Dewey did well at this job. In the spring of 1935 a grand jury in New York, investigating racketeering, became so dissatisfied with the way in which the evidence was presented to it by the Tammany District Attorney that it rose up in wrath and asked Governor Lehman to appoint a special prosecutor. Governor Lehman appointed the valiant Dewey and on July 29, 1935, he set to work.

There followed one of the most extraordinary performances in the history of criminal detection and prosecution. Dewey mobilized an able staff of young lawyers and accountants in a highly protected office in the Woolworth Building, sent them out to get the evidence about racketeering, and to everybody's amazement got it, despite the terrified insistence of the very people whom he was trying to protect that they knew nothing at all. This evidence Dewey marshaled so brilliantly that presently he began a series of monotonously successful prosecutions. He put out of business the restaurant racket, to which at least 240 restaurants had paid tribute. He sent to prison Toots Herbert, who in the guise of a labor leader, head of Local 167, had collected large sums from the poultry business. He convicted Lucky Luciano, who had levied toll upon the prostitutes and madams of New York (with such smooth-running political protection that although during 1935 no less than 147 girls who worked for this combination had been arrested, not one of them had got a jail sentence). Within two years Dewey had indicted 73 racketeers and convicted 71 of them: and all this despite the unwillingness of witnesses to talk, the constant need of protecting against violence those who agreed to talk, and constant attempts at bribery and intimidation. Elected District Attorney in 1937, Dewey continued his onslaught, and in 1939 he secured the conviction of an important Tammany leader, James J. Hines. (Hines appealed, and at the end of the decade his case was still pending.)

The intimidation industry was not destroyed, of course, any more than kidnapping and bank robbery had been ended; but Dewey, like the G-men, had shown that crime could be successfully combated, and the lesson was widely noted. When the worthy members of the National Economic League, who in 1930 and 1931, as we have previously seen, voted that "Administration of Justice" and "Crime" and "Lawlessness" were—along with Prohibition—the important issues before the country, voted again in 1937, they decided that "Crime" offered a less important problem than "Labor," "Efficiency and Economy in Government," "Taxation," or "The Federal Constitution."

The drive against crime had won at least a temporary victory.

§ 5

Through the years 1934 and 1935, President Roosevelt was sore beset.

Economic recovery was lagging badly. For a measure of what was happening, let us return once more to the Federal Reserve Board's Adjusted Index of Industrial Production, which gives perhaps the best general indication of economic health. We have seen that the index figure had dropped from its prosperity peak of 125 in 1929 all the way to 58 in the summer of 1932, and again to 59 in the bank-panic month of March, 1933; that it had then bounded to 100 during the New Deal Honeymoon, and slid down to 72 in November, 1933, as the Honeymoon came to an end. Slowly it crept up again, but only to 86 in the spring of 1934. Back it slipped to a discouraging 71 in the fall of 1934. Once more it gained, till at the beginning of 1935 it had reached 90. Then during the spring of 1935 it receded to 85. Not until the last month of 1935 had it fought its way up again to the hundred mark it had attained during those first frenzied months of the New Deal—and this despite the pouring of billions of dollars of relief money into the bloodstream of trade.

The President's confident proposals for new legislation could not altogether distract public attention from the administrative difficulties which tangled the agencies he had already set up. The NRA appeared to be stimulating dissension rather than production. On the one hand it had virtually invited labor to organize; on the other hand it had turned over the formulation and administration of its hundreds of codes mainly to employers, and was unable to require these employers to recognize the rapidly mushrooming unions, dominated in many cases by inexperienced and over-combative leaders; hence it could not make good on its promise. Disillusioned auto workers were saying that NRA stood for "National Run Around." A fierce dock strike on the Pacific Coast grew into an attempt to tie up the whole city of San Francisco by a general strike in July, 1934. When the textile code authority called for a cut in production that same summer—a cut which meant grievous reductions in hard-driven textile workers' wages—another great strike began, with flying squadrons of strikers driving from mill town to mill town in the South, with National guardsmen called out in seven states, and with a list of dead and wounded growing ominously day by day. That fall General Johnson left the NRA under a storm of criticism—or, as he delicately put it himself, a "hail of dead cats."

The AAA was a storm center too, and its effect upon the farmers' income was a matter of dispute, since the rise in farm prices in 1934 might be partly attributed to the deadly drought which was blighting the prairies and the Great Plains. Unemployment and the resulting drain upon the national budget continued almost unabated.

Politically, the President came through the Congressional elections of 1934 with flying colors; the Democrats gained nine seats in the Senate and even enlarged slightly their big majority in the House. But how long would this supremacy last? Cannon were being unlimbered not only to the right of Roosevelt, but to the left of him too. That the forces of capital and management—bankers, investors, big business men, and their sympathizers—should have closed ranks against him was natural in view of his reform legislation, his monetary unorthodoxy, his huge spendings for relief, his intermittent hostility to big business, and his expansion of the area of government authority. But what if he could not hold the support of the have-nots, and found himself the leader of a centrist minority, raked by a cross fire from both sides?

On the left Roosevelt must reckon with Huey Long, the Kingfish of Louisiana, who had always been a maverick in national politics and had definitely quit the New Deal since that day in June, 1933, when he had called at the White House, had kept his jaunty straw hat on throughout most of his interview with the President, had been told that the Administration could not appoint some of his nominees for office, and had remarked to Jim Farley as he left, "What the hell is the use of coming down to see this fellow? I can't win any decision over him." Long was one of the most extraordinary figures in all American political history. He was of the stuff of which dictators are made, and he ruled Louisiana with an iron hand, smashing opposition as ruthlessly as a racketeer. Blatant, profane, witty, unscrupulous, violent; possessed of the demagogue's habit of promising the impossible, together with the statesman's ability to provide good roads, better schools, free schoolbooks, and a generally better standard of living among the poor, both black and white, and at the same time to keep the state government solvent—Huey had blustered and bludgeoned his way into a stormy national prominence.

No use for Senators to try to silence him in Washington by leaving the Senate Chamber when he began to speak; his invective was the one thing the crowds in the galleries wanted most to hear.

When Huey toured the South in the spring of 1935, ten thousand people gathered in Atlanta to hear him denounce the Administration. "Pour it on 'em, Kingfish!" they yelled in delight. He was getting the headlines that spring by calling for an investigation of Postmaster General Jim Farley, of whom he said later, by way of explanation, "Jim was the biggest rooster in the yard, and I thought that if I could break his legs the rest would be easy." Radio audiences chuckled with delight at Huey's barnyard wit, as when he said, commenting on Herbert Hoover's call for a militant Republicanism, "Hoover is a hoot owl. Roosevelt is a scrootch owl. A hoot owl bangs into the roost and knocks the hen clean off and catches her while she's falling. But a scrootch owl slips into the roost and scrootches up to the hen and talks softly to her. And the hen just falls in love with him, and the next thing you know, there ain't no hen." Had there ever been before, in American political life, a man who could rule a state with machine guns, subdue a legislature completely to his will, and yet produce the sort of hilarity represented by a remark in the course of his comment on the Mardi Gras: "Once I got invited to one of their balls. I went down to a pawn shop and bought a silk shirt for six dollars with a collar so high I had to climb up on a stump to spit"?

Huey Long had a fantastic, utopian "Share Our Wealth" program for the country, very explicit as to objectives but very vague as to methods. It began with "Every family to be furnished by the government a homestead allowance, free of debt, of not less than one-third the average family wealth of the country, which means, at the lowest, that every family shall have the reasonable comforts of life up to a value of from $5,000 to $6,000." It ended with a clause proclaiming, "The raising of revenue for the support of this program to come from the reduction of swollen fortunes from the top." No wonder the New Deal, champion of the "forgotten man," feared Huey's rising power! When during 1935 the Democratic National Committee conducted a secret poll on a national scale, it found that on a third-party ticket Long would be able to command between three and four million votes for the Presidency. And nobody could tell how much further he might go.

Roosevelt must reckon also with another one-time ally who, like Long, had left the New Deal reservation: Father Coughlin of the Shrine of the Little Flower, whose eloquence over the radio had gained for his National Union for Social Justice an immense following, somewhat similar to Huey Long's. Father Coughlin's voice was raised in behalf not only of "a living annual wage" but of "nationalization of banking and currency and of national resources." How much strength might this prophet of the air waves command by 1936, if recovery continued to lag, and how would he dispose it?

Even more portentous, for a time, seemed the incredible organization headed by Dr. Francis E. Townsend of Long Beach, California. Not until the first of January, 1934, had this elderly physician announced his plan for a government allowance of $200 a month to every citizen 60 years of age or older, the pension to be financed by a sales tax—and to be spent by each recipient within 30 days, thus assuring (so the argument ran) such a wave of spending that business would boom and the sales tax would easily be borne. Yet so glowing was the appeal of the Townsend Old Age Revolving Pensions plan, and so clever was Townsend's aide Robert L. Clements in organizing Townsend Clubs, welding them into a hierarchic national system, and providing the faithful with a *Townsend National Weekly* and with speakers' manuals, Townsend buttons, stickers, tire covers, and automobile plates, that within a year the Townsend planners were said to possess the balance of political power in eleven states west of the Mississippi and were entrenched even in Ohio, Indiana, Illinois, and Massachusetts.

Smile as one might at the naïve devotion of these embattled old folks, in their annual convention, as they heard Townsend and Clements likened to George Washington and Alexander Hamilton, and rose to sing

> Onward, Townsend soldiers,
> Marching as to war,
> With the Townsend banner
> Going on before.
> Our devoted soldiers
> Bid depression go;
> Join them in the battle,
> Help them fight the foe!

it was no smiling matter for the Democratic general staff that the number of Townsend Club members was conservatively estimated at three million, and that the movement, by the end of 1935, had gained at least ten million supporters. Old age, it appeared, must be served.

And what of the communists? They were few in number compared with these other groups, but the influence of their scattered agents in provoking labor disputes and offering aggressive labor leadership was disproportionately great, the intellectual offensive waged by their journalists and writers was powerful, and they formed the spearhead for a wide-ranging attack upon the New Deal from the left—an attack epitomized in such books as *The Economic Consequences of the New Deal*, by Benjamin Stolberg and Warren Jay Vinton, which denounced Roosevelt for trying to "organize scarcity" instead of "organizing abundance" and for trying merely to shore up the vicious and doomed system of capitalism, instead of wholeheartedly siding with the proletariat in the coming "irreconcilable conflict between capital and labor." To the communists and their allies, in 1934 and early 1935, a liberal who did not stand for unrelenting war in this conflict was a fascist in sheep's clothing. Alien to the American temper and American habits of thought as the communist credo was, it had a boldness, a last-resort ferocity, that might commend itself to millions of desperate men.

What of the future possibilities of some such movement as Upton Sinclair's EPIC (End Poverty in California) campaign? Sinclair had recommended that the unemployed be set to work producing for one another, setting up—by an extension of the barter plans which had been so hopefully tried at the bottom of the Depression—a sort of economy-within-the-going-economy. Sinclair had scared prosperous Californians half to death in the elections of 1934, and had been defeated only with the aid of motion pictures faked by the Hollywood studios, showing dreadful-looking bums arriving in California by the carload to enjoy the new Eden that Sinclair promised.

And what of the farmer-labor movement in the Northwest, and of the aggressive Governor Floyd Olson of Minnesota as a possible leader?

In dealing with these various political menaces on the left the quarterback showed himself to be a brilliant broken-field runner. Roosevelt smiled upon Sinclair—without embracing him. Pushing forward the Social Security Bill, he gave implicit assurance to the Townsendites that he intended to secure for them at least half a loaf. Not without a side glance at Huey Long and Father Coughlin, he suddenly produced in the summer of 1935 a proposal to increase the taxes upon the rich—to levy a big toll upon inheritances and large incomes and a graduated tax upon corporation incomes. The tax did not produce much revenue and its effect upon the wealthy was apoplectic; but Huey was so delighted that he moved back on the New Deal reservation—for how long, nobody could predict.

Yet all the broken-field dodging in the world could hardly have got Roosevelt past all these captains of dissent had not luck, too, intervened on his side. The luck assumed strange guises. Who would have guessed that Stalin, fearing the rise to power of Hitler and Mussolini, would have called upon good communists everywhere to join forces with liberal democrats in Popular Fronts—as he did in the summer of 1935—and that the advice from Moscow would soon spike the guns which the communists had been leveling at Roosevelt? Or that the powerful Olson of Minnesota would fall fatally ill and be unable to head a third party? Or that Huey Long, walking down the corridor of his own State Capitol in Baton Rouge in the evening of September 8, 1935, would be shot by a young physician, Carl Austin Weiss, Jr., and fatally wounded—while Huey's bodyguards, leaping too late to his defense, drilled the assassin with sixty-one bullets?

§ 6

While these assorted threats were still menacing the New Deal from the left, there fell from the right such a body blow that almost its whole program seemed in danger of annihilation. In a unanimous decision on May 27, 1935, the United States Supreme Court invalidated the NRA.

By implication, furthermore, the Court did much more

than that. Had it struck down the NRA alone, the blow would not have been staggering; for the NRA, as we have seen, had long since been recognized as the problem child of the New Deal. Had the Court's objection simply been to the drafting of the statute, the blow would not have been staggering; for Congress and the Executive were accustomed to being reminded that he who legislates in haste must expect to be invalidated at leisure. Had the Court even been content with objecting—as it did object—to the way in which the National Industrial Recovery Act had delegated law-making powers to trade associations, the blow would not have been staggering. What was lethal about the decision was that—as Charles and Mary Beard have put it—"In the opinion that supported the decision, the Chief Justice seemed to block every loophole for the regulation of procedures, hours, and wages in industries by Federal law."

The decision implied that it would be unconstitutional for the Federal government to deal with a national industrial or social or agricultural problem by dictating to individual factories, stores, or farmers what they should do. For the operation of a factory, according to the Court's reasoning, was an intrastate operation—even if the raw materials which it manufactured came from another state, and the factory competed with factories in other states. The operation of a store was intrastate, even if this store was operated by a national chain incorporated in another state, sold goods made in other states, and was at a hundred other points affected by the economic conditions in other states. The growing of crops was an intrastate process, even if when grown they moved into interstate commerce and the price which the farmer received was dependent upon a national market. No, said the Court: under the Constitution the Federal government may regulate only interstate commerce, and none of these things are interstate commerce as we interpret it. Not even in a national emergency may the

Federal government deal with them. "Extraordinary conditions do not create or enlarge constitutional power."

If the decision of May 27, 1935, was remarkable, so was the President's manner of replying to it. Four days later, more than two hundred newspaper men crowded into the Executive Offices at the White House to hear what he had to say. Jammed shoulder to shoulder in the hot room—for it was a warm day outside—and too cramped for ready note-taking, they listened to a discussion of the decision which lasted for an hour and twenty-five minutes. While Mrs. Roosevelt, sitting beside the President, knitted steadily on a blue sock, Roosevelt began by reading a few of the telegrams that had reached him since the decision—telegrams asking whether there wasn't something he could do to "save the people"—and then, placing a fresh cigarette in his holder, began a measured and carefully thought-out, if informal, analysis of the meaning of the decision, which he said was "more important than any decision probably since the Dred Scott case." Only two or three times did his voice rise in anger, but it thrilled with intensity throughout, and the reporters could have no doubt that he was profoundly moved.

"The big issue," said the President, "is this: Does this decision mean that the United States Government has no control over any economic problem?" And again—after a long analysis of the changes in the nature of the national economy since the Interstate Commerce Clause was written, and of the increase in economic interdependence since the days of the early Court decisions interpreting that clause strictly—"We have been relegated to the horse-and-buggy definition of interstate commerce." A great question, he said, had been raised for national decision—"The biggest question that has come before this country outside of time of war, and it has to be decided. And, as I say, it may take five years or ten years."

Before the correspondents filed out, there came a question from one of them: "You made a reference to the necessity of the people deciding within the next five or ten years. Is there any way of deciding that question without voting on a constitutional amendment or the passing of one?"

"Oh, yes, I think so," said the President. "But it has got to come, in the final analysis."

"Any suggestion as to how it might be made, except by a constitutional amendment?"

"No; we haven't got to that yet."

Nor was he to get to it for nearly two years.

Chapter Eight

WHEN THE FARMS BLEW AWAY

§ 1

IT WAS on Armistice Day of 1933 that the first of the great dust storms swept across South Dakota.

"By mid-morning a gale was blowing, cold and black. By noon it was blacker than night, because one can see through night and this was an opaque black. It was a wall of dirt one's eyes could not penetrate, but it could penetrate the eyes and ears and nose. It could penetrate to the lungs until one coughed up black. If a person was outside, he tied his handkerchief around his face, but he still coughed up black; and inside the house the Karnstrums soaked sheets and towels and stuffed them around the window ledges, but these didn't help much.

"They were afraid, because they had never seen anything like this before. . . .

"When the wind died and the sun shone forth again, it was on a different world. There were no fields, only sand drifting into mounds and eddies that swirled in what was now but an autumn breeze. There was no longer a section-line road fifty feet from the front door. It was obliterated. In the farmyard, fences, machinery, and trees were gone, buried. The roofs of sheds stuck out through drifts deeper than a man is tall."

I quote from an account by R. D. Lusk, in the *Saturday Evening Post*, of the way in which that first great storm of blowing dust hit the 470-acre Karnstrum farm in Beadle County, South Dakota. But the description might apply equally well to thousands of other farms on the Great Plains all the way from the Texas Panhandle up to the Canadian border, and to any one of numberless storms that swept the Plains during the next two years. For the "great black blizzard" of November 11, 1933—which darkened the sky in Chicago the following day and as far east as Albany, New York, the day after that—was only a prelude to disaster. During 1934 and 1935 thousands of square miles were to be laid waste and their inhabitants set adrift upon desperate migrations across the land.

Long afterward, an elderly farm woman from the Dust Bowl—one of that straggling army of refugees whose predicament has been made vivid to hundreds of thousands of readers in Steinbeck's *The Grapes of Wrath*—told her story to Paul Taylor and Dorothea Lange in California. She described how her family had done pretty well on their Arkansas farm until the Depression, when prices had fallen and they had found themselves in hard straits. "And then," said she, "the Lord taken a hand."

To many others it must have seemed as if the Lord had taken a hand in bringing the dust storms: as if, not content with visiting upon the country a man-made crisis—a Depression caused by men's inability to manage their economic affairs farsightedly—an omnipotent power had followed it with a visitation of nature: the very land itself had risen in revolt. (To other people, omnipotence may have seemed to be enjoying a sardonic joke at the expense of the New Deal's Agricultural Adjustment program: "So it's crop-reduction you want, is it? Well, I'll show you.") Yet this was no blind stroke of nature such as that of the hurricane which, wandering far from the paths usually followed by hurricanes, tore across New England in the fall of 1938, swamping towns, ripping up forests, and taking nearly seven hundred lives. There was a long story of human error behind it.

During the latter part of the nineteenth century the Great Plains—a region of light rainfall, of sun and high winds, of waving grasses, "where seldom is heard a discouraging word, and the skies are not cloudy all day"—had been the great cattle country of the nation: a vast open area, unfenced at first, where the cowboys tended the cattle-kings' herds. Before the end of the century this range had been badly damaged by over-grazing, according to contemporary Federal reports, and the land was being heavily invaded by homesteaders, who tried manfully to wring a living from the semi-arid soil. But it was not until the Great War brought a huge demand for wheat, and tractors for large-scale machine farming became available, that the Plains began to come into their own as a crop-producing country, and the sod-covering which had protected them was plowed up on the grand scale. Throughout the nineteen-twenties the area devoted to big wheat farms expanded. A new power era had come, it was said, to revolutionize American agriculture; factory methods were being triumphantly applied to the land.

To be sure, there wasn't much rain. The mean annual rainfall was only between 10 and 20 inches on the Plains (as compared with, for example, 20 to 40 in the Mississippi Valley region, 40 to 50 in the North Atlantic region, 40 to 60 in the Ohio and Tennessee basins, and 75 and more in the Pacific Northwest). But there was a pretty favorable series of years during the nineteen-twenties and the farmers were not much disturbed.

In a recent report of the National Resources Committee there is a revealing map. It shows—by means of black dots scattered over the United States—the regions where there was an increase, between 1919 and 1929, in the acreage of land in harvested crops: in short, it shows the regions newly invaded by the crop farmer. Easily the most conspicuous feature of the map is an irregular blur of those black dots running from north to south just a little east of the Rocky Mountains—running from the Canadian border at the northern edge of Montana and North Dakota, down through the Dakotas, western Kansas and Nebraska and eastern Colorado, and then into Oklahoma and northern Texas. This, very roughly, was the next region of promise—and the region of future tragedy.

Nineteen-thirty was a bad year in parts of this territory— and worse elsewhere; it was then, you may recall, that President Hoover was agitated over the question whether Federal money should be granted to drought-distressed farmers. Nineteen-thirty-one was worse in the Dakotas; 1932 was better. Then came 1933: it was a swinger, hot and dry. During that first summer of the New Deal, farmers in South Dakota were finding that they couldn't raise even enough corn to feed the livestock. In western Kansas not a drop of rain fell for months. Already the topsoil was blowing; there were places in Kansas where it was said that farmers had to excavate their tractors before they could begin to plow. That fall came the Armistice Day black blizzard.

But it was during 1934 and 1935—the years when Roosevelt was pushing through his financial reforms, and Huey Long was a national portent, and the languishing NRA was put out of its misery by the Supreme Court—that the thermometer in Kansas stayed week after week at 108 or above and the black storms raged again and again. The drought continued acute during much of 1936. Oklahoma farms became great dunes of shifting sand (so like seashore dunes, said one observer, that one almost expected to smell the salt). Housewives in the drought belt kept oiled cloths on the window sills and between the upper and lower sashes of the windows, and some of them tried to seal up every aperture in their houses with the gummed paper strips used in wrapping parcels, yet still the choking dust filtered in and lay in ripples on the kitchen floor, while outside it blew blindingly across a No Man's Land; roads and farm buildings and once green thickets half-buried in the sand.

It was in those days that a farmer, sitting at his window during a dust storm, remarked that he was counting the Kansas farms as they came by.

Retribution for the very human error of breaking the sod of the Plains had come in full measure. And, as often happens, it was visited upon the innocent as well as upon the guilty—if indeed one could single out any individuals as guilty of so pervasive an error as social shortsightedness.

§ 2

Westward fled the refugees from this new Sahara, as if obedient to the old American tradition that westward lies the land of promise. In 1934 and 1935 Californians became aware of an increasing influx into their state of families and groups of families of "Okies," traveling in ancient family jalopies; but for years the streams of humanity continued to run. They came along U. S. Highway 30 through the Idaho hills, along Highway 66 across New Mexico and Arizona, along the Old Spanish Trail through El Paso, along all the other westward trails. They came in decrepit, square-shouldered 1925 Dodges and 1927 La Salles; in battered 1923 Model-T Fords that looked like relics of some antique culture; in trucks piled high with mattresses and cooking utensils and children, with suitcases, jugs, and sacks strapped to the running boards. "They roll westward like a parade," wrote Richard L. Neuberger. "In a single hour from a grassy meadow near an Idaho road I counted 34 automobiles with the license plates of states between Chicago and the mountains."

They left behind them a half-depopulated countryside. A survey of the farmhouses in seven counties of southeastern Colorado, made in 1936, showed 2878 houses still occupied, 2811 abandoned; and there were also, in that area, 1522 abandoned homesites. The total number of drought refugees who took the westward trek over the mountains was variously estimated in 1939 at from 200,000 upwards—with more coming all the time.

As these wanderers moved along the highways they became a part of a vast and confused migratory movement. When they camped by the wayside they might find themselves next to a family of evicted white Alabama sharecroppers who had been on the move for four years, snatching seasonal farm-labor jobs wherever they could through the Southwest; or next to tenant families from the Arkansas Delta who had been "tractored off" their land—expelled in order that the owner might consolidate two or three farms and operate them with tractors and day labor; or next to lone wanderers who had once held industrial jobs and had now for years been on relief or on the road—jumping freights, hitchhiking, panhandling, shunting back and forth across the country-side in the faint hope of a durable job. And when these varied streams of migrants reached the Coast they found themselves in desperate competition for jobs with individuals or families who for years had been "fruit tramps," moving northward each year with the harvests from the Imperial Valley in southern California to the Sacramento Valley or even to the apple-picking in the Yakima Valley in Wash-ington.

Here in the land of promise, agriculture had long been partly industrialized. Huge farms were in the control of absentee owners or banks or corporations, and were accus-tomed to depend upon the labor of migratory "fruit tramps," who had formerly been mostly Mexicans, Japanese, and other foreigners, but now were increasingly Americans. Those laborers who were lucky enough to get jobs picking cotton or peas or fruit would be sheltered temporarily in camps consisting typically of frame cabins in rows, with a water line between every two rows; they were very likely to find in their cabin no stove, no cots, no water pail. Even the best of the camps offered a way of life strikingly different from that of the ruggedly individualist farmer of the American tradition, who owned his farm or else was preparing, by working as a resident "hired man," or by renting a farm, for the chance of ultimate ownership. These pickers were homeless, voteless nomads, unwanted anywhere save at the harvest season.

When wave after wave of the new migrants reached California, the labor market became glutted, earnings were low, and jobs became so scarce that groups of poverty-stricken families would be found squatting in makeshift Hoovervilles or bunking miserably in their awkward old Fords by the roadside. Being Americans of native stock and accustomed to independence, they took the meager wages and the humiliation bitterly, sought to organize, talked of striking, sometimes struck. At every such threat, something like panic seized the growers. If this new proletariat were permitted to organize, and were to strike at picking time, they might ruin the whole season's output of a perishable crop. There followed anti-picketing ordinances; the spectacle of armed deputies dislodging the migrants from their pitiful camps; violence by bands of vigilantes, to whom these ragged families were not fellow-citizens who had suffered in a great American disaster but dirty, ignorant, superstitious outlanders, failures at life, easy dupes for "red" agitators. This engulfing tide of discontent must be kept moving.

Farther north the refugees were likely to be received with more sympathy, especially in regions where the farms were small and not industrialized; here and there one heard of instances of real hospitality, such as that of the Oregon town which held a canning festival for the benefit of the drought victims in the neighborhood. The well-managed camps set up by the Farm Security Administration were havens of human decency. But to the vast majority of the refugees the promised land proved to be a place of new and cruel tragedy.

§ 3

These unhappy wanderers of the West were only a small minority of the farmers of the United States. What was happening to the rest of them?

We have already seen the AAA beginning the colossal task of making acreage-reduction agreements with millions of farmers in the hope of jacking up the prices of crops and thus restoring American agriculture to economic health. We have seen it making credit available to farmers and trying, through the Farm Mortgage Moratorium Act and other legislation, to free them of the immediate hazards of debt. Just how successful the AAA program could be considered was still, at the end of the decade, a subject of ferocious controversy, if only because one could not separate its effect upon prices from the effects wrought by the drought and by the general improvement in economic conditions after 1933. But certainly farm prices rose. For example, the farmer who had received, on the average, only 33 cents a bushel for wheat in 1933 received 69 cents in 1934, 89 cents in 1935, 92 cents in 1936, $1.24 in 1937, and 88 cents in 1938. The cotton farmer who had received an average price of 5.6 cents a pound for his cotton in 1933 received between 10 and 13 cents during the next four years, and 7.9 cents in 1938. And certainly there was a general improvement in the condition of those farmers who owned their own farms—and lived outside the worst drought areas. A survey of 3,000 farms in various parts of the country—mostly better-than-average farms—made by the Department of Agriculture in 1938 showed a distinct gain in equipment and in comfort; more of these farms had electricity than in 1930, more had tractors and trucks, more had bath-

rooms, automobiles, and radios. But this was not a complete
picture of what had happened.

To begin with, quantities of farmers had lost their farms
during the hideous early years of the Depression—lost them
by reason of debt. These farms had mostly fallen into the
hands of banks or insurance companies, or of small-town
investors who had held the mortgages on them, or were
being held by government bodies for non-payment of taxes,
or had been bought in at tax sales. As early as 1934, the
National Resources Board stated that nearly thirty per cent
of the total value of farm land in the West North Central
States was owned by "creditor or government agencies which
have been compelled to take over the property." At the
small prairie city, the local representative of a big New
York insurance company was a very busy man, supervising
the management of tracts of property far and wide. The
tentacles of the octopus of metropolitan financial control
reached more deeply than ever before into the prairie country—though one must add that this octopus was a most
unwilling one, and would have been only too glad to let go
if it could only get its money back. (As time went on, the
Metropolitan and other insurance companies made determined efforts to find buyers for their farm properties,
financing these buyers on easy terms.) In the callous old
Wall Street phrase, the farms of the United States had been
"passing into stronger hands"; and that meant that more
and more of them, owned by people who did not live on
them, were being operated by tenants.

For over half a century at least, farm tenancy had been
on the increase in the United States. Back in 1880, only 25
per cent of American farms had been run by tenants. Slowly
the percentage had increased; now, during the Depression,
it reached 42. The growth of tenantry caused many mis-
givings, for not only did it shame the fine old Jeffersonian
ideal of individual landholding—an ideal in which most

Americans firmly believed—but it had other disadvantages. Tenants were not likely to put down roots, did not feel a full sense of responsibility for the land and equipment they used, were likely to let it deteriorate, and in general were less substantial citizens than those farmers who had a permanent share in the community. In 1935, less than two-thirds of the tenant farmers in the United States had occupied their present land for more than one year! In the words of Charles and Mary Beard, "Tenants wandered from farm to farm, from landlord to landlord, from region to region, on foot, in battered wagons, or in dilapidated automobiles, commonly dragging families with them, usually to conditions lower in the scale of living than those from which they had fled."

The passing of farms into "stronger hands" was accompanied by another change. More and more the farm owner, whether or not he operated his own farm, was coming to think of himself as a business man, to think of farming as a business. He was less likely to use his farm as a means of subsistence, more likely to use as much of it as possible for the growing of crops for sale. He was more interested in bookkeeping, more alert to the advantages of farm machinery, and especially of operating with tractors on the largest possible scale. A striking example of this trend was the appearance of the "suitcase farmer"—a small-town business man who bought a farm or two, cleared them of houses and barns, spent a few weeks of each year planting and harvesting them (using his own tractor or a hired one), and otherwise devoted himself to his business, not living on the land at all. A Kansas banker told Ladd Haystead, toward the end of the decade, that he estimated that between twenty and thirty per cent of the land in western Kansas was owned by suitcase farmers. This was what was happening to the territory whence the victims of drought had fled!

In certain parts of the South and Southwest this trend

toward making a mechanized business of farming took a form even more sinister in the eyes of those who believed in the Jeffersonian tradition. In these districts farm tenancy was becoming merely a way station on the road to farm industrialism. The tenants themselves were being eliminated. Furthermore, the AAA, strangely enough, was unwittingly assisting the process.

How easy for an owner of farm property, when the government offered him a check for reducing his acreage in production, to throw out some of his tenants or sharecroppers, buy a tractor with the check, and run his farm mechanically with the aid of hired labor—not the sort of year-round hired labor which the old-time "hired man" had represented, but labor engaged only by the day when there happened to be work to be done! During the nineteen-thirties large numbers of renters and sharecroppers, both black and white, were being displaced in the South—to the tune of angry protests by the Southern Tenant Farmers' Union, equally angry retaliation by the landlords and their allies, and a deal of the sort of barbarous cruelty which we have noted in California. In the areas where large-scale cotton farming with the aid of machinery was practicable, tenants were expelled right and left. *Fortune* told of a big Mississippi planter who bought 22 tractors and 13 4-row cultivators, evicted no less than 130 of his 160 sharecropper families, and kept only 30 for day laborers. During the years 1930-37, the sales of farm tractors in ten cotton states increased no less than ninety per cent—and the indications were that at the end of that period the increase was accelerating. While the number of farms operated by tenants was growing elsewhere in the country between 1930 and 1935, it actually declined a little in the West South Central States. In two cotton counties of the Texas Panhandle, studied by Paul S. Taylor in 1937, it declined sharply. And here was the reason: "Commonly, the landlord who purchases a tractor throws two 160-acre farms operated by tenants into an operating unit, and lets both tenants go. Sometimes the rate of displacement is greater, rising to 8, 10, and even 15 families of tenants."

Where did the displaced tenants go? Into the towns, some of them. In many rural areas, census figures showed an increased town population and simultaneously a depopulated countryside. Said the man at a gas station in a Texas town, "This relief is ruining the town. They come in from the country to get on relief." Some of them got jobs running tractors on other farms at $1.25 a day. Some went on to California: out of farming as a settled way of life into farming as big business dependent on a large, mobile supply of labor.

So far this new pattern was only fragmentary and was confined mostly to the South and West, though the number of migratory farm workers was growing fast even along the Atlantic seaboard. Perhaps the onrushing agricultural industrialism would prove as short-lived as the earlier epidemic of tractor farming which had promised so much for the Great Plains during the nineteen-twenties—would lead once more to depletion of the soil and thus to its own undoing as well as the land's. Perhaps those agrobiologists were right who believed that the trend of the future would be toward smaller farms and more intensive yields. The relatively new science of farm chemurgy was revealing all sorts of new industrial uses for farm products; du Pont, for example, was using farm products in the making of cellophane, Duco, motion-picture film, rayon, pyralin, plastecele, fabrikoid, sponges, window shades, hair ornaments, handbags, alcohols, and a lot of other things which one would hardly associate with the old-fashioned farm. Yet even if the farmer of the future who applied new methods to the growing of specialized crops for specialized uses would be able to operate best with a small tract of land, as some people expected, would he be able to operate without more capital than most farmers possessed? That question was still unanswered.

Meanwhile large-scale tractor farming was spreading fast, and was repeating the harshnesses of mid-nineteenth century industrialism—as if America had learned nothing in the interim.

How far would the new trend go? Would great mechanized farm corporations, perhaps controlled from the metropolitan cities, gradually put out of business the smaller farms of those rolling areas, such as abounded in the Old Cotton South, where tractors could not readily be used? Would the cotton picker invented by the Rust brothers of Memphis accelerate this change? What would become, then, of the already miserable sharecroppers? Were other parts of the country destined sooner or later to go through the same sort of transition that was taking place in the South and West, producing a huge, roving, landless proletariat of the land, helpless if unorganized, menacing if organized because it had no stake in the land and its settled institutions? These questions, too, waited for answers.

§ 4

For a generation or more the conservationists had been warning the country that it was squandering its heritage of land and forests and fields and minerals and animal life: that in effect it was living riotously on its capital of national resources. But to most citizens the subject had seemed dull, academic. Now, in the Dust Bowl, the Lord had "taken a hand" in instruction. And hardly had the black blizzards blown themselves out when—as if distrustful whether the country properly realized that droughts and floods were not incompatible phenomena, but were associated results of human misuse of the land—the Lord drove the lesson home. The rivers went on a rampage.

"In 1936"—I quote from Stuart Chase's summary—"the Merrimac, Connecticut, Hudson, Delaware, Susquehanna, Potomac, Allegheny, and Ohio all went wild. The Potomac was up twenty-six feet at Washington and long barriers of sandbags protected government buildings. . . . Pittsburgh was under ten to twenty feet of water and was without lights, transport, or power. The life of 700,000 people was paralyzed. The food supply was ruined, the steel industry at a standstill." The following January, the unseasonably warm and rainy January of 1937, the Ohio River produced what was perhaps, all things considered, the worst flood in American history.

The bare facts of that flood are impressive. The Ohio rose 7.9 feet higher than it had ever risen before at Cincinnati, 6.8 feet higher than it had ever risen before at Louisville. Nine hundred people were estimated to have lost their lives by drowning or by other casualties resulting from the flood. The number of families driven from their homes was set at 500,000; the number still homeless a month after the worst of the crisis was set by the Red Cross at 299,000.

But these figures give no impression whatever of what men and women experienced in each town during the latter days of January as the swirling waters rose till the Ohio seemed a great rushing muddy lake full of floating wreckage, and the cold rain drizzled inexorably down, and every stream added its swollen contribution to the torrent. Railroad tracks and roads washed away. Towns darkened as the electric-light plants were submerged. Business halted, food supplies stopped, fires raging out of control, disease threatening. The city of Portsmouth, Ohio, opening six great sewer valves and letting seven feet of water rush into its business district, lest its famous concrete flood wall be destroyed. Cincinnati giving City Manager Dykstra dictatorial powers. The radio being used to direct rescue work and issue warnings and instructions to the population as other means of communication failed: a calm voice at the microphone telling rescuers to row to such-and-such an address and take a family off the roof, to row somewhere else and help an old woman out of a second-story window. Breadlines. The Red Cross, the Coast Guard, the WPA aiding in the work of rescue and reorganization. Martial law. Churches above the water line being used as refuges. Dead bodies of horses and cattle—yes, and of men and women—floating through the streets, along with tree branches, gasoline tanks, beams from collapsed houses. Mud everywhere, as the waters receded—mud and stench. Most dramatic of all, perhaps, the triumphant fight to save Cairo, Illinois: men piling more and more sandbags atop the levee, standing guard day and night, rushing to strengthen the wall of defense wherever it weakened, as the waters rose and rose—and did not quite break over.

By this time everybody with any capacity for analysis was ready to begin to understand what the government technicians had long been saying in their monographs; what Stuart Chase and Paul B. Sears and David Cushman Coyle, the Mississippi Valley Committee and the National Resources Committee, and Pare Lorenz's very fine films, "The River" and "The Plough that Broke the Plains," were repeating in more popular terms: that floods as well as dust storms were largely the result of reckless misuse of the land. Indeed, as early as the beginning of 1936, when the Supreme Court threw out the Agricultural Adjustment Act, Congress took account of the new understanding in revamping its farm program. The new law was labeled a Soil Conservation and Domestic Allotment Act, and the new crop adjustments were called "soil-erosion adjustments."

Already at many points the government was at work restoring a deforested and degrassed and eroded countryside. In the CCC camps, young men were not only getting healthy employment, but were renewing and protecting the forest cover by planting trees, building firebreaks, removing inflammable underbrush, and building check dams in gullies. The experts of the Soil Conservation Service were showing farmers how to fight erosion by terracing, contour plowing, rotation of crops, strip cropping, and gully planting. After the dust storms, for example, they demonstrated how the shifting dunes of Dalhart, Texas, could be held in place by planting them with milo, Sudan grass, and black amber cane. Under the supervision of the Forest Service, the government between 1935 and 1939 planted 127,000,000 trees to serve as windbreaks on the Great Plains. The Taylor Grazing Act of 1934 stopped homesteading on the great range and gave the Department of the Interior power to prevent over-grazing on eighty million acres.

PWA funds were going into the construction of dams which would aid in flood control (and also extend navigation), such as that at Fort Peck in eastern Montana, which was to create a lake 175 miles long. The TVA—that most combative and most remarkable of New Deal agencies—was not simply creating a new electric-light and power system in competition with privately owned utilities (though this part of its work stirred up ten times as much excitement as all the rest put together); its dams were also controlling floods, and it was showing farmers how to deal with erosion, how to use phosphates. (In 1937, during the Ohio River flood, the Tennessee River did not misbehave.) Other PWA funds were providing a better irrigation system for parts of Utah where water was running short. The colossal dam at Grand Coulee, Washington—the biggest thing ever built by man—was getting ready to pump water for the irrigation of 1,200,000 acres of desert land, as well as to provide hydroelectric power in quantity (like its sister dam at Bonneville) for the future development of the Northwest. These were only a few of the numerous enterprises going ahead simultaneously.

Nor was the government undertaking these enterprises in a wholly piecemeal manner: through its National Resources Committee and other agencies it was making comprehensive studies of the country's resources and equipment, so that the movement of restoration and regeneration could proceed with a maximum of wisdom.

§ 5

With the aid of these studies—and of the lessons taught by drought and flood—more and more Americans, during the latter nineteen-thirties, were beginning to see the problem of their country's future in a new light. They were beginning to realize that it had reached maturity. No longer was it growing hand-over-fist.

Immigration was no longer adding appreciably to its numbers: indeed, during the years between 1931 and 1936, the number of aliens *emigrating* from the United States had been larger each year than the number *immigrating*: the tide had actually been trickling in reverse. If, beginning in 1936, the incoming tide had increased again as Europeans sought to escape from the shadow of Hitlerism, even so the total remained tiny in comparison with those of pre-war years. Ellis Island was no longer a place of furious activity. The time was at hand when the number of foreign-born people in the United States would be sharply diminished by death, and the sound of foreign languages would be heard less and less in the streets of American cities. Already the schools, the manufacturers of children's clothing, and the toy manufacturers were beginning to notice the effects of the diminished birth rate (accentuated by the sharp drop during the early Depression years). Writing in the spring of 1938, Henry Pratt Fairchild reported that there were over 1,600,000 fewer children under 10 in the United States than there had been five years earlier. School principals, confronting smaller entering classes of children, could well understand what the population experts were talking about when they predicted a slower and slower population growth for the country, with an increasing proportion of old people and a decreasing proportion of young ones. They could see the change taking place before their own eyes.

That the frontier was closed was not yet quite true, a generation of historians to the contrary notwithstanding; for the Northwest was still a land of essentially frontier possibilities. Yet for a long time past, young men and women bent on fortune had mostly been going, not west, but to the cities. If the victims of the Dust Bowl and the tractor had pushed west, their fate had been ironic. The brief return to the country of great numbers of jobless city dwellers during the early Depression years had only temporarily slowed down the movement from farm to city and town. For a long time past, the fastest-growing communities had been, by and large, not Western boom towns but the suburbs which ringed the big cities—and during the nineteen-thirties these suburbs were still adding to their numbers. Industry, by and large, was no longer moving westward; the great bulk of the country's manufacturing was still done along the north Atlantic seaboard and in the strip of territory running thence out through Pennsylvania and Ohio to Chicago and St. Louis—and some observers even believed they detected during the nineteen-thirties a slight shift back toward the East.

American individuals and families were becoming more nomadic. This was partly due to the omnipresence of the automobile; there were three million more cars on the road in 1937 than in 1929, for though fewer cars were sold, more old ones were still in use. Partly, as we have seen, it was due to the Depression search for jobs and to the eviction of farm tenants. But American *institutions* appeared, geographically, to be settling down.

Still there was a chance for a far richer development of the country, and the chance was most visible west of the Great Plains. Yet if this development was to be durable, the new pioneering must be more disciplined than the old. The hard fact that the days were over when Americans could plunder and move on, stripping off forests, ripping out minerals, and plowing up grasslands without regard to the long consequences, was now penetrating the public consciousness—even while the men and women whose farms had blown away were still wandering homeless through the land.

Chapter Nine

THE VOICE WITH THE SMILE WINS

§ 1

DANCE orchestras were blaring forth "The Music Goes 'Round and 'Round" and one could hardly turn a radio dial without hearing the ubiquitous refrain. Major Bowes was the current radio sensation, so warmly did he inquire into the life histories of the yodelers and jews-harp-players on his Amateur Hour, and so spontaneous and unexpected seemed the well-rehearsed programs. At the movie houses Fred Astaire and Ginger Rogers were dancing nimbly in "Follow the Fleet." Gary Cooper was about to introduce his audiences to the word "pixillated" in the hilarious court-room scene of "Mr. Deeds Goes to Town." Seven-year-old Shirley Temple was becoming the rising star of Hollywood. She had no such income-tax troubles as had Mae West, whose salary of $480,833 for the preceding year had been second only, in all the United States, to that of William Randolph Hearst; nor could any Shirley Temple picture attract at its opening such crowds as greeted Charlie Chaplin's "Modern Times"; but her curls and her childish smile made the great American heart throb with sentiment. (She was about to appear in "Captain January.")

To scores of thousands of readers, *Life with Father* was still offering an acquaintance with the rambunctious Clarence Day, senior; *North to the Orient,* an air ride with the Lindberghs. Among best-selling novels, *Vein of Iron* and *It Can't Happen Here* were yielding their leadership to *The Last Puritan,* and people who believed in the finer things of life were expressing pleasure that a genuine hundred-per-cent philosopher like George Santayana should have been able to hit commercial success on the nose. In the fastnesses of the publishing house of Macmillan the editors were wondering whether a forthcoming novel of theirs, Margaret Mitchell's *Gone with the Wind*, might possibly sell as well as *Anthony Adverse*. (It would not only do that but within its first six months would sell over a million copies—a prodigious record—and would set ladies' luncheon tables from coast to coast buzzing with the question whether Scarlett O'Hara really got Rhett Butler back—and who ought to play Scarlett on the screen.)

It was a cold winter in the North, with heavy drifts of snow. Sales of skiing equipment were noteworthy, and the snow trains bore away to the uplands innumerable incipient experts in the slalom—or in the lesser art of teetering safely down a very small hill. Over in Germany the Olympic winter sports were being held, as a prelude to that monstrous summer carnival of athletics in which it was to be revealed to the eyes even of Adolf Hitler that Nordics, whatever their transcendent virtues, could not run as fast as black Jesse Owens. (The Germans, however, would have their reply ready: had not their Max Schmeling confounded the sports writers by defeating Joe Louis at the Yankee Stadium by a technical knockout in the twelfth round?)

If the zest of ladies and gentlemen for corporate finance was being circumscribed by the SEC, they at least could undertake imaginary feats of financial daring in the parlor game of "Monopoly." The time was approaching when a popular if short-lived diversion among otherwise reasonable Americans would be the exchange of such curious pleasantries as these: "Knock, knock." "Who's there?" "Eskimo, Christian, and Italian." "Eskimo, Christian, and Italian who?" "Eskimo, Christian, and Italian no lies."

In short, the year 1936 was getting under way—the year when President Roosevelt's New Deal would have to face the voters.

How much water had gone under the bridge since 1932, when Roosevelt had first been a candidate for the White House! Gone was the prospect of imminent financial catastrophe. Gone was popular distrust of the solvency of the banks: bank failures now were few and far between. Gone was any real hope of collecting the war debts (except from Finland); was it possible that only five years previously, Herbert Hoover had tried to halt the Depression by proposing a year's delay in payments? Gone was any hope of early return to the traditional international gold standard: managed currencies had become the order of the day. Waning at least, if not gone, was the fear of immediate headlong inflation of the currency. (Although the huge Federal deficits—larger than any in Hoover's time—caused grave headshakings, nevertheless people went right on buying government bonds.) Yet waning also was any real expectation of an abrupt economic upsurge which would eliminate speedily the unemployment problem. Although people still talked of "the emergency" or "the crisis," clearly they were no longer thinking of any "sudden juncture," any "moment of danger," such as dictionary definitions of those terms would imply; this "emergency" had become semi-permanent. The economic system had pulled out of its sinking spell of 1929-33 only to become a chronic invalid, whose temperature was lower now in the mornings but showed no signs of returning quickly to normal. Americans were getting used to the fact that nine or ten million of their fellow-countrymen were out of work.

No longer was there any question, in the minds of most Americans capable of realistic thought, that the government must carry a heavy responsibility for the successful or unsuccessful working of the economic system. Having once intervened, it could not extricate itself even if it would. The debate was only about the extent to which the intervention should go. The economic headquarters of the country had not only moved from Wall Street to Washington, but apparently had settled down there for an indefinite stay. If, as we have seen, economic authority still tended to gravitate from the countryside to the cities and from the lesser cities to New York, until great tracts of land in the Mississippi Valley were subject to the dictates of New York executives, no longer did those executives issue their dictates as they pleased; when Washington spoke, they knew they heard their master's voice. Even the great House of Morgan—head, front, and symbol of the one-time sovereignty of Wall Street—had been forced to divide itself into two concerns, one for commercial banking, the other for investment banking. No major decision could any longer be made in Wall Street without the question being asked, "What will Washington say to this?"

The government was growing in size and complexity as well as in power. Whenever a new fever attacked the body politic, new Federal agencies multiplied—like white corpuscles in the blood—to fight it. The custom of the time decreed that each agency must be known by the initials of its title, but soon there were so many that only an expert could identify them by these alphabetical designations. RFC, NRA, and WPA might be easy even for the elementary class in governmental nomenclature; AAA, CCC, SEC, and TVA for the intermediate class; but what did HOLC stand for, and FHA, and FCA and NYA—to mention only a few?

Because the riddles which the New Deal faced were beyond its ability (or, probably, anybody's ability) to solve with real success, and because anyhow it was easier to hand out subsidies to the victims of a maladjustment than to bring the maladjustment to an end, this swelling government establishment had become a huge subsidizing machine—handing out Federal relief payments, farm allotment payments, and other "emergency" benefits innumerable, to say nothing of war bonuses and such venerable subsidies as kept the color in the wan cheeks of the merchant marine; until by 1936 an appropriation of a hundred million dollars looked like small change, and even a billion seemed no bigger than a light-year seems to an astronomer.

All this development of the Federal power the Republicans viewed with loud alarm; yet with such an air of inevitability did the growth take place that one wondered whether the Republicans, should they come to power, would be able to reverse the trend. It seemed likely that the difference between the two parties would be that one of them, in moving toward the concentration of power in Washington, would move with the throttle open; the other, with the brakes on.

In the world outside the United States the changes between 1932 and 1936 were even more striking. No longer could France be thought of as the pre-eminent power on the Continent. British diplomacy was beginning that series of surrenders and evasions which was presently to reduce sharply the prestige of the Empire. The League of Nations, which had failed to make Japan regret its invasion of Manchuria in 1931, and was now failing to make Mussolini regret his invasion of Ethiopia in 1935, was in its death throes. The Nazi government of Germany, though only three years old, was already alarming the Continent; and was about to begin, with its march into the Rhineland, that series of bold territorial moves which were to keep all Europe in fear of immediate general war. Mussolini, the father of fascism, was shifting from opposition to Hitler to alliance with this younger and more furious disciple of the totalitarian idea. The European center of gravity was moving definitely toward Berlin.

No longer were vital economic decisions made at international conferences of bankers; now they were made only by the political leaders of states. That trend toward concentration of national authority in the government which was noticeable in Washington was noticeable almost everywhere else—even in Britain and France. Russia was becoming less and less the exponent of a revolutionary form of economic and social organization and more and more a nation whose dictatorial government pursued nationalist ends in a world of national rivalries. In Germany, the central power was now absolute. National Socialism had become the most dynamic religion of the day, and the head of the state was rapidly becoming an object of worship. Watching the German spectacle, American observers were wondering whether the world was irresistibly due for an era of political, racial, religious, and intellectual intolerance.

It had been expected that the economic barriers between nations would gradually be lifted after the worst of the Depression was over. But now these barriers were stronger than ever. In Germany the objective of the Nazi government was no longer primarily to solve the insoluble economic problems which confronted every government in the nineteen-thirties, but to give its people the thrill and pride of conquest; and to achieve prosperity incidentally by putting the unemployed to work (as in a vast public-works campaign) at armament-making, and by controlling its inflated currency and well-nigh every other economic activity through the exercise of central authority. The Nazis were defying half the economic axioms of the days of free business enterprise and—at least temporarily—getting away with it. They were in fact abolishing economics entirely, in the sense that the word implies an organization of the decisions of free men, and were substituting for it an organization of compulsions and conquests.

As Germany re-armed, so did the other governments. By 1936 an international armaments boom was in full swing. Indeed, so dependent were the various national economies becoming upon arms manufacturing that some observers were beginning to wonder which would be worse, the general war which so many people dreaded, or the true peace which so many people longed for and which would put out the fires in hundreds of factories and might light the fires of rebellion in millions of hungry men.

Whenever people thought of "the danger of war," they thought of such a general headlong conflict as had broken out in 1914. Experts on foreign affairs had been predicting at intervals ever since the early nineteen-twenties that such a conflict would surely break out next month or next year or within two or three years at the most; and now their predictions were more urgent than ever. Yet the pattern of international relations which was being established in Europe was a pattern neither of general war nor of true peace. It was a pattern of continuous half-war: of nations remaining partially mobilized, partially on a war footing; making quick sallies to grab this territory or that, knowing that the dread of another 1914 would prevent anybody from stopping them until it was too late; of nations gaining new spheres of influence by subsidizing revolts in other countries (or even aiding these revolts by force of arms) as the Italians and Germans were shortly to aid Franco's revolt in Spain. In short, it was a pattern of shifting, localized, undeclared, unceasing conflict. War? Peace? This was neither, by the vocabulary even of 1932: it was something in between, to which the words of an earlier day no longer applied.

Truly it was a new world upon which Americans were looking in 1936: a world full of the wreckage of the verities not merely of 1929 but even of 1932.

§ 2

At last business conditions in the United States were definitely improving. The Federal Reserve Board's Adjusted Index of Industrial Production (which as you may recall had sunk as low as 58 and 59 in the crises of 1932 and early 1933, had leaped to 100 during the New Deal Honeymoon, had then slipped back to 72 by November, 1933, and had obstinately hung in the seventies and eighties throughout 1934) had now begun to show a pretty definite upward trend. By the beginning of 1935 it had risen as far as 90. By the end of 1935 it had reached 101. And after a brief relapse into the nineties, it swept on during 1936 to 104 in June, 108 in July and August, 109 in September, 110 in October, 114 in November, and 121 in December—within striking distance of the record figure of 125 which had been set in 1929.

A very pretty picture indeed—yet one could not appraise it rightly without noting several disquieting facts. One was that the production figure would have to rise much higher than 125 to absorb the bulk of the unemployed. Labor-saving machinery, speed-up methods of work, and executive efficiency had now made it possible to produce more goods with less workers. Perhaps there was significance also in the fact that as a result of the drop in the birth rate and the closing down of immigration, a larger proportion of the people of the country than ever before were of working age. Another disquieting fact was that the improvement was being secured at a price—the price of a rising Federal debt. The net deficits of the United States government had been running as follows:—

Fiscal year ending June 30, 1933 (which strad-
   dled the Hoover and Roosevelt Adminis-
   trations): $2,602,000,000
Fiscal year ending June 30, 1934: $3,630,000,000
Fiscal year ending June 30, 1935: $3,002,000,000
To which was now being added the 1936 figure
   of $4,361,000,000

This latter enormous figure for 1936 was by no means attributable solely to New Deal policies; for it was not only affected by the destruction by the Supreme Court of the processing taxes levied by the AAA, but was also very gravely enlarged by Congress's voting of the Bonus over Roosevelt's veto. On June 15, 1936, the postmen sallied forth to distribute over a billion and a half dollars in bonds and checks. Most of these were cashed within the next three months. What wonder that the deficit was larger than ever before—and that, with these new funds being spent all over the country, the business index was rising?

Throughout these early years of the New Deal the levels of prices and wages and the structure of corporate and private debt were being artificially supported by government spending—or, to put it another way, by the failure of the government to levy high enough taxes to take care of the spending. If it had been possible for the law of supply and demand to work unhindered, prices and wages—and the volume of corporate and private debt—would theoretically have fallen to a "natural" level and activity could have been resumed again. But it was not possible for the law of supply and demand to work unhindered. In a complex twentieth-century economy, deflation was too painful to be endured. Hoover had set up the RFC because the banks couldn't take it; Roosevelt had set up the Federal relief system because human beings couldn't take it. Some of Roosevelt's advisers, embracing the theory of John Maynard Keynes (and also making a virtue of necessity), had been arguing for some time that when the government, by over-spending, poured new money into the economic bloodstream, business would be stimulated and a new adjustment would be reached at a higher level, thus rendering the anguish of deflation unnecessary. The new money would "prime the pump" of business; presently all sorts of new businesses would be undertaken, there would be a boom, the unemployed would be absorbed in industry, and all would be well. Roosevelt hoped that this would happen, and so far the process seemed to be beginning. Business was picking up. But where, oh, where, were the new enterprises?

During the preceding year there had been a considerable volume of capital flotations, but chiefly these flotations had been undertaken merely to refund old issues of securities at lower interest rates: interest rates having gone down, corporations had been seizing the happy opportunity to substitute 3¾ per cent bonds for 5 per cent bonds. Few of the flotations had represented the investment of money in the expansion of old businesses or in the inauguration of new ones. Uninvested money was piling up in the banks instead of being spent in building and equipping new factories. In short, the pump was not working right.

Of course it was not working right, argued most business men. The trouble was that investors were frightened. Naturally they were distrustful of the New Deal's reformist zeal and of the very spending policy which was supposed to entice their money into the capital markets. Surely the pump would work really well before long, replied the New Dealers; and how could they cut expenses without destroying buying power and perhaps starving their fellow-citizens? Eagerly they continued to prime the pump. Year after year, in his Budget messages, the President who had berated Hoover in 1932 for failing to balance the Budget expressed the hope that next year, or the year after, the balance would at last be achieved; but like the man who swears that this little drink is positively his last one, presently he began to sound as if he did not convince even himself.

There were other somewhat unsettling facts about this recovery, too. The Lynds noticed, for example, that in "Middletown" it was harder now for a man to start a small business than it had been even a decade before. "The Middletown tradition is all in favor of an enterprising man with an idea and a shoestring of capital," they noted. "But it is this type of small enterprise that has gone under in Middletown in the Depression." Personal savings had been eaten up, bankers were cautious, the trend in manufacturing was toward such large and expensively equipped shops that the small manufacturer was at a disadvantage, and the going concerns in many lines of business were inclined, with or without the aid of their trade associations, to make things hot for a newcomer. It was the big corporations, by and large, which were making the profits; small ones were lucky indeed to break even. Here was a barrier to new investment (which will be noted more fully in the last chapter of this book): the odds were against making money in fledgling enterprises.

Even inside going businesses, as the Lynds also pointed out, the ladder of opportunity was not so readily climbed as it once had been. The skilled laborer was finding that the higher-paid and more important positions were going to a different class of specially trained men. "In other words," said the Lynds, "Andrew Carnegie's advice to enterprising young men to begin at the bottom no longer appears to be sound advice. Men of his type are advising young men today to get a toehold in one of the managerial or technical departments halfway up the ladder."

Was this a sign of a gradual crystallization of class structure in American society? Certainly it was hard for reliefers to get themselves out of the relief class. It was hard for dispossessed farmers to get back on the land. If it was also harder than it had been for the man without a higher education or influential friends to get a job in the upper ranks of business, how would fare the American dream of a classless democracy in which anyone could go to the top?

§ 3

But how welcome was even this modest and dubiously founded recovery of 1936! The railroads, to be sure, were not getting much of it; but the automobile companies were selling more cars than in any previous season save 1928 and 1929, the steel industry was operating close to capacity at last, the consumers' goods industries and chain stores were mostly going strong, and even the building industry—which had come to a prolonged and almost complete halt during the worst of the Depression—was climbing briskly (with government aid) up the lower foothills of recovery. (No longer was it inevitably embarrassing to ask an architect what he was doing these days.) There seemed to be plenty of free-and-easy spending among the prosperous: Miami was having its best season since the collapse of the Florida boom in the distant days of Calvin Coolidge, there were lavish débutante parties in the big cities, the race tracks were crowded, the cash registers were tinkling in the night clubs. Apparently the men of means, looking ruefully back on what had happened to their investments under Hoover and meditating fearfully on what might happen to them under Roosevelt, were putting their money where they could enjoy it right away.

There were visible promises, too, if one looked about one, of what might prove to be a new industrial age. A few of the more progressively managed railroads, shaking themselves out of their long technological nap, were running slick new streamlined trains made of duralumin, stainless steel, or corten. The Union Pacific had started the new movement by completing a dural train early in 1934, the Burlington had followed with a stainless steel Zephyr, and by the end of 1936 there were 358 cars made of these new materials in operation or under construction for the Class I railroads of the country. Whenever one of the fancy new trains was put on exhibition, crowds surged through it, entranced: here was a symbol of the new America they wanted. Air-conditioning was coming in fast, too, not only in the movie theatres and railroad trains but in restaurants and shops and offices as well. As for streamlining, it had become a briefly overworked fad. In 1934 and 1935 some of the automobile companies had produced cars so bulbous, so obesely curved as to defy the natural preference of the eye for horizontal lines; the city streets were being invaded by new busses streamlined against the terrific air resistance built up while edging through urban traffic at ten miles an hour; and the streamline idea was being applied by designers even to quite stationary buildings and to objects of furniture which would never have to confront a stronger draft than that of an electric fan.

New ocean liners were breaking records for size and speed. In June, 1935, the New York waterfront had been lined with crowds and the harbor had resounded with tootings of welcome as the *Normandie* arrived; a year later the reception was to be repeated as the *Queen Mary* swept in from England. As for airplanes, one had only to compare the great silvery Douglas DC3 of June, 1936, which had a cruising speed of 200 miles an hour, with the 110-mile-an-hour transport planes of 1932. Coast-to-coast travel in overnight air sleepers had become a matter of routine. In October, 1936, the China Clipper finished its first scheduled round-trip passenger flight across the Pacific to Manila and back. Not yet was there any passenger service across the Atlantic by plane, but there was service by air nonetheless: Germany's newest dirigible, the *Hindenburg*, began in 1936 a regular series of flights—nor did any one then guess what would happen to that graceful ship of the air on May 6, 1937.

The motorist too could get, here and there, a glimpse of the promise of a new world when he found himself cruising at 60 miles an hour on a huge well-banked highway, with underpasses and majestic clover-leaf intersections—a highway which smoothly skirted the towns in which, a few years before, his car would have been clogged in local traffic. It was all new and exciting, this world of beautiful speed, as exciting as it was to follow a guide about Rockefeller Center, New York, the one and only skyscraper group to rise in the United States during the nineteen-thirties, and to see how a combination of cool design and gay planting and shining new materials could brighten the metropolitan scene.

New materials? Why, it was beginning to seem as if the chemists and metallurgists could produce any sort of substance that was needed. Lighter, tougher steels, made with nickel, chromium, tungsten, vanadium, molybdenum. Plastics suited to the making of anything from automobile steering wheels to tableware, from radio cabinets to dice. New artificial fibers made from cellulose, and new processes for extracting cellulose from Southern pines. Plywood with absurdly un-woodlike qualities. Certainly the technical men were making ready the materials for the world of tomorrow, however discouragingly the production of these marvels lagged. What boundless possibilities might be locked in the development of tray agriculture? What marvels of efficiency might not the photo-electric cell make possible? What would television do to entertainment and news distribution in the future? Would the two-cycle Diesel engine revolutionize the production and transmission of power? And how would people live when the pre-fabricated house moved out of the phase of experiment into the phase of mass production? Questions like these were running through people's minds; the American imagination was beginning to break loose again.

Was there, perhaps, some new machine, some new gadget the furious demand for which would set in motion a new boom—something like the automobile or the radio? In the spring and summer of 1936 a great many people thought they had found one. Way back in the summer of 1929, just before the Panic, a bacteriologist named Arthur G. Sherman had built for his family a little house on wheels which could be towed behind his car on vacations. It attracted so much favorable attention wherever he went that he built a few more, and exhibited one of them at the Detroit Automobile Show in 1930. Presently he was manufacturing them on an expanding scale, other manufacturers were leaping in, householders with a knack for tools were building their own trailers in their backyards. By 1936 the number of house trailers on the road was estimated by *Automotive Daily News* at 160,000. On New Year's Day, 1937, Florida observers reported that these contrivances were crossing the state line at the rate of 25 an hour. Roger Babson declared that within twenty years half the population of the United States would be living in them. What more lovely vision could there be—provided one did not focus one's attention on real-estate values, taxes, steady jobs, schooling for the children, sanitation problems, and other such prosy details—than the vision of the coming of a carefree era when the restless American could sell his house, climb into his trailer, and go forth to live the life of the open road?

§ 4

The amount of money which was going into new things like the trailer industry, however, was but a fraction of what was needed. What was holding back the rest?

However economists might disagree upon this point, there was very little disagreement among the potential investors themselves, the possessors of capital, the well-to-do, and especially the very rich. What was wrong, they were sure, was "lack of confidence"—and this lack of confidence was caused by the arbitrary rule of an Administration which spent money recklessly, followed unsound and inflationary principles of public finance, yielded to the advice of semi-communist brain-trusters, burdened business with grievous taxes, wasted the tax money on crazy boondoggling schemes for the pampering and political bribing of the unenterprising poor, harassed business men with hasty and unpredictable and paralyzing reforms and with government competition, slaughtered little pigs to win votes from the farmers, encouraged labor agitators to tie up industry, generally opposed the "profit system," and threatened American freedom by dictating to Congress, discrediting the Supreme Court, and undermining the Constitution.

On these and other charges against the Administration endless changes were rung in the conservative press, in the speeches of conservative business men and political leaders, in the circulars of such varied organizations as the Liberty League, the Crusaders, the Defenders, and the American Nationalists, Inc., and above all in the private conversation of the well-to-do.

That the large property owners and the managers of large businesses should have become indignant was not at all surprising. Buffeted and frightened by the Depression, they had at first hailed Roosevelt as a deliverer. Presently they had discovered that he did not intend the "recovery" for which he was working to be a recovery of things as they had been in 1929; he wanted things changed. He not only continued to press for reforms, he tore to bits the fiscal promises of the 1932 Democratic platform and of his own campaign speeches. He set out to champion the less fortunate, to denounce such financiers and big business men as stood in his way; and as their opposition to him hardened, so also did his opposition to them. Raymond Moley has told how Roosevelt, sitting with a group of men discussing the tenor of an impending Presidential speech, would listen to their accounts of the derogatory Roosevelt stories that were going the rounds of Wall Street and State Street and Chestnut Street and La Salle Street, and how his face would stiffen, till it became clear that the speech would be—as Moley said—"more like a thistle than an olive branch."

It was natural, then, that men and women of means should feel that the President had changed his course and singled them out as objects of the enmity of the government. It was natural that they should have become confirmed in this feeling when, with half an eye to undermining Huey Long's "Share Our Wealth" offensive, he backed in the summer of 1935 a revenue bill which stepped up taxes on the rich. It was even natural that they should have felt so strongly about what had happened since 1933 as to seem to forget that there had been anything wrong with the country before 1933.

Yet the lengths to which some of them went in their opposition, and the extent to which this opposition became concentrated, among a great many of them, into a direct and flaming hatred of Roosevelt himself, constituted one of the memorable curiosities of the nineteen-thirties.

All the fumblings of a government seeking to extricate the country from the world-wide Depression which had followed the slackening of nineteenth-century expansion; all the maneuvers of an Administration trying to set right what seemed to have gone wrong in the financial world during the previous decade, to redress the disadvantages under which the common man labored, and simultaneously to maintain its political appeal to this common man—all these things were reduced, in the minds of thousands of America's "best people," to the simple proposition that Franklin D. Roosevelt was intent upon becoming a dictator at their expense. Much that Roosevelt did lent a color of justification to this version of history; yet in reducing so much to so little these people performed one of the most majestic feats of simplification in all American history.

This hatred of Roosevelt was strong, though far from unanimous, among the well-to-do in all sections of the country. It was strongest and most nearly unanimous among the very rich and in those favored suburbs and resorts where people of means were best insulated against uncomfortable facts and unorthodox opinions. (To live in Locust Valley or Greenwich, let us say, to work in Wall Street, and to read only the New York *Herald Tribune* in the morning and the New York *Sun* at night, offered excellent insulation, especially if one concentrated devotedly upon the daily lamentations of Mark Sullivan and the uniformly sour interpretations of Administration policies in the financial columns of the *Sun*.) In general, the hatred was most intense in the cities along the Atlantic seaboard, with the exception of Washington, where there were moderating opportunities to see New Dealers in the flesh and to discover that they were human after all. It flared higher and higher during 1934 and 1935 and continued at a high temperature until about 1938, when it appeared to weaken somewhat, if only through exhaustion.

Sometimes the anti-Roosevelt mood was humorous. On the commuting trains and at the downtown lunch clubs there was an epidemic of Roosevelt stories, like that of the psychiatrist who died and arrived in Heaven to be whisked off to attend God Himself: "You see, He has delusions of grandeur— He thinks He's Franklin D. Roosevelt." But there was nothing humorous in the attitude of the gentlemen sitting in the big easy chairs at their wide-windowed clubs when they agreed vehemently that Roosevelt was not only a demagogue but a communist. "Just another Stalin —only worse." "We might as well be living in Russia right now." At the well-butlered dinner party the company agreed, with rising indignation, that Roosevelt was "a traitor to his class." In the smoking compartment of the Pullman car the traveling executives compared contemptuous notes on the President's utter ignorance of business. "He's never earned a nickel in his life—what has he ever done but live off his mother's income?" In the cabañas at Miami Beach the sun-tanned winter visitors said their business would be doing pretty well if it weren't for THAT MAN. In the country-club locker room the golfers talked about the slow pace of the stock market as they took off their golf shoes; and when, out of a clear sky, one man said, "Well, let's hope somebody shoots him," the burst of agreement made it clear that everybody knew who was meant.

There was an epidemic, too, of scurrilous Roosevelt gossip. Educated and ordinarily responsible people not only insisted, but sincerely believed, that "everybody in Washington knew" the whole Roosevelt family was drunk most of the time; that the reason why Mrs. Roosevelt was "so all over the place" was that she was planning to succeed her husband in the Presidency "until it's time for the sons to take over"; and that Roosevelt was insane. Hadn't a caller recently sat with him and tried to talk public affairs, only to be greeted with prolonged and maniacal laughter? From this point the gossip ran well over the line into the unprintable.

A good deal of the bitter anti-Roosevelt talk could not, of course, be taken at its face value. Often it was a form of conscious self-indulgence in the emotional satisfaction of blaming a personal scapegoat for everything that went wrong. When, as in a *New Yorker* cartoon, a group of ladies and gentlemen sallied forth to the trans-lux theatre "to hiss Roosevelt," they enjoyed the sort of release that many liberals had enjoyed when they blamed all the ills of the economic system on the personal wickedness of bankers, or that Nazis enjoyed when they blamed all the ills of Germany on the Jews. To find a scapegoat is to be spared, for the moment, any necessity for further examination of the facts or for further thought.

Yet to the extent that it stopped factual inquiry and thought, the Roosevelt-hating was costly, not only to recovery, but to the haters themselves. Because as a group (there were many exceptions) the well-to-do regarded the presence of Roosevelt in the White House as a sufficient explanation for all that was amiss and as a sufficient excuse for not taking a more active part in new investment, they inevitably lost prestige among the less fortunate. For the rich and powerful could maintain their prestige only by giving the general public what it wanted. It wanted prosperity, economic expansion. It had always been ready to forgive all manner of deficiencies in the Henry Fords who actually produced the goods, whether or not they made millions in the process. But it was not disposed to sympathize unduly with people who failed to produce the goods, no matter how heart-rending their explanations for their failure. Roosevelt-hating thrust the owners and managers of business into inaction—into trying to resist the tide of affairs, to set back the clock. It made them conservatives in the sense that they were trying to hold on to old things, whereas before 1929 they had been, in their own way, innovators, bringers of new things. It made them, as a group, sterile.

And they were soon to learn that sterility does not stir public applause.

§ 5

The Presidential campaign of 1936 was approaching. Whom would the Republicans nominate to embody and galvanize the widespread indignation against the New Deal, not only among the rich but also among the majority of business men, and a host of others who regarded Roosevelt as dangerously radical, extravagant, or untrustworthy?

Hoover? No, his name recalled too many bitter memories of economic and political defeat. Borah? He had strong popular backing, especially in the West, but he was fiscally unorthodox and too old and too much of a maverick. Frank Knox of Chicago? Senator Vandenberg of Michigan? All were passed over. As the time for the Cleveland convention drew near, the Republican choice settled upon a candidate who had been virtually unknown to the country before 1936 but who seemed supremely "available"—Governor Alfred Mossman Landon of Kansas.

A successful independent oil producer, Landon should appeal, the Republican leaders felt, to business men. A Governor who had balanced his State budget in trying times, he should be a fitting standard-bearer in a fight against Federal spending (though his opponents pointed out that he had had to balance the budget anyhow because the Kansas Constitution decreed it; and also that Kansas had leaned heavily on the Federal government for relief funds). A former Bull Mooser, a man of generally liberal views, Landon should invite the support of men and women in the middle of the political road. (The conservative diehards were his anyhow: they would vote for the Devil himself to beat Roosevelt.) An adroit political adjuster, Landon should be amenable to the suggestions of men on the Hill who thought Roosevelt too dictatorial toward Congress. A friendly, likable person, with an attractive family, he should personally be a good vote-getter. If his record contained little evidence of brilliance, he could be presented as an unassuming average man, a regular fellow who didn't set himself up to be a superman but possessed plain common sense and would stick to "the American way." As the delegates assembled in Cleveland, Landon was clearly so far in the lead that no other name was even placed in nomination. Landon was nominated with a whoop. The "Kansas Coolidge," "the Careful Kansan," with a Kansas sunflower as his emblem, was sent forth to do battle with Roosevelt.

Landon was provided with a platform likewise intended to appeal to those in the middle of the road. Though it bristled with denunciations of the New Deal, in certain respects it wore a surprisingly liberal aspect. It did not utterly decry Federal participation in relief, though it advocated the "return of responsibility for relief administration to non-political local agencies." It did not utterly decry Federal participation in agricultural regulation, but proposed a national land-use plan not wholly different from the Democratic scheme—with, however, a greater reliance upon the state governments. It did not call for the repeal of the Securities Act, the Stock Exchange Act, or the Public Utility Holding Company Act, upon which the men of Wall Street had poured such vitriol, but called for "Federal regulation, within the Constitution, of the marketing of securities to protect investors," and added, "We favor also Federal regulation of the interstate activities of public utilities." Indeed, if a visitor from Mars had compared the two party platforms of 1936, concentrating his attention not on the denunciations and pointings-with-pride but merely upon the positive recommendations which they contained, he might have wondered why feeling ran so high in this campaign.

If the Republicans demanded a balanced budget and "a sound currency to be preserved at all hazards," the Democrats also spoke of their "determination to achieve a balanced budget" and "approved the objective of a permanently sound currency." Both platforms inveighed against monopolies, approved collective bargaining, promised to protect civil liberties, approved the merit system in the civil service, and spoke friendly words about old-age security (though the Republicans proposed an altered Social Security system). And if the Republicans hammered at the Democrats for "flaunting" the "integrity and authority of the Supreme Court" and for "insisting on passage of laws contrary to the Constitution," if they pledged themselves to "resist all attempts to impair the authority of the Supreme Court of the United States," the Democrats also proposed "to maintain the letter and spirit of the Constitution," explaining that if national problems could not be "effectively solved by legislation within the Constitution, we shall seek such clarifying amendment as will assure to the Legislatures of the several states and the Congress of the United States, each within its proper jurisdiction, the power to enact those laws which the State and Federal Legislatures, within their respective spheres, shall find necessary. . . ." Surely, the visitor from Mars would have said, these parties which so denounce each other are virtually as Tweedledum and Tweedledee.

The reference in the Democratic platform to the possible need of a "clarifying" amendment to the Constitution was a master-stroke of rhetorical precision. For during the preceding year the Supreme Court had emerged as the one conservative force able and ready to withstand the New Deal offensive. Not only had it thrown out the NRA, unanimously; in January, 1936, it had thrown out the AAA too, by a vote of 6 to 3; it had also vetoed the Farm Mortgage Moratorium Act, the Guffey Coal Act, and several other measures; and in these decisions it had interpreted so narrowly the interstate commerce clause of the Constitution that almost every important New Deal law seemed likely in due course to fall before its scythe. Only two of the Court's decisions thus far had favored the Administration —a 5 to 4 Gold Clause verdict and an 8 to 1 verdict on certain limited phases of the TVA. Under the circumstances the New Dealers' opinion of the "nine old men" of the Court—or, more particularly, of the right-wing justices —was blistering; and by contrast the Court had become to conservatives an object of unprecedented veneration. (Above the rear number plate of the conservative's Cadillac was now affixed a plate reading SAVE THE CONSTITUTION, in the very place where, four years before, had been affixed a plate reading REPEAL THE EIGHTEENTH AMENDMENT.)

Roosevelt was deeply indignant at the Court and longed to checkmate it, but had not yet decided how to attempt to do this. He did not want to propose during the campaign to amend the Constitution, for it would have been difficult to frame any amendment of the interstate-commerce clause which might not be represented by the Republicans as a wide-open door to complete government regimentation of business. He wanted to dodge the issue of the Court for the time being. That word "clarifying"—so innocent-looking, so suggestive of a mere attempt to prevent misinterpretation— helped in the dodging.

Luck helped Roosevelt, too, and in ironical fashion. For just as the elder Republicans were packing their bags to go to Cleveland for the convention, the Supreme Court did a strange thing. Previously it had thrown out Federal wages-and-hours legislation. Now, taking the bit in its teeth, it threw out *State* wages-and-hours legislation by ruling against a New York State minimum wage law for women. The result was staggering: *nobody* could legislate on wages and hours! Not even the Republican leaders could swallow that and remain smiling. As a result, after the Republicans had declared in their platform that they would "protect women and children with respect to maximum hours, minimum wages, and working conditions" by state laws, adding somewhat lamely, "We believe that this can be done within the Constitution as it now stands," Governor Landon felt it necessary to inform the convention that if necessary he would seek an amendment to make this possible. Somehow this took the edge off the Republican championship of the Court. Unwittingly the nine gentlemen in black had scored a point for the embarrassed President.

In other ways fortune favored Roosevelt. One of Landon's earliest discoverers had been William Randolph Hearst, and by 1936 the support of Hearst was less than an asset. At the beginning of 1936 Al Smith, once Roosevelt's good friend and mentor, had threatened to "take a walk" and had urged other Democrats to join him in leaving the New Dealers; but the threat had been made at a dinner of the Liberty League, an organization so studded with millionaire industrialists as to become a political liability for the Republicans. (Even in Republican politics, millionaires are customarily kept in the background, behind a convincing front of small business men and "plain people.") Adroitly seizing the opportunity thus offered, the Democratic strategists conducted their campaign as though they were opposed merely by the millionaire Liberty League, not the Republican party. When at the close of the Democratic convention in Philadelphia—a rubber-stamp, Roosevelt-controlled convention which was dragged out for five days to make the merchants and hotel-keepers of Philadelphia happy and to fill the ears of radio listeners with triumphant if vacuous New Deal oratory—Roosevelt went to Franklin Field to accept renomination, he made a ringing speech in which the Republicans were not even once mentioned. The

enemy, according to this speech, was the "economic royalists," who "complain that we seek to overthrow the institutions of America" when "what they really complain of is
that we seek to take away their power." Whether one calls
such a phrase good demagoguery or good politics, it scored
with the voters. The phrase became as popular as an earlier
Roosevelt's reference to "malefactors of great wealth."

Even the elements favored the President. During the
summer of the campaign he made an ostensibly non-political
tour of inspection of the drought-stricken Great Plains—
and as he went he was preceded by such torrents of rain
that one of the reporters on the Presidential special, wak-
ing one morning to look out a streaming train window at a
soaking countryside, remarked, "What's this? A flood-con-
trol trip?"

But the President's greatest advantage lay in his superior
personal appeal to the voters. Whether or not the Republicans, succumbing to old habit, had selected an available
candidate when they needed a crusader, the fact was that
Landon did not throw out sparks. He spoke sensibly,
thoughtfully, moderately, including among his campaign
speeches a fine defense of freedom; but his voice was harsh
compared to Roosevelt's, especially over the radio, where
Roosevelt could swing thrillingly from apparently confidential persuasion to sharp-edged exhortation; and though
Landon had an amiable smile, it lacked the contagious
expansiveness of Roosevelt's. Whatever may have been Landon's potential abilities, as a campaigner—in opposition to
one of the master politicians of American history—he was
hardly a man to encourage the van or to harass the foe from
the rear.

§ 6

Roosevelt, by contrast, was in his element as the battle
cries began to resound.

The group of aides which surrounded him during this campaign was different from the Brain Trust which had surrounded him in 1932. Sam Rosenman, to be sure, was still unobtrusively at his side in policy-making discussions. Raymond Moley, although supposedly he had left the New Deal as well as his office in the State Department in the fall of 1933, had remained a confidential Presidential adviser, though with waning influence and growing exasperation at the President's offensive against big business. Throughout 1934 and 1935 Moley had been a constant back-door visitor to the White House, and he remained in close touch with Roosevelt until the time of the Democratic convention of 1936. But the divergence between their views had become so patent that after the "economic royalists" speech Moley was definitely through. Tugwell was no longer so close to the throne as he had been; nor was Berle. And although Jim Farley was still on hand to direct the political management of the campaign, the devoted and astute Louis Howe was not. After a lingering illness in the White House, Howe had died in April, 1936.

The leading newcomer to the ranks of Presidential aides and intimate advisers was a young man named Tom Corcoran, an Irishman from Pawtucket, Rhode Island, who had been a protégé of Felix Frankfurter's since his Harvard Law School days, had been recommended by Frankfurter to Moley to draft the Securities Act of 1933, along with James M. Landis and Benjamin Cohen, and had subsequently, with Cohen, drafted both the Stock Exchange Act and the Public Utility Holding Company Act. Corcoran's skill in bill-drafting, his indefatigable energy, his devotion to the New Deal and to a high ideal of public service, his gay brilliance, and his knack for playing the accordion had all endeared him to Roosevelt, and now within a year he had become one of the innermost circle. His acquaintance among the liberals in the Administration was large; he became a natural leader of the young liberal lawyers and a sort of unofficial employment officer for them inside the government; and already he and his close ally, the shy, rumpled, unobtrusive, clear-headed Ben Cohen, who lived with Corcoran and other young New Dealers at a little red house on R Street, were men of mark in the new Washington.

They were by no means the extreme radicals which current conservative opinion made them out to be (their draft of the Public Utility Holding Company Act, for example, was the mildest of three submitted to the President). They wanted the government to hold big business in check, to discipline it, and if necessary to take over some of its functions, but largely in order to clear the way for small business, which, they believed, was being crowded out of the economic race by big business. Corcoran and Cohen were closer to the elder La Follette in their economic philosophy, or to Woodrow Wilson, than to Moscow. This philosophy, however, involved them in hostility to the great corporations and great financial interests; and they readily stimulated a similar hostility in Roosevelt, who—though he had never formulated a consistent economic policy—was angry at the rich men's hatred for him and also believed that only by inveighing against "economic royalists" could he hold in his own ranks the disaffected millions who had followed leaders like Huey Long. Moley, on the contrary, wanted no continuing onslaught upon the power of concentrated wealth, wanted collaboration between it and the government. There was real significance in the fact that during the campaign of 1936 Corcoran succeeded Moley as one of the chief Presidential speech-drafters (along with Stanley High, Ben Cohen, William C. Bullitt, and others) and as an intimate (along with Relief Administrator Harry Hopkins, Secretaries Morgenthau and Ickes, Judge Rosenman, and others). The apostles of ever-strict business regulation (and also of spending for recovery) had definitely gained the Presidential ear.

During the campaign, one or more of the inner group would prepare drafts of a speech for Roosevelt. At a White House conference a number of them would argue out with him questions of policy and epigram. Then the President would dictate his own draft from the others, utilizing an idea here, a telling phrase there. The copy would be revised, perhaps again and again, and then Roosevelt would sally forth to deliver it. The main themes of his speeches were that the whole country was bound together and what benefited one interest, one locality, benefited all; that only a beginning had been made in the work of national conservation, not only of physical but of human resources; that if the public debt was rising, so also was the national income; that things were demonstrably better in 1936 than in 1932. On awkward points such as budget-balancing Roosevelt was agile if not actually slippery in his logic. On past government measures he was explicit; on future ones, vague—for the truth was that his legislative program, so far as it had been thought out, had been completed. He had no future program but only a sense of direction. His demeanor was generally friendly; only in the Madison Square Garden speech at the end of the campaign—when he had been enraged by some misguided Republican propaganda about Social Security—did he turn to bitterness (with no Moley or Louis Howe at hand to tone down his wrath). It was in that philippic that he cried, "I should like to have it said of my first Administration that in it the forces of selfishness and of lust for power met their match. I should like to have it said of my second Administration that in it these forces met their master." During the rest of the campaign he appeared a happy man reporting encouraging progress and almost completely neglecting to take notice of Landon or the Republican party.

Nor did the long, exhausting journeys of the campaign—the sleeping-car nights, the goldfish-bowl publicity, the incessant speechmaking, the hand-shaking, the hurried conferences, the incessant uproar of cheering—seem to tire Roosevelt in the least, cripple though he was, unable to walk alone. On the contrary, he wore out his companions and emerged from every day of his ordeal fresher than ever, like an Antaeus renewed in strength by every contact with the political element. Smiling, always smiling, the silver voice ringing, he swung through the country in a triumph.

Where were the rivals on the left who a year or two before had looked so menacing? Huey Long was dead. Father Coughlin and the Townsendites, together with a remnant of the Huey Long following, had joined in backing for the Presidency Representative Lemke of North Dakota; but it was early apparent that the Lemke opposition would be weak. Governor Olson of Minnesota was dead. The socialists, nominating Norman Thomas as was their habit, were weak. And as for the communists, though they nominated Earl Browder for the Presidency, so anxious were they to be true to the Popular Front principle dictated by Moscow, and so anxious to defeat Landon, whom they called the "fascist" candidate, that one could hardly be sure whether they were really revolutionary Marxians or just another group of New Dealers. The contest had become Roosevelt against Landon, with no important third-party opposition.

Bitterly the campaign progressed. Not since 1896, certainly, had public feeling run so high over an election. To hear angry Republicans and angry Democrats talking, one would have supposed the contest was between a tyrant determined to destroy private property, ambition, the Constitution, democracy, and civilization itself, and a dupe of Wall Street who would introduce a fascist dictatorship.

Who would win? The *Literary Digest*, which for years had been conducting election straw votes on a huge scale, predicted a Landon victory, with Roosevelt getting only 161 electoral votes as against Landon's 320. Dr. George Gallup, whose American Institute of Public Opinion had been reporting the results of its more scientific polls since October 20, 1935—thereby inaugurating a new kind of political measurement, with unguessable possibilities for the future—showed Roosevelt in the lead throughout the campaign, and gaining through most of it: Gallup predicted that Roosevelt would get 477 electoral votes, that Landon would get 42 (with two states left in the doubtful column). Jim Farley predicted that Roosevelt would get 523 electoral votes, carrying every state but Maine and Vermont—but who ever believes a campaign manager's prophecies? Doggedly, the Republicans held to their hope that Landon would carry the country.

Then came Election Day, and as they gathered by their radios that evening to hear the returns, they were thunderstruck. For Jim Farley had been right. The Roosevelt landslide was overwhelming. The old political adage had to be altered to "As Maine goes, so goes Vermont." The Democrats won every state but those two. Roosevelt's popular vote was 27¾ millions to Landon's 16 2/3 millions. Congress was now to be more than three-quarters Democratic in both Houses—a terrific majority. The New Deal had been upheld by the great electorate, and in no uncertain terms.

Why did this happen? Some reasons have already been suggested. But there were two which have not hitherto been mentioned in this account. One was that the New Deal was a vast dispenser of pecuniary aid to individuals, chiefly in the form of relief. In some areas these payments were crassly used for political advantage. In most, they were not. To argue that the billions spent for relief were in essence a vast Democratic campaign fund, paid for by the taxpayers, was to exaggerate cynically. Nevertheless the argument for the

New Deal was implicit in every payment, whether spoken or not: "We are looking after you. Maybe these other people won't. Better vote for us." The momentum of governmental subsidies is tremendous; anybody who suggests reducing them does so at his political peril.

The other reason was that although Roosevelt was bitterly hated by most of the well-to-do, he was genuinely admired and trusted by most of the poorer people of the country. Between the lines of his speeches as well as of the legislation which he sponsored they read a genuine friendliness toward them, a genuine desire to help them. Part of the failure of the press (which, in the cities, was overwhelmingly pro-Landon) either to sway the small voters or to predict their vote undoubtedly lay in the failure of editors to understand the impress on these people's minds of the New Deal relief policy and of Roosevelt's own personality. Newspaper articles about the scandalous waste of relief funds or about nonsensical boondoggling were discounted by these small voters, not simply because some of them were getting money themselves and wanted the flow of cash to continue, but because they saw in the New Deal a badly needed angel of mercy which stood sincerely ready to help them. Above all, they saw in Roosevelt himself a friend who did not talk down to them, did not patronize them, but respected them as American citizens and wanted his Administration to serve them. What did they care what the papers said? They knew what the McGarritys in the next block, what the Nelsons on the next farm, had been up against, and what the Federal government had done for them; they had heard Roosevelt's friendly voice themselves, over the radio, again and again. They felt that they *knew*, and they voted accordingly.

§ 7

Gradually Europe was drawing nearer.

During 1936 Hitler's armies had marched unopposed into

the Rhineland. Mussolini's armies, completing their Ethiopian campaign, had marched into Addis Ababa. Civil war had broken out in Spain, and by the time of Roosevelt's re-election the forces of Francisco Franco, backed by German and Italian support, were drawing close to Madrid. With more and more disquiet the American people were taking note of an outside world whose orderly foundations were crumbling as the aggressors of the new German-Italian Axis moved step by threatening step toward domination.

But the event which was presently to bring the average American man and woman closer to the European theatre than they had been since Versailles, and which for days on end was to overshadow in interest anything that was happening on the American continent, leaping into the American headlines and becoming the predominant topic of American conversation, was no affair of armies or conquests. Though this event might be regarded as a sign of the weakness of the British Empire—or, conversely, of the ability of that Empire to adjust its weaknesses, close ranks, and carry on—to most observers it was simply a personal drama on an imperial stage: the drama of a king forced to choose between his kingdom and a woman. That the king should be Edward VIII of Great Britain and Ireland and of the British Dominions Beyond the Seas, King, Defender of the Faith, Emperor of India, and that the woman should be a Baltimore girl, Wallis Warfield Simpson, heightened the drama into what H. L. Mencken called "the greatest news story since the Resurrection."

All through the summer and fall of 1936, while Roosevelt and Landon had been stumping the United States, the American press had been conspicuously aware of the royal romance. Americans had seen photographs of Edward and Wallis together on a Mediterranean cruise, he (in swimming trunks) paddling in a rubber boat, she (in a bathing suit) sitting on a pier-end above him. When on October 27 she was granted a divorce from Ernest Simpson, the news from the Ipswich Assizes made the front pages in the United States. Not for weeks thereafter were the great mass of the English people even to learn of the existence of Mrs. Simpson, so strict was the unofficial censorship on news uncomfortable to royalty; not, in fact, until after the Bishop of Bradford, on December 1, spoke (at a diocesan convention) of the King's need of God's grace, said he hoped the King was aware of this need, and added sadly, "some of us wish he gave more positive signs of such awareness." This sentence, indirect and discreet as it was, opened the way to the revelation in England. But in America the way did not need to be opened. Americans had been asking one another for weeks whether the King and Mrs. Simpson were really to be married; and as the drama unfolded to its climax, the dispatches from Downing Street and Westminster and Fort Belvedere let loose a tumult of argument from one end of the United States to the other.

"Good for him. Best thing he's ever done. Let him marry her. Can't a king be a human being?" "No, no, no. He accepted a responsibility and now he's chucking it. If he was going to welsh on his job, why did he ever take it in the first place?" "Well, he never was good for much but nightclub work anyhow. Did you see the bawling-out Westbrook Pegler gave him in his column?" "Kind of a sock for Wallis, I guess. She was all set to be Queen—and now where is she?" "I'll bet it was the Archbishop of Canterbury that spoiled the thing. Those divorces of hers, you know." "Nonsense—they'd have swallowed the divorces all right if she hadn't been an American. Now if she'd been a duchess . . ." "You have to hand it to her at that—a Baltimore girl who can bring about an imperial crisis single-handed."

Endlessly the talk buzzed, till Wallis Warfield Simpson had fled England for the seclusion of the Rogers' villa at Cannes, and Stanley Baldwin had told the House of Commons the long story of his activities as a match-breaker, and the headlines had shrieked, THE KING QUITS, and millions of Americans had gathered at their radios on the afternoon of December 11, 1936, to hear, above the crackle of static, the slow, measured words of Edward himself:

"At long last I am able to say a few words of my own. I never wanted to withhold anything, but until now it has not been constitutionally possible for me to speak. . . . (*Try another station—I can't hear. What was that he said?*) . . . I have found it impossible to carry the heavy burden of responsibility and to discharge my duties as King as I should wish to do, without the help and support of the woman I love. . . . (*There, that's better. No, try the other one again.*) . . . And now we all have a new King. I wish him and you, his people, happiness and prosperity with all my heart. God bless you all! God save the King!"

With this last speech of Edward's, so perfect in its eloquent simplicity, the curtain fell upon the drama of British royalty. Now Americans could turn their minds again to what was happening at home. Their own chief of state, reelected, had been given virtually a blank check. What would he write upon it?

Chapter Ten

WITH PEN AND CAMERA THROUGH DARKEST AMERICA

§ 1

IF IN the year 1925 (or thereabouts) you had gone to a cocktail party in New York attended by writers, critics, artists, musicians, and professional men and women interested in the newest ideas and the newest tendencies in the arts, you would probably have heard some of the following beliefs expressed or implied in the conversation screamed over the Martinis:—

That there ought to be more personal freedom, particularly sex freedom.

That reformers were an abomination and there were too many laws.

That Babbitts, Rotarians, and boosters, and indeed American business men in general, were hopelessly crass.

That the masses of the citizenry were dolts with thirteen-year-old minds.

That most of the heroes of historical tradition, and especially of Victorian and Puritan tradition, were vastly overrated and needed "debunking."

That America was such a standardized, machine-ridden, and convention-ridden place that people with brains and taste naturally preferred the free atmosphere of Europe.

If after a lapse of ten years you had strayed into a similar gathering in 1935 (or thereabouts) you would hardly have been able to believe your ears, so sharp would have been the contrast. It is unlikely that you would have found anybody showing any conversational excitement over sex freedom, or the crudeness of Babbitts, or the need for debunking Henry Wadsworth Longfellow. (It was characteristic of the nineteen-thirties that the Queen Victoria with whom Strachey had dealt sharply in the previous decade became a popular heroine as portrayed on the stage by Helen Hayes, and that Longfellow himself and other worthies of Victorian Boston were largely restored to favor in Van Wyck Brooks's *The Flowering of New England* in 1936.) In the conversation screamed over the somewhat more palatable Martinis of 1935 you would probably have heard some of the following beliefs expressed or implied:—

That reform—economic reform, to be sure, but nevertheless reform by law—was badly needed, and there ought to be more stringent laws. (Some members of the company might even scout reform as useless pending the clean sweep of capitalist institutions which must be made by the inevitable Communist Revolution.)

That the masses of the citizenry were the people who really mattered, the most fitting subjects for writer and artist, the people on whose behalf reform must be overtaken. (Indeed, if you had listened carefully you might have heard a literary critic who had been gently nurtured in the politest of environments referring to *himself* as a proletarian, so belligerently did he identify himself with the masses.)

That America was the most fascinating place of all and the chief hope for freedom; that it was worth studying and depicting in all its phases but particularly in those uglier phases that cried most loudly for correction; and that it was worth working loyally to save, though perhaps it was beyond saving and was going to collapse along with the rest of civilization.

"What has happened in these ten years?" you might have asked. "Have these people got religion?"

They had. The religion, of course, was not the religion of the churches; one of the few points of resemblance between the prevailing attitude of such a group in 1925 and its prevailing attitude in 1935 was that at both times its members were mostly agnostic if not atheist. What animated these men and women was the secular religion of social consciousness to which a reference was made in Chapter VI of this book. Deeply moved by the Depression and the suffering it had caused; convinced that the economic and social system of the country had been broken beyond repair, that those who had held the chief economic power before 1929 had been proved derelict and unworthy, and that action was desperately needed to set things right; wrung by compassion for the victims of economic unbalance, these men and women no longer set such store as formerly upon art as art. They wanted it to have a social function, to illuminate the social scene, to bring its darkest places clearly into view. "What's the use of being a connoisseur of the arts when people are starving?" cried a New York woman of means who had prided herself on her judicious purchases of modern paintings; "I feel as if I'd been wasting my money." "What's the use of writing pretty novels about ladies and gentlemen?" thought the young fiction-writers of 1935. "If we write about the sharecroppers we're getting at the sort of thing that matters—and we may accomplish something."

To understand the thrust of American literature during the nineteen-thirties one must realize how strong was this mood of social evangelism among writers and critics and the intellectual élite generally.

§ 2

At this point careful qualification is necessary. The new mood was most widespread in New York, which had long been the center of intellectual ferment in the United States and an extremely sensitive barometer of the pressure of new and radical ideas. It was more widespread among the young and rising—and frequently jobless—intellectuals than among the older and better-established. Many successful practitioners of the craft of writing to sell were quite untouched by it. It was not strikingly prevalent among well-to-do "nice people" of culture who had always been surrounded with books and had always subscribed to the more decorous magazines, or among academic gentry remote from the fever of new creative effort in the arts. It was likely to bewilder and perhaps frighten the clubwoman who enjoyed literary lectures and wanted to beautify her town and subscribed to all the best concerts and belonged to the Book-of-the-Month Club. As for the banker who was a college trustee and helped to make up the annual deficit of the symphony concerts and had every right to be considered a sustainer of the arts, he was likely to be angered by it—if indeed he was aware of it at all.

Now and again some expression of the mood leaped into wide popularity. There was, for example, the play "Tobacco Road," written by Jack Kirkland from a novel by Erskine Caldwell. Produced in New York on December 4, 1935 (just as Prohibition gave way to Repeal), this study of a poverty-stricken and depraved Southern tenant family seemed at first about to fail but gradually found its public and, to the amazement of Broadway, ran on and on, year after year, until by the autumn of 1939 it had easily broken the phenomenal record for successive New York performances set by "Abie's Irish Rose" in the nineteen-twenties. Undoubtedly the success of "Tobacco Road" was due in part to its frank and profane dialogue, its exhibitions of uninhibited love-making, and James Barton's fine gift for both comic and tragic effects as Jeeter Lester; but at least the success was not prevented by the fact that the play showed relentlessly and compassionately the interworking of poverty and degeneracy—showed it without blinking the fact that the Lesters had become a dirty, irresponsible, mentally defective, disreputable family.

Another quite different embodiment of the mood was the musical revue "Pins and Needles," produced on November 27, 1937, by Labor Stage, Inc., a company of garment workers (of which no actor was paid more than $55 a week). This revue likewise went on and on until late in 1939 it had broken all previous musical-show endurance records. Playfully pleading the cause of the labor unions and satirizing their enemies, "Pins and Needles" was different from anything previously seen on the musical stage. Who would have imagined, in the nineteen-twenties, that a revue would run for years whose catchiest air was called "Sing Me a Song of Social Significance"?

Only one or two books which could fairly be said to reflect the mood of social consciousness reached the top of the best-seller list during the nineteen-thirties. One was Sinclair Lewis's *It Can't Happen Here*, published late in 1935, which showed how fascism might come to the United States. A still better example was John Steinbeck's *The Grapes of Wrath*, a very vivid and finely wrought account of the plight of a family of migrant "Okies" in California, which not only met with thunders of critical applause when it appeared early in 1939 but jumped at one bound to the top of the list. Here, even more than in "Tobacco Road," the components of the young intellectuals' credo were brought together: a sense of the way in which economic and social forces worked together to bring tragedy to innocent people; a deep sympathy for those people, combined with a willingness to reveal all their ignorance, their casual carnality, their inability to understand their own plight; a sense of the splendor of America, its exciting challenge to artist and to social engineer alike; and a resolve to arouse an indifferent public by showing the worst in poverty and cruelty that America could offer.

Otherwise an examination of the annual best-seller lists would seem to suggest how limited in size was the public which wanted social documents. To command the attention of two or three hundred thousand readers in its original full-price edition, a book succeeded best by addressing itself to other impulses.

There was, for example, the desire to escape from the here and now of Depression and anxiety. May not *The Good Earth*, by Pearl S. Buck, which led the fiction list in 1931 and 1932, have had an additional appeal because it took its readers away to China? May not the appearance of *The Fountain*, by Charles Morgan, on the best-seller list for 1932 have been partly due to the fact that it told of a man who escaped from the outward world of ugly circumstance into a world of inward reflection? Surely the success of *Shadows on the Rock*, by Willa Cather (1931), the even greater success of *Anthony Adverse*, by Hervey Allen (which led all comers in 1933 and 1934), and the superlative success of *Gone with the Wind*, by Margaret Mitchell (which was the overwhelming favorite in 1936 and 1937)—to say nothing of Stark Young's *So Red the Rose* (1934), Kenneth Roberts's *Northwest Passage* (1937), and a number of other books, was the greater because they offered an escape into history. For a time the likeliest recipe for publishing profits was to produce an 800-page romance in old-time costume.

Indeed, it is possible that *The Grapes of Wrath*, if it had appeared a few years earlier, would not have been the big popular hit that it was in 1939. It would have seemed to many readers too painful, too disturbing. By 1939 they had become accustomed to unemployment—even complacent about it—and had acquired new worries to be diverted from (Hitler and the threat of war). They could now take the Steinbeck medicine with less flinching.

There were suggestions of other moods, too, in the best-seller lists. The fact that *The Strange Death of President Harding* in 1930 and *Washington Merry-Go-Round* in 1931 both stood high may be regarded as an indication of the growing public disillusionment with the government as the Hoover Administration battled vainly with the Depression. *The Epic of America,* best-selling non-fiction book of 1932, may have appealed to a mood of inquiry into the background and traditions of a nation which could get itself into such a fix. When the economic tide turned in 1933, what more natural than that men and women whose dreams of a career had been thwarted by the Depression and who now began to hope that they could make a second start should have rushed to buy *Life Begins at Forty* by Walter B. Pitkin (first on the non-fiction list in 1933, second in 1934)?

Americans have always wanted guideposts to personal success and the more rewarding life, and it might be pushing inference too far to suggest that the big sales of *Live Alone and Like It* by Marjorie Hillis in 1936, *Wake Up and Live* by Dorothea Brande in 1936, and *How to Win Friends and Influence People* by Dale Carnegie in 1937 had any close relation to the state of business, or that the rise of *The Importance of Living,* by Lin Yutang, to the top of the list in 1938 was a sign that during the business Recession there was once more a wish to learn how to be happy by denying the need for worldly advancement. But the popularity of Vincent Sheean's *Personal History* (1935), Negley Farson's *Way of a Transgressor* (1936), John Gunther's *Inside Europe* and *Inside Asia* (1936 and 1939), and other books on foreign affairs (not to mention *It Can't Happen Here*), surely re-

ROOSEVELT RIDES IN TRIUMPH
Returning with Mrs. Roosevelt from the rainy Inauguration of
January 20, 1937

Otto F. Hess

BENNY GOODMAN IN ACTION
At a "Battle of Swing" at the Savoy Ballroom, Harlem, New York City

flected the rising excitement over the news from Europe as the Nazis and fascists advanced through crisis after crisis to ever greater power.

Some books during the decade rode high with the aid of very special circumstances. The best-selling non-fiction book of 1934 was Alexander Woollcott's *While Rome Burns,* a collection of anecdotes and whimsies which would hardly have fared so well had its author not invented a new sort of radio program well adapted to the intelligence of bookish people, and had he not been delighting huge audiences on the air by collecting old poems and old eyeglasses, telling stories about Katharine Cornell, and extolling Kipling, Harpo Marx, Laura E. Richards, and the wonderful dogs of the Seeing Eye. (To Mr. Woollcott's audible enthusiasm was also due in no small measure the success of *Goodbye Mr. Chips.*) *North to the Orient* (1935) and *Listen, the Wind* (1938) sold in great volume not simply because they were exquisitely written but also, perhaps, because Anne Morrow Lindbergh was the wife of an idolized hero and was admired in her own right. No correlation between the successful books of any given period and the general trend of opinion and taste during that period can be pushed far: there is always a vast diversity of talent among the writers, a vast diversity of taste among the readers, and an element of chance in the whole process. For example, throughout most of the decade there was an undeniable public interest in economic problems and a considerable sale of economic treatises. Yet no book on the economic condition of America got to the top of the best-seller list, although there were big sales for *100,000,000 Guinea Pigs* (a diatribe for consumers on the difference between what they thought they were buying and what the manufacturers were actually selling them) and fairly big sales for several of Stuart Chase's lively simplifications of the economic dilemma. Perhaps economics was, after all, the dismal science—or, let us say, the dismal area of disagreement, assumption, and conjecture.

§ 3

Limited in size as were their audiences, the writers who were engaged in the search for social significance produced perhaps the most vital and certainly the most characteristic work of the decade. John Dos Passos with his *U.S.A.* trilogy, in which he suggested the hollowness and wastefulness of pre-Depression American life, interlarding his passages of fiction with impressionistic portraits of famous Americans (in which, of course, J. P. Morgan was roundly condemned, Woodrow Wilson sharply satirized, and Thorstein Veblen extolled), and closing the trilogy with a word-picture of an unemployed man trying hopelessly to thumb his way down a fine American highway; Erskine Caldwell packing his pages with the cruelty and misery of the lower ranges of Southern life; Ernest Hemingway trying (not very successfully) to make a proletarian lesson out of the story of Harry Morgan, a disreputable Key West rumrunner; James T. Farrell showing how environment got the best of Studs Lonigan, a lower-middle-class Irish Catholic boy of Chicago; Albert Halper presenting the factory workers of *The Foundry*; Robert Cantwell dealing with striking fruit pickers; and John Steinbeck later following the Joads from drought-ridden Oklahoma to vigilante-ridden California—these and others like Fielding Burke and Grace Lumpkin were the pace-setters for the period in fiction (though of course there were very able novels produced by writers of different intent, such as Thomas Wolfe, Pearl Buck, Ellen Glasgow, Margaret Mitchell, and William Faulkner). Even Sinclair Lewis engaged in the politico-social battle, though not on the side of rebellion; in *The Prodigal Parents* his effort was to show that the Babbitt whom he had once satirized was a kindlier and better man than the youngsters of the radical left.

Among the poets, Archibald MacLeish and Edna St. Vincent Millay were turning likewise to political and social themes; Carl Sandburg was writing

> Stocks are property, yes.
> Bonds are property, yes.
> Machines, land, buildings are property, yes.
> A job is property,
> no, nix, nah, nah.

and numerous younger men and women were struggling with the almost impossible task of writing sagas and songs of the masses in idioms intelligible only to those who had learned to follow the abstruse indirections of T. S. Eliot and Ezra Pound.

In the theatre, Clifford Odets made energetic use of proletarian themes; Maxwell Anderson, in "Winterset," turned social injustice to the uses of poetic tragedy; as the decade grew older and fascism became more menacing, Robert E. Sherwood epitomized the democratic faith in his moving tableaux from the life of "Abe Lincoln in Illinois"; the Federal players dramatized current politics in "Triple A Plowed Under" and "One Third of a Nation."

At the same time ardent historians and literary sociologists were bringing out harsh biographies of the robber barons and Mellons and Morgans of the American past; delving into aspects of the history of American cities and regions which had been carefully neglected by chambers of commerce; taking to pieces the life of American communities and assembling their findings in statistical and graphic profusion. With more amiable intent, the Writers' Project of the WPA was going over the country inch by inch for a series of guidebooks. Surveys supported by the Federal government or by foundations were analyzing every public problem in exhaustive detail. The nineteen-thirties were a golden age of literary sociology. America had discovered itself to be a fascinating subject for exploration, dissection, and horrified but hopeful contemplation.

§ 4

At the heart of the literary revolt against the America that had been stood the communist intellectuals. Numerically they were hardly important, but from them the revolt caught the fire of burning conviction, and from the curious nature of the communist position it derived most of its weaknesses. Many an author was handicapped by his conviction that, as a Marxian, he must take for his hero a kind of American he did not really know, or that he must make his characters conform to a Marxian pattern and argue the Marxian case, or that he must depict his proletarians both as men rendered cruel and vicious by their lot and as the heroic standard-bearers of a glorious revolution, or that he must present anybody with more than $3,000 a year only in caricature, or that he must preach a collective uniformity which ran counter to his own natural instinctive preference for individual dissent. Especially in the early years of the decade, the Marxian pattern was a strait jacket into which American literature could not readily be fitted. As Malcolm Cowley has remarked, in those early years at least six novels and two plays were based on a single actual strike (at Gastonia in 1929), and "strike novels began to follow a pattern almost as rigid and conventional as that of a Petrarchan sonnet. The hero was usually a young worker, honest, naïve and politically undeveloped. Through intolerable mistreatment, he was driven to take part in a strike. Always the strike was ruthlessly suppressed, and usually its leader was killed. But the young worker, conscious now of the mission that united him to the whole working class, marched on toward new battles." (Later, especially after the communists accepted the idea of the Popular Front, the bonds of doctrine became progressively less constricting.)

The truth was that many of the young rebels had embraced—or at least dallied with—communism chiefly because they saw it as the end-station of the road of disillusionment. First one saw that the going order was not working right; then one progressed to the consideration of reforms, one read *The Autobiography of Lincoln Steffens*, and decided that half-measures would not suffice to redeem America; one went on to the idea that nothing short of revolution would serve; and there at the terminus of one's journey sat Karl Marx waiting to ask one's unquestioning devotion, there was the Communist Party promising to make a clean sweep of all that was hateful in American life. How welcome to find the end of the road, how easy to be able to ascribe everything one disliked to capitalism! (Did not Robert Forsythe, in *Redder Than the Rose*, a book of left-wing comment which succeeded in being both vehement and humorous, argue that Dillinger was a product of capitalism, that the vulgarities of the Hauptmann trial were American capitalism's "own narcotic to deaden its death pains," that Mae West showed "in her frank cynical way the depths to which capitalistic morality has come"?) Yet how hard, nevertheless, to swallow the belief that any deceit was justified by the cause—even if the cause appealed to one's most generous instincts—and to follow unquestioningly the twists and turns of the Moscow party line, now damning Roosevelt as the best friend of the rich, now embracing him as a partner in the Popular Front!

During the latter nineteen-thirties there appeared a crop of autobiographies full of nostalgic memories of the Bohemian Greenwich Village of the early nineteen-hundreds, when young intellectuals were manning the silk strikers' picket lines, seeing Big Bill Haywood plain, cheering for the Armory Show of independent art, and experimenting with free verse and free love. Perhaps the day would come when a new crop of autobiographies would recall the dear dead days of the nineteen-thirties when the young rebels saw themselves as soldiers in the class war, regarded Union Square as their G.H.Q., debated endlessly about "ideology," were lashed into their wildest furies of controversy over the "trial" of Trotsky in Mexico City, and were heartened every day by the knowledge that as capitalism withered, communism was inevitably rising to take its place.

§ 5

Through the ranks of the painters, too, swept the contagion of social concern and of enthusiasm for putting American life on record. Thomas H. Benton's muscular and turbulent groups, Grant Wood's formalized Midwestern landscapes and satirical portraits, John Stuart Curry's scenes of farm life on the plains, Charles Burchfield's gaunt mansions of the Rutherford B. Hayes era, Edward Hopper's grim streets and cool New England lighthouses, Reginald Marsh's pageants of New York slum life attracted many disciples. The Federal government, wisely including artists among its relief beneficiaries, put scores of them to work painting murals on post-office walls; and presently the young painter's model found that she was no longer simply to lie on a couch while he experimented with the treatment of planes of color and bulges of significant form, but was to strike a pose as a pioneer mother or embody the spirit of America insisting upon slum clearance. The value of the new trend was debatable, but at least it promised to decrease the wide gap between the artist and the general public, which at last began to feel that it knew what was going on. Simultaneously there was a sharp increase in the number of young people who, at places like the School of Fine Arts of the University of Iowa, were actually learning to paint; and there, too, was hope for the future of American art.

Not altogether unrelated to this change in emphasis in American painting, perhaps, was the rise to sudden popularity of an art hitherto seldom regarded with serious attention—the art of photography. It rose on the crest of a camera craze of remarkable dimensions—a craze which otherwise served chiefly as a new and amusing hobby, with aesthetic values and satisfactions thrown in for good measure.

During the early years of the Depression one began to notice, here and there, young men with what appeared to be leather-cased opera glasses slung about their necks. They were the pioneers of the camera craze who had discovered that the Leicas and other tiny German cameras, which took postage-stamp-size pictures capable of enlargement, combined a speed, a depth of focus, and an ability to do their work in dim light which opened all sorts of new opportunities to the photographer. The number of "candid camera" addicts grew rapidly as the experts showed how easily an executive committee or a table-full of night-club patrons might be shot sitting. During the eight years from 1928 to 1936 the importation into America of cameras and parts thereof—chiefly from Germany—increased over five-fold despite the Depression.

By 1935 and 1936 the American camera manufacturers and the photographic supply shops found their business booming. Candid cameras were everywhere, until before long prominent citizens became accustomed to having young men and women suddenly rise up before them at public events, lift little cameras to one eye, and snap them— of course without permission. At intermissions during theatrical openings and gala concerts the aisles would sometimes be full of camera sharpshooters. Schoolboys were pleading with their parents for enlargers and exposure-meters. Camera exhibitions were attracting unprecedented crowds.

During the two years 1935-37 the production of cameras in the United States jumped 157 per cent—from less than five million dollars' worth in 1935 to nearly twelve and a half million dollars' worth in 1937. An annual collection of distinguished photographic work, *U. S. Camera,* became a bestseller. A flock of new picture magazines appeared and a few of these jumped to wide popularity, led by the more dignified *Life* and the less dignified *Look.* One had only to lay *U. S. Camera* beside the camera magazines of a few years before, with their fancy studies of young women in Greek draperies holding urns, their deliberately blurred views of sailboats with rippled reflections, and their sentimental depictions of cute babies, to realize how this art had grown in range, imagination, and brilliance.

Some of the new photographers centered their interest upon snapping friends and relatives (including, of course, their children) and immortalizing their travels; some of them tried to capture the sentimental loveliness of scenes that they had enjoyed; and some went on to experiment in the making of abstract patterns of light and shade. But a great many others found themselves becoming unsentimental reporters—of events, of the social scene, even of the uglier parts of the social scene. Able professionals like Margaret Bourke-White, like Dorothea Lange of the Farm Security Administration, like Walker Evans, often worked with the same sort of sociological enthusiasm that had caught the young novelists and was here and there catching the young painters. When S. T. Williamson, reviewing for the *New York Times* a book of Walker Evans's uncompromising pictures (brought out by the Museum of Modern Art in 1938), denied that Mr. Evans had revealed the physiognomy of America and insisted that it would be "nearer the mark to say that bumps, warts, boils, and blackheads are here," he was saying the sort of thing that might be said about half the novels written by the devotees of social significance. What was significant about this aspect of the camera craze was that photographers like Mr. Evans with their grim portrayals of dismal streets, tattered billboards, and gaunt, sad-eyed farm women, were teaching the amateur—whose name was legion—that the camera need not necessarily be shut up in its case until a beauty spot was reached, that there was excitement in catching characteristic glimpses even of the superficially ugly manifestations of life, that these too could be made beautiful in their way, and that when one began to see the everyday things about one with the eye of an artist who was simultaneously a reporter or a sociologist, one began to understand them.

§ 6

One morning in the winter of 1937-38 a crowd began to gather outside the Paramount Theatre in Times Square, New York, as soon as it was light. By 6 A. M. there were three thousand people assembled in the otherwise empty streets—mostly high-school boys and girls in windbreakers and leather jackets. By 7:30 the crowd had so swelled that ten mounted policemen were sent from the West 47th Street station to keep it under control. At 8 o'clock the doors of the theatre were carefully opened to admit 3,634 boys and girls; then the fire department ordered the doors closed, leaving two or three thousand youngsters out in the cold.

Benny Goodman and his orchestra were opening an engagement at the Paramount. Benny Goodman was the King of Swing, and these boys and girls were devotees of swing, ready to dance in the aisles of the theatre amid shouts of "Get off, Benny! Swing it!" and "Feed it to me, Gene! Send me down!" They were jitterbugs, otherwise "alligators," equipped with the new vocabulary of swing ("in the groove," "spank the skin," "schmaltz," "boogie-woogie," "jam session," "killer-diller," and so on endlessly); members of that army of young swing enthusiasts all over the country who during the next year or two knew the names and reputations of the chief band leaders and instrumentalists of swingdom—Goodman, Tommy Dorsey, Artie Shaw, Gene Krupa, "Count" Basie, Teddy Wilson, Louis Armstrong, Jack Teagarden, Larry Clinton, and others without number—as a seasoned baseball fan knows his professional ball players.

To trace fully the origins of this craze one would have to go back very far. Suffice it to say here that during the nineteen-twenties, the jazz craze—which had begun long before in the honky-tonks of New Orleans and had burst into general popularity with the success of "Alexander's Ragtime Band" and the rising vogue of the one-step and fox-trot as dances between 1911 and 1916—had become tamed into decorum and formality; but that even during this time there were obscure jazz bands, mostly of Negro players, which indulged in a mad improvisation, superimposing upon the main theme of the dance music they were playing their own instrumental patterns made up on the spur of the moment (and sometimes later committed to writing). During the early years of the Depression there was little popular interest in this "hot jazz" in the United States; what a worried public wanted was "sweet" music, slow in rhythm and soothingly melodious, like "Some Day I'll Find You" (1931) and "Star Dust" (very popular in 1932), or poignantly haunting, like "Night and Day" (1932) and "Stormy Weather" (1933). But Europe had acquired a belated enthusiasm for jazz rhythms and in France there grew up something of a cult of "le jazz hot." Phonograph records of the playing of such experts as Louis Armstrong and his band sold well abroad. In the fall of 1933—at about the time of the NRA parades and the coming of Repeal—an English company arranged with a young New Yorker who was crazy about hot jazz to try to get some good records made by a band of American whites; and young John Henry Hammond, Jr., persuaded the scholarly-looking clarinetist, Benny Goodman, who was playing in a radio orchestra, to gather a group of players for this purpose.

The resulting records not only sold well in England but made an unexpected hit in the United States; and thus began a public enthusiasm for "swing"—as the hot jazz full of improvisation came to be called—which welled to its climax in the winter of 1937-38, when the bespectacled Mr. Goodman, playing at the Paramount and later in Boston and elsewhere, found that the boys and girls so yelled and screamed and cavorted when his band began to "send" that a concert became a bedlam. When in the spring of 1938 a Carnival of Swing was held at Randall's Island in New York, with twenty-five bands present, over 23,000 jitterbugs listened for five hours and forty-five minutes with such uncontrollable enthusiasm that, as a reporter put it in the next morning's *Times*, the police and park officers had all they could do to protect the players from "destruction by admiration."

Among many of the jitterbugs—particularly among many of the boys and girls—the appreciation of the new music was largely vertebral. A good swing band smashing away at full speed, with the trumpeters and clarinetists rising in turn under the spotlight to embroider the theme with their several furious improvisations and the drummers going into long-drawnout rhythmical frenzies, could reduce its less inhibited auditors to sheer emotional vibration, punctuated by howls of rapture. Yet to dismiss the swing craze as a pure orgy of sensation would be to miss more than half of its significance. For what the good bands produced—though it might sound to the unpracticed ear like a mere blare of discordant noise—was an extremely complex and subtle pattern, a full appreciation of which demanded far more musical sophistication than the simpler popular airs of a preceding period. The true swing enthusiasts, who collected records to the limit of their means and not only liked Artie Shaw's rendering of "Begin the Beguine" but knew precisely why they liked it, were receiving no mean musical education; and if Benny Goodman could turn readily from the playing of "Don't Be That Way" to the playing of Mozart, so could many of his hearers turn to the hearing of Mozart. It may not have been quite accidental that the craze for swing accompanied the sharpest gain in musical knowledge and musical taste that the American people had ever achieved.

This great gain in the appreciation of good music was one of the most remarkable phenomena of the nineteen-thirties. Some credit for it belongs to the WPA, which, doing valiant work in music as in literature and the theatre and the plastic arts, not only offered music classes and other aids to the potentially musical, but maintained no less than 36 symphony orchestras. But the chief credit probably must go to the radio, which had been demonstrating the ancient truth that if you throw at people enough of the products of any art, good, bad, and indifferent, some of these people will in time learn to prefer the good.

For a long time the radio had been spilling into the ears of millions of Americans an almost continuous stream of music of all sorts, mostly trite. At the beginning of the nineteen-thirties it was still accepted as axiomatic by most radio people—and particularly by those business executives whose task it was to approve the programs devised by advertising agencies to promote the sale of their goods—that good music was not widely wanted. Long before this, however, the broadcasting companies had been experimenting with putting music of high quality on the air, partly for the sake of prestige, partly to convince the people who wanted the radio to be more educational that the radio companies themselves were hot for culture. The National Broadcasting Company had put on the New York Symphony Orchestra as early as 1926, the Boston Symphony in 1927, the Philadelphia in 1929. By 1929 the Philadelphia Orchestra program had actually secured an advertising sponsor: Philco took the plunge. In 1930 the Columbia Broadcasting System began a series of concerts of the New York Philharmonic on Sunday afternoons, and the next year the NBC began putting the Metropolitan Opera on the air on Saturday afternoons. Before long the opera broadcast, too, acquired sponsors: a cigarette company and a mouth-wash company signified their willingness to pay for it if only a few well chosen words about the advantages of the right sort of smoke or gargle might accompany the works of Wagner and Puccini. What was happening was that these classical programs were obviously attracting listeners and more listeners.

So the movement swept on until on the first day of February, 1937—just a little while before President Roosevelt brought out his plan for the enlargement of the Supreme Court—an emissary of David Sarnoff of the National Broadcasting Company, calling upon Arturo Toscanini in his native Milan, told him that the NBC wanted him to conduct a radio orchestra the following winter.

"Did you ever hear of the NBC?" the emissary, Samuel Chotzinoff, is said to have begun.

"No," replied Toscanini.

Some explanation was required; and then Chotzinoff handed over a memorandum which suggested several alternative plans for Toscanini concerts on the air. The great conductor peered at it nearsightedly, ran his finger down the list, and presently stopped.

"I'll do this," said he. He was pointing at a suggestion of a concert a week for ten weeks.

He did it—with an orchestra especially recruited to do him justice. When, at Christmas time of 1937, he stepped upon the podium in the biggest broadcasting studio in the NBC Building in New York, facing a visible audience of a thousand or so men and women (equipped with satin programs guaranteed not to make crackling noises) and an invisible audience of millions more at their radios all over the country, it was clear that a milestone had been reached. Things had come to the point where the huge radio public was ready to be given the best that could be got, and given it direct—not simply granted a chance to overhear what was intended in the first place for the musically elect.

The remarkable rise in American musical appreciation may best be measured, perhaps, by citing a few figures collected by Dickson Skinner in *Harper's Magazine* in the spring of 1939. Here they are:—

In 1915 or thereabouts there had been 17 symphony orchestras in the United States. By 1939 there were over 270.

It was estimated that in 1938-39 the combined audiences on the air for the Metropolitan Opera on Saturday afternoon, the NBC symphony on Saturday evening, and the New York Philharmonic and Ford hour on Sunday, numbered 10,230,000 families *each week*. (Figure for yourself how many families had been able—and willing—to hear music of such calibre before 1930.)

As evidence that these audiences were increasing, it was estimated by the Coöperative Analysis of Broadcasting that the audience for the Ford Sunday evening hour, offering the Detroit Symphony, was 118 per cent larger in 1937 than in 1935; and that by 1938 it was fifth among all radio programs in national popularity, being exceeded only by the news broadcast and by three other commercial programs.

The NBC Music Appreciation Hour, conducted by Walter Damrosch, was being heard each week in 1938 by more than seven million children in some 70,000 schools—and probably by three or four million adults also.

And finally, during 1938, broadcasts of symphony orchestras and of grand opera were being carried by the two NBC networks at a rate which averaged more than an hour a day.

After reciting these statistics, it would seem hardly necessary to add that the biggest phonograph company reported that its sales of records increased 600 per cent in the five years 1933-38. The phonograph, once threatened with virtual extinction by the radio, had come into its own again, not only because of the swing craze but even more importantly because of the widespread desire to hear "classical" music of one's own choice without having to wait till a radio orchestra got round to playing it.

Thus far very little benefit from the growth of this huge audience had come to American composers. But that time would presumably arrive before long. For the testimony of concert performers who found that their audiences now wanted not simply the old sure-fire favorites, but the less familiar symphonies and concertos; the number of school and college glee clubs that now preferred to sing valid music; the growing number of listeners to Station WQXR in New York, which specialized in good music; the demeanor of the crowds who came to such music festivals as that held each summer in the Berkshires: these were among the accumulating fragments of evidence that a great American musical public of real discrimination was being built up.

§ 7

One does not expect a piece of music to carry a political or economic message, but one might well expect newspapers, magazines, the radio, and the movies to do so. These were the chief agencies of day-to-day adult instruction and entertainment, reaching audiences vastly bigger than even the most popular book or play could command. What was their function in the struggle over the future of America?

Inevitably the influence of the newspapers tended to be conservative. Newspaper publishing had become a branch of big business, obedient to the economic law which concentrated power into fewer and fewer hands. Although the tendency of newspapers to be combined into chains under a single ownership seemed to have been halted during the nineteen-thirties (during the latter years the Hearst chain actually showed signs of weakening), the tendency toward monopoly or duopoly of newspaper control in each city but the very largest continued. By 1938 a number of good-sized American cities—such as Denver, Des Moines, Grand Rapids, Hartford, Louisville, Memphis, Nashville, Omaha, Toledo, and St. Paul—had each only one morning and one afternoon paper; several of the biggest cities—Baltimore, Buffalo, Cleveland, Detroit, Kansas City, Pittsburgh, St. Louis, and Seattle—had only one morning and two afternoon papers; and in three of these latter cities the one morning paper was under the same ownership as one of the two afternoon papers. So complex and expensive an enterprise did a city newspaper have to be to survive that its controlling owners were perforce capitalists on a considerable scale, and their influence was likely to be exerted on behalf of property rights, of big business, and of the interests of important advertisers.

Not that the newspaper editors and reporters were conservative by preference. Many if not most of these, in fact, were aggressive supporters of the underdog. Indeed, the decrease in the number of newspapers, the increasing use of syndicated material, and the drastic economies required by the Depression had thrown so many newspaper men out on the street that what had once been hopefully spoken of as the "profession of journalism" had become one of the most crowded and ill-paid of all white-collar occupations, and the reporter might well regard *himself* as an underdog. Out of these circumstances emerged such anomalies as newspapers whose editors and reporters were mostly New Dealers (or even communists) and members of the Newspaper Guild affiliated with the CIO, yet whose editorial pages warred fiercely against Roosevelt and whose news columns were

THE HINDENBURG BURSTS INTO FLAME

This photograph was taken just as the fire broke out while the dirigible was approaching her mooring-mast at Lakehurst, N. J., at dusk on May 6, 1937

THE SOUTH CHICAGO "RIOT," MEMORIAL DAY, 1937
Police routing a picket-line outside the Republic Steel plant in the Little Steel
strike: 10 dead, 90 wounded

"slanted" against labor. Where the tradition of factual, objective reporting was strong, as on the *New York Times*, the slanting was only minor and occasional; where this tradition was weaker, as on the Chicago *Tribune*, it was sharp.

But if the newspapers tended toward conservatism, at least they did not tend toward evasion of political and economic issues. One of the most striking phenomena of the decade was the rising importance of the political columnist whose writings were syndicated all over the country and whose audiences were numbered by the millions. The readers of a small-city newspaper might find on their breakfast tables not only the advice of Dorothy Dix on affairs of the heart, the gossip of Walter Winchell, the Broadway talk of O. O. McIntyre, but also the opinions on national affairs of people like Walter Lippmann, David Lawrence, Frank Kent, Dorothy Thompson, Drew Pearson and Robert S. Allen, and Westbrook Pegler (and also Eleanor Roosevelt, whose "My Day" seldom touched national issues directly but had an indirectly persuasive effect). Being permitted usually more latitude of expression than a local editor, these syndicated columnists—who incidentally were mostly conservative—became national oracles. When Walter Lippmann turned against the New Deal he carried thousands of readers with him; when Westbrook Pegler took issue with a political adversary, people from coast to coast watched the fur fly. Lippmann in 1932, Dorothy Thompson in 1937, were among the most influential of all Americans. Strange that the old tradition of personal journalism, so nearly killed by the transformation of the American newspaper into a standardized corporated entity, should thus reassert itself on the grand scale!

In the magazine world—if one excepts such liberal weeklies of small circulation as the *New Republic* and the *Nation* and such organs of the solid intellectuals as *Harper's* —the tendency was toward a very timid discretion in the treatment of public affairs. This discretion was relaxed somewhat in 1932 and 1933, when readers clamored to know what was wrong with the management of American business and the upholders of the status quo were too bewildered to offer confident resistance, but reasserted itself after the New Deal Honeymoon. Among the big popular magazines with circulations of two or three million the only sort of militancy likely to be manifest thereafter was a militancy such as that of George Horace Lorimer of the *Saturday Evening Post*, who risked considerable losses in circulation (but, of course, few losses in advertising) by his incessant hammering at the Roosevelt Administration. Otherwise these magazines—particularly the women's magazines—touched controversial issues timidly if at all and confined themselves mostly to highly expert fictional entertainment and to the discussion of matters to which neither their owners, their advertisers, nor their more tenderminded readers could conceivably take exception. When an attempt was made to provide, in *Ken*, a liberal-radical periodical of large circulation, advertisers held off and thus condemned it to an early death. But on the whole it would be inexact to say that direct pressure from advertisers affected very largely the policy of the successful big-circulation magazines. What chiefly affected them was the desire of their owners to see their own opinions echoed, to make money by pleasing and flattering their advertisers, and at the same time to provide agreeable and innocuous entertainment.

That there was money to be made nevertheless by the sharp presentation of facts, and particularly of facts about America, was shown by the growing success of *Time*—an expertly edited, newsy, and withal irreverent (though not at all radical) weekly—and its younger sister *Fortune* (founded in 1930), which although edited by liberals for the benefit chiefly of the rich, developed such a brilliant technic of team-research and team-authorship and trimmed its sails so skillfully to the winds of conservatism that it not only became a mine of factual material for future historians but subtly broadened reactionary minds. None of the other periodical successes of the decade promised to have so acute an effect upon the status of the writer as this adventure in writing a magazine inside the office; there were those who saw in it a threat of extinction to the free-lance journalist, a threat of the coming of the day when the magazine writer would have to look for an office job or be shut out from publication. (The rise of the *Reader's Digest* to huge popularity appeared to prove chiefly that readers liked to save time, if their reading could be ably condensed and reassuringly simplified; the rise of the picture magazines, led by *Life* and *Look,* proved chiefly that the camera craze had produced enough good photographers to satisfy a public that always liked pictures.) Yet even such new successes as these hardly affected the basic generalization that the way of the popular magazines was the way of evasion and sheer entertainment.

Of radio's coming-of-age during the nineteen-thirties something has already been said. We have noted its contribution to the cause of music. But it developed in other ways also. As a news agency it invaded more and more successfully a field in which the press had stood alone. During the early and middle years of the decade the "commentators" of the air waves became rivals in influence of the political columnists of the press: men like Edwin C. Hill, William Hard, Lowell Thomas, Boake Carter, and H. V. Kaltenborn interpreted national affairs to huge numbers of auditors. Summary, explanation, and interpretation were in demand, especially on the crises in Europe. But personal opinion was likely to be dampened unless safely conservative. The radio commentators added little to the fires of domestic revolt.

Otherwise perhaps the most significant development in radio was the improvement and standardization of the variety show of the air, an hour's or half-hour's program of alternating light music and humorous dialogue, featuring such national favorites as Jack Benny, Rudy Vallee, Fred Allen, George Burns and Gracie Allen, Bing Crosby, and Edgar Bergen and Charlie McCarthy. Throughout most of the decade, unless there was an election, a prize fight, a European crisis, or a Presidential "fireside chat" to demand brief attention, it was the variety shows which commanded the biggest audiences. Their chief rivals for popularity were the numerous serial stories of the air, ranging from Amos 'n' Andy (which reached its biggest number of listeners in 1930 but continued *ad infinitum*) to the Lone Ranger, a wild West thriller, which first was heard on January 30, 1933, and rose in favor until by 1939 it was a three-times-a-week treat to some twenty million people who received it from 140 stations.

Almost without exception both the variety shows and the serials were innocent of any political or economic or social import whatever, save for the announcer's occasional interposition with a suave tribute to the products and policies of the corporation which footed the bill for the entertainment. Charlie McCarthy, for instance, took one into a safe little world of small boys' pranks, a world in which nothing more distressing happened than that Edgar Bergen grew bald, a world in which there were no unemployed men, no budget deficits, no marching dictators. How close were the heroic exploits of the Lone Ranger to observed reality may be suggested by the fact that—according to J. Bryan, III, in the *Saturday Evening Post*—neither Fran Striker, who wrote the innumerable scripts, nor Earle W. Graser, whose voice made "Hi-Yo, Silver!" familiar the country over, had ever been west of Michigan.

§ 8

As for the movies, so completely did they dodge the dissensions and controversies of the day—with a few exceptions, such as the March of Time series, the brief newsreels, and an occasional picture like "I Am a Fugitive from a Chain Gang" or "They Won't Forget"—that if a dozen or two feature pictures, selected at random, were to be shown to an audience of 1960, that audience would probably derive from them not the faintest idea of the ordeal through which the United States went in the nineteen-thirties.

Upon these movies were lavished huge sums of money. For them the stage was robbed of half its ablest actors and playwrights; the literary world, of many of its ablest writers—to say nothing of the engineering and photographic skill which brought to adequacy that cacophonous novelty of 1929, the talking picture, and which toward the end of the decade was bringing more and more pictures in reasonably convincing color. A large number of excellent pictures were produced, with capital acting—whether comedies like "It Happened One Night," or adventure stories like "Mutiny on the Bounty," or historical dramas like "The Life of Emile Zola," or picturizations of fictional classics like "A Tale of Two Cities"; and there was a far greater number of pictures which, whatever their unreality, served as rousing entertainment for an idle evening. But although the secular religion of social consciousness was rampant in Hollywood—especially in 1937 and 1938, when numerous script-writers and actors and technical men were ready to do or die for their guilds, for Tom Mooney, for the Spanish Loyalists, or even for the communist version of the Popular Front—nevertheless in the pictures upon which they worked there was hardly a glimpse of the real America.

The movies took one to a never-never land of adventure and romance uncomplicated by thought.

The capital invested in the movies preferred to steer clear of awkward issues, not to run the risk of offending theatre-goers abroad or at home. The moralists must be placated; as a result of the campaign of the Legion of Decency in 1934, Joseph Breen had been installed in the office of the Motion Picture Producers and Distributors of America, ready to censor before production any picture which showed too prolonged a kiss, which showed small boys bathing naked, which permitted a character to say "damn" or "hell." (The immediate effect of the Legion of Decency campaign, oddly enough from the point of view of censorship-haters, appeared to be salutary; it frightened the producers into launching, during 1935 and 1936, some of the best pictures yet seen.) Foreign opinion must be placated lest foreign sales be lost: when "Idiot's Delight" was adapted from stage to screen, it must be set in an anonymous country whose inhabitants spoke not Italian but Esperanto; when "Beau Geste" was refilmed in 1939, the villains of the original silent version must be given Russian names rather than Italian and Belgian names because film trade with Russia was comparatively small. Neither capital nor labor, neither the Administration nor its enemies, must be given any opportunity to criticize. If one wanted to show a crusading reformer, better to make him a Frenchman of the past, like Emile Zola, than an American of the present: for how could an American engage in a crusade without implying that something was wrong?

It was significant that the pre-eminent artist of the motion picture during the nineteen-thirties, Walt Disney, was a maker of fantasies, and that the motion-picture event in January, 1938, which Westbrook Pegler called "the happiest thing that has happened in this world since the armistice" was the production of "Snow White," a fairy story of the screen. Only in unreality could genius have free rein.

The Disney film was a huge popular success; it set the whole country humming "Heigh-ho" and "Whistle While You Work" and incidentally was a godsend to the toy business: during the bleak first third of 1938, when the Recession was at its worst, over $3,000,000 worth of Disney toys were sold, and that summer, when the wheels of most factories were turning intermittently, the Sieberling-Latex plant near Akron was three weeks behind orders (after running 24 hours a day for months)—making rubber statuettes of Dopey and the other dwarfs!

Not merely did the movies avoid temptations to thought about the condition of the country; in effect their producers played, half unwittingly, a gigantic joke upon the social salvationists, and particularly upon those men and women who would have liked to make the American masses class conscious. For the America which the movies portrayed—like the America of popular magazine fiction and especially of the magazine advertisements—was devoid of real poverty or discontent, of any real conflict of interests between owners and workers, of any real ferment of ideas. More than that, it was a country in which almost everybody was rich or about to be rich, and in which the possession of a huge house and a British-accented butler and a private swimming pool not merely raised no embarrassing questions about the distribution of wealth, but was accepted as the normal lot of mankind. So completely did the inveterate movie-goer come to take this America for granted —at least during his two hours in the theatre—that he was unlikely to be surprised to find a couple of stenographers pictured as occupying an apartment with the newest built-in kitchen equipment and a living-room 35 feet long and 20 feet wide; or to hear Bette Davis, in "Dark Victory," expressing satisfaction that she had given up the life in which she "had had everything" for a life in which she "had nothing"—"nothing," in this case, being a remodeled Vermont farmhouse which (according to the careful computations of E. B. White in *Harper's Magazine*) must have cost at least $11,000 or $12,000 a year to live in.

While the writers and artists in whom burned a fierce desire to reveal to their fellow-countrymen the inequalities and miseries of their lot were resolutely addressing a public numbered in the thousands, another public numbering *eighty-five millions each week* was at the movies watching Gary Cooper, Clark Gable, Myrna Loy, Katharine Hepburn, Ronald Colman, Carole Lombard, and the other gods and goddesses of Hollywood disporting themselves in a dreamland of wide-sweeping stairways, marble floors, and magnificent drawing-room vistas. And these eighty-five millions were liking it.

Was not the lesson of all this that America was not—or not yet, if you prefer—proletarian-minded? True, its citizens were capable of organizing hotly to redress wrongs and secure themselves benefits, were quite ready to have these wrongs redressed and these benefits provided by the government if no other agency would do it; and some Americans might even fight, if need be, to get what they wanted. Yet still in the back of their minds there was room for an Horatio Alger paradise where young men of valour rose to the top and young women of glamour married the millionaire's son, and lived happily ever after.

Chapter Eleven
FRICTION AND RECESSION

§ 1

IN A cold rain which slanted viciously down upon sodden throngs before the Capitol, Franklin D. Roosevelt, standing with head bared to the gusts, took the oath of office for his second term as President of the United States and began his Inaugural Address.

It was an eloquent address. Describing in glowing terms the improvement in national conditions which had taken place since 1933, he went on to ask, "Shall we pause now and turn our back upon the road that lies ahead?" His answer, of course, was No; and he proceeded in biting sentences to summarize the poverty and wretchedness that still remained to be defeated. "I see one-third of a nation ill-housed, ill-clad, ill-nourished," said he. "It is not in despair that I paint for you that picture. I paint it for you in hope, because the nation, seeing and understanding the injustice in it, proposes to paint it out. We are determined to make every American citizen the subject of his country's interest and concern, and we will never regard any faithful law-abiding group within our borders as superfluous. The test of our progress is not whether we add more to the abundance of those who have much, it is whether we provide enough for those who have too little."

Down in the crowd below, New Dealers tried to hold on to their streaming umbrellas and clap simultaneously—and cheered anyhow. This was the sort of fighting humanitarianism they liked. Yet everybody in the crowd, New Dealer or skeptic or opponent, was listening intently for something more specific. How did Roosevelt propose to proceed along the "road that lies ahead," and in particular how did he propose to deal with the Supreme Court, which stood right in the middle of that road as Roosevelt saw it? During the almost twenty months that had elapsed since the Court had smashed the NRA he had been biding his time. All through the 1936 campaign he had left the Court issue severely alone. Now, with the seal of majority approval upon him, would he speak?

Twice already today he had drawn the minds of the crowd to the overarching question. When he took the oath of office he had not been content to answer Chief Justice Hughes with a simple "I do," but with his left hand upon the Bible and his right hand upraised he had repeated the whole historic oath, with sharp emphasis upon the word "Constitution." Early in the Inaugural Address he had remarked, "The Constitution of 1787 did not make our democracy impotent." What more would there be? The crowd waited, the rain beating down upon them. There was no further reference to the Court, direct or indirect.

The deluge from the heavens on that twentieth of January, 1937, might have been taken as an unhappy omen. In a direct physical sense it was indeed to be one; for that rainstorm, following previous rains and being followed by others, was presently to set in motion the great Ohio River flood. Already down a thousand hillsides from Pennsylvania to Arkansas were coursing the muddy rivulets which would join to inundate Cincinnati, Louisville, and many another city and town. And in another, broader sense those who regarded the storm as an ill omen were to be justified. For the new year of 1937 was to be marked by discords and disappointments. At that very moment, in Flint, Michigan, thousands of sit-down strikers were occupying the factories of the General Motors Corporation in what was to prove the first major conflict of a widespread and ugly industrial war. By the time this war waned, the national economy was to slide down into a new crisis which would dash, for a long time to come, the high hopes set forth in the Inaugural Address. As for the President himself, even at that moment—though only his Attorney-General and perhaps three or four other men had an inkling of what was afoot—he had formulated and was having drafted in detail a plan of campaign against the Supreme Court, a plan which, although in the end it would bring him an indirect victory, would in the meantime lead him to a painful and damaging defeat.

§ 2

The General Motors Corporation was one of the mightiest of American economic principalities. It employed nearly a quarter of a million men and annually produced, in factories and assembly plants all over the country and abroad, some two million cars and trucks—over two-fifths of all those made in the United States, and well over a third of all those made in the whole world. Its management was theoretically answerable to over a third of a million stockholders, but was actually free from any direction or restraint by any but a handful of the biggest of them. (This army of stockholders wanted dividends; when dividends are not forthcoming, the innumerable small stockholders of such a monster corporation do not revolt—they sell.) The Corporation's net earnings, though they had dwindled to the vanishing point in 1932, had swelled in 1936 to nearly a quarter of a billion dollars—just about a thousand dollars per employee. The Corporation was half immune to competition of the traditional sort, for now it shared with Ford and Chrysler well over 90 per cent of the American automobile business; only those two other monster organizations could combat it. It had become virtually independent of the banking houses of Wall Street, since it could finance out of earnings and depreciation allowances not only replacements and improvements and additions to its plants, but all manner of adventures in other economic fields; the building of ice boxes, airplane engines, Diesel locomotives, and so on; engineering research more effective than private inventors could manage. All in all, the General Motors inner management—a few men in New York and Detroit—exercised a power in American life probably greater than that of any state government.

Yet since the end of December, 1936, this principality had been paralyzed by groups of employees who had seized its key plants by simply sitting down at their jobs and defying all who would dislodge them. The stream of car production, dammed at these vital points, slowed to a halt; while the little city of Flint, Michigan, where most of the key plants were situated, became the scene of something close to civil war.

Behind the defiance of these workers lay a long story of business regimentation, labor insurgency, and government inefficacy.

When the New Deal, in 1933, had given to business managements the permission to organize, it had also, as we have seen, acknowledged the right of labor to organize. There was nothing revolutionary about this acknowledgement: previous laws such as the Clayton Act and Norris-La Guardia Act had included similar provisions—though the courts tended to whittle them down. But the express permission, written into Section 7a of the National Industrial Recovery Act and into the resulting NRA codes, had started a rush to join labor unions.

With this rush most of the leaders of the American Federation of Labor—slow-moving, inflexible, conservative-minded men, devoted to old-fashioned craft unionism and

jealous of their jurisdictional rights—had been quite unable
to cope. A few of them, however, had been galvanized
into sudden activity, and one in particular, John L. Lewis,
the beetle-browed boss of the United Mine Workers, had
seemed to become a new man. In previous years Lewis
had been noted chiefly for his dictatorial and obstructive
ways and had become unpopular among the Mine Workers
themselves, but now he staked every last penny in the union
treasury upon a whirlwind organizing campaign, sent out
bands of organizers to tell the miners that "The law is on
our side," and signed them up by the hundreds of thousands.

Presently the transformed Lewis became the strong
leader of an aggressive group inside the Federation, a group
which stood for industrial unionism—for collecting in a
single organization all the workers in a given industry,
whatever special crafts they might be engaged in. Along
with Lewis the group included such men as Sidney Hill-
man, the astute head of the International Garment Workers; Charles P. Howard of the International Typographers;
and David Dubinsky of the International Ladies Garment
Workers. Believing that the craft-unionists of the Federation were consistently muffing opportunities to mobilize the
workers in the yet-unorganized mass-production industries
—steel, automobiles, rubber, and so on—these men gathered
on October 9, 1935, to form a special organization of their
own, inside the A. F. of L. They called it the Committee
for Industrial Organization: the CIO. The rift deepened
and the next year, 1936, the CIO was read out of the A. F.
of L. and became, under Lewis's leadership, a competing
federation—more alert, more headlong, better able to undertake rapid, large-scale organization, and quite prepared
to go into party politics: its fast-growing unions contributed
nearly half a million dollars to help Roosevelt defeat Landon.

Meanwhile the NRA had been tossed into the wastebasket by the Supreme Court. Congress had quickly passed a new law, the Wagner Labor Relations Act, to supplant Section 7a and specifically authorize collective bargaining, and had set up a National Labor Relations Board to enforce the Act. From the outset this Board faced a well-nigh impossible task. Many employers were coolly proceeding as if there were no Wagner Act at all, driving away union organizers and firing union members in the confident hope that the Supreme Court would upset the new law and things would return to the *status quo ante*. Other employers were setting up "company unions"; and though some of these were really representative agencies for genuine conciliation and adjustment, others were essentially fake unions, under the management's thumb. There was an ugly temper in the industrial towns, where men who had suffered acutely during the Depression, and had lost all respect for the princes of industry who hired and fired them, were ready to make trouble just as soon as they had full stomachs and a glimmer of hope. With labor in a rebellious mood, many unions inexperienced and undisciplined, racketeers and adventurers making hay as union organizers, jurisdictional disputes frequent, the labor high command divided, the status and meaning of the law uncertain, the attitude of the government shifting and ambiguous, many employers openly heedless of the law, and conflicting propagandas misrepresenting the issues, there was confusion everywhere. Anger deepened and strikes multiplied.

Among the automobile workers the militancy became especially hot. They complained of their low wages, arguing that although the hourly rates were higher than in most other industries, employment was spasmodic and the annual wage uncertain and unsatisfactory. They complained of the inexorable speed of the factory assembly lines. Especially they were angry at the way in which the corporations spied on union members and found pretexts to discharge them in order to break the union movement. According to the official summary of the report of the La Follette Committee of the Senate, during the period of a little over two and a half years between January 1, 1934, and July 31, 1936, the General Motors Corporation alone "paid $994,-855.68 to detective agencies for spy services." Union leaders were shadowed, there were stool pigeons in the unions, and no man in the assembly line knew whether a casual reference to the union in a conversation with a fellow-workman might not be followed by his discharge on the ground of inefficiency.

An industrial union, the United Automobile Workers, had been formed among these men. In 1936 it was taken under the wing of the CIO and thereafter it grew with angry speed. In December, 1936, its new head, an energetic ex-minister, Homer Martin, tried to arrange a meeting with William S. Knudsen, the vice-president of General Motors, only to be told that labor matters should be taken up with the heads of the various plants; the vast General Motors principality, so well integrated in many respects, preferred not to act as if labor policy were a matter for integration. The plant managers were indisposed to negotiate. Thereupon the dispute boiled over.

John L. Lewis wanted no strike then in General Motors. He had his hands full organizing other industries, particularly steel. An automobile strike now might wreck the CIO in its infancy. Besides, the General Motors Corporation was far from unpopular with the general public, which liked its cars and thought of it as paying high wages. But the rebellion was irrepressible.

In plant after plant the men abruptly sat down—in the Cleveland Fisher Body plant, in Fisher Body No. 1 and Fisher Body No. 2 at Flint, in the Fleetwood and Cadillac plants at Detroit, and elsewhere. They kept enough men inside each factory to hold it as a fortress, and while these men idled, played cards, and stood guard at doors and windows, food was sent in to them from union kitchens outside. Thus began one of the most gigantic industrial conflicts in American history.

The sit-down strike was not a new phenomenon. It had been tried, briefly but successfully, by employees of the Hormel Packing Company in Austin, Minnesota, as far back as 1933. There had been several sit-downs in Europe in 1934, and subsequently the method had been utilized on an immense scale in France and to a limited extent in the United States, particularly at Akron. But the General Motors strike was the first to bring it forcibly to the attention of the great American public, and the country buzzed with indignation, enthusiasm, and bewilderment, according to its various predilections, as it read the news from Flint.

Pretty clearly the sit-down was illegal. Liberal observers might point out that the traditional concepts of ownership did not seem quite applicable to a colossal corporation the ownership of which rested, not with the management, but with a third of a million stockholders, very few of whom were anywhere near as close to it as the workmen whose daily lives were bound up with it; but no new legal concepts applicable to such a principality had been formulated. And anyhow the angry men at Flint were beyond bothering about the law. They had discovered that the sit-down gave them new strategic advantages. Not only did it enable them to capture and hold the corporation's productive machinery; it also removed from them the usual temptation to violence, or the appearance of violence, which would alienate the general public. From the moment they sat down they were on the defensive, and the temptation to attack rested with the management. Behind the walls of the great factories they had only to sit and wait while Governor Murphy of Michigan and Secretary of Labor Frances Perkins sought tirelessly to induce the General Motors management to sit down at a table with the United Automobile Workers.

On January 11 the management took the offensive. It turned the heat off in one of the besieged plants, Fisher Body No. 2, and the police gathered to prevent food from being sent in. The union leaders sent a sound truck to the scene, and with the magnified voice of an organizer to cheer them on, rushed food past the police to their friends inside. A few hours later the police stormed the plant, and were beaten off in a pitched battle in which the weapons included buckshot and tear gas (on the part of the police) and door hinges, metal pipes, and soda-pop bottles (on the part of the strikers). The sit-downers remained in possession. The National Guard was called out; but Governor Murphy—who was willing to let the law go unenforced if only he might prevent further violence—forbade the troops to attack. Still the sit-downers remained in possession.

The management turned to the courts for aid, securing an order that the factories must be evacuated—an order which failed of its moral effect when the judge who had issued it was revealed to be a large stockholder in General Motors. Again the management secured an evacuation order, from another judge, which threatened the strikers with imprisonment and a fine of no less than fifteen million dollars if they did not get out by three o'clock on the afternoon of February 3. The men, inflamed now by the sort of spirit which sends soldiers over the top, had no intention of getting out; and as three o'clock on that fiercely cold winter afternoon approached, and thousands of CIO members and sympathizers gathered from Detroit and Toledo and Akron and massed in the streets, armed with clubs, pokers, and crowbars, while the soldiers of the National Guard waited grimly for the order to advance, one could see impending a tragic battle the scars of which might remain for generations.

But there was no battle. Instead, there was hilarious square dancing on the frozen lawns outside Fisher No. 1. For at the last moment Governor Murphy wired that he had induced Knudsen to confer, and told the sheriff to make no move. After an anxious week of conferences, the Governor was able to announce that a settlement had been reached. General Motors recognized the United Automobile Workers as the exclusive bargaining agency in seventeen of its plants, and would negotiate for a contract with it.

The strike was over—after lasting 44 days, involving 44,000 workers directly and 110,000 indirectly, and paralyzing 60 factories in 14 states. Governor Murphy had succeeded in settling it—at the expense of the prestige of the law—with a minimum of bloodshed. And the CIO had won a great victory: a chance to participate in the government of the General Motors principality.

What wonder that after this intoxicating triumph workers all over the country caught the sit-down fever and stopped work in factories, ten-cent stores, restaurants, all manner of workplaces, until the total of sit-down strikers in America from September 1936, through May, 1937, was brought to almost half a million? Or that partisanship for and against the CIO reached the boiling point? Or that John L. Lewis became the man of the hour, sagely discussed as a looming presidential candidate for 1940—a portentous dictator-in-the-making in the eyes of the conservatives, a hero immaculate in those of the liberals?

§ 3

Where would the next struggle come? In United States Steel?

That was what men were asking one another. But they were due for a surprise. For already the drama of the CIO and United States Steel was far advanced—in complete secrecy.

On Saturday, January 9, 1937—when the General Motors strike was still young—John L. Lewis had been lunching with Senator Guffey of Pennsylvania at the Mayflower Hotel in Washington when Myron C. Taylor, the dignified chairman of the board of United States Steel, entered the dining-room with Mrs. Taylor. Taylor bowed to the Senator and the big labor leader as he threaded his way past their table; a moment later he came back to chat with them briefly; and after Lewis and Senator Guffey had finished lunch and the Senator had left, Lewis went over to the Taylors' table and remained with them for twenty minutes or so, in what appeared to be the most affable conversation. Other luncheon guests throughout the room were agog at the spectacle of the leader of the CIO and the leader of the most famous corporation in the country hobnobbing agreeably. They would have been much more surprised had they guessed that during the conversation the labor leader had said he would like to have a leisurely talk with Taylor, and Taylor had suggested that they confer the next day—Sunday—at his suite at the Mayflower. When Lewis arrived at the Mayflower the next day and took the elevator, nobody in that hotel lobby in news-hungry Washington had an inkling of where he was bound.

There followed a series of conferences, most of them at Taylor's house in New York—still without anybody's being the wiser. The result of these conferences was an agreement upon a formula by which the Steel Corporation would recognize and sign contracts with the Steel Workers Organizing Committee, a unit of the CIO. Taylor submitted this agreement to his astonished directors and won their consent to it; and on Monday, March 1, the news broke that Steel and the CIO were signing up.

"One of the steel workers just came in and said he heard

over the radio that U. S. Steel was meeting with the CIO," said an organizer over the telephone to Philip Murray of the SWOC; "I told him he was crazy and kicked him out of the office." "I can't believe you!" cried the president of one of the lesser steel companies when President Irwin of U. S. Steel called him on the telephone to tell him the news. No reconciliation during the nineteen-thirties until the reconciliation of Stalin and Hitler in 1939 caused more amazement. The steel industry as a whole had gone on record against the CIO unionization drive only the preceding summer. The Steel Corporation had been historically noted as an implacable foe of organized labor. The CIO's attitude toward corporation properties during the General Motors strike had brought most conservative industrialists almost to the point of apoplexy. Yet here was the Corporation making friends with the CIO—running up the white flag of surrender, cried the angry industrialists—without even a struggle! The news was too good to be true, cried the partisans of labor; surely there must be a catch in it somewhere! But there was no catch. The chairman of the Steel Corporation had simply recognized that the SWOC had already signed up enough workers—even out of the Corporation's own company unions—to cause a very ugly strike; that such a strike would cost the Corporation money, for foreign orders for steel for armaments were booming; that it would also cost the Corporation good will, for U. S. Steel had had a bad labor record in the past; and that the way of conciliation was the way of prudence.

Would there, then, be peace throughout the steel industry? There would not. "Little Steel"—the Bethlehem, Republic, National, Inland, and Youngstown Sheet and Tube companies—refused to sign contracts with the CIO. A strike was called that spring, for the insurgent workers could not be held back; and the companies fought it with all the weapons at their command. "Loyal workers" were protected with riot guns and gas grenades. These "loyal workers" were fed inside company plants with supplies sent them by airplane and by parcel post. "Back-to-work" movements were organized and well publicized. Local police and deputies broke up picket lines (a crowd of picketers in South Chicago were pursued and shot down as they ran, leaving behind them four killed, six fatally injured, and ninety wounded, some thirty of them by gunfire). And there was a barrage, throughout the strike, of persuasive publicity, which represented the steel companies as defending the "right to work," as protecting men who wanted to work from the "intimidation, coercion, and violence" of "outside agitators" sent into peaceable and contented communities by the CIO. "I won't have a contract, verbal or written," said Tom M. Girdler, head of the Republic company and leader of the managements' side in the conflict, "with an irresponsible, racketeering, violent, communistic body like the CIO, and until they pass a law making me do it, I am not going to do it."

The strike was broken. The CIO was defeated.

Already the sit-down epidemic and the strike epidemic generally were waning, somewhat to the relief of most of the general public, which had become sick and tired of reading about riots, plug-ugly strikebreakers, and new strikes started by new labor factions after settlements had been reached; sick and tired of picket lines, vigilantes, and all the discords of industrial friction. And presently the ubiquitous disputes were to be almost automatically subdued by the approach of the business Recession of 1937-38.

§ 4

During the very months in the spring and summer of 1937 when the country was most sharply divided by the disputes over the CIO, it was torn also by another major conflict. For on February 5—when President Roosevelt's second term was hardly more than two weeks old, and the receding flood waters of the Ohio were leaving wreckage and slime in the streets of Louisville and Cincinnati, and Governor Murphy was beginning his conferences with Knudsen and Lewis for the settlement of the General Motors strike—the President almost nonchalantly tossed to Congress his plan for the liberalization of the Supreme Court. It was like tossing a cannon cracker into a munitions dump.

No President who was not buoyed up by a great confidence in the willingness of the majority of Congress and of the public to follow him wherever he might lead, and who was not by nature both daring and impulsive, would have gambled on such a plan without a preliminary sounding of opinion. For nearly two years Roosevelt had shown by his caution that he knew there was dynamite in the Supreme Court issue. But now he walked blithely up and set off the charge almost single-handed.

On the afternoon of February 4 the President asked the Speaker of the House, the Democratic leaders in the Senate and House, and the chairman of the two judiciary committees of Congress to meet with the Cabinet the following morning; and when, on the morning of the 5th, these gentlemen assembled in the Cabinet room at the White House, he explained to them briefly his new proposal and dismissed them with the word that he had a press conference to attend and would be sending his message to Congress, together with a draft of the proposed bill, at noon. Nobody in the room, according to the best evidence available at this writing, had had the least foreknowledge of the proposal except Attorney-General Homer Cummings, who had drafted it in consultation with the President. To all the rest of the Cabinet, and to the Congressional leaders, it came as a complete surprise. In the current vernacular, the President was not asking them, he was telling them.

It seems that some time in December, 1936, Cummings remembered that he had once found in the files of the Department of Justice a document drafted back in 1913 by Attorney-General McReynolds, who subsequently had become the most violently anti-New-Deal justice on the Supreme bench: this document was a suggestion that younger men be provided for the Federal judiciary by appointing a new judge for each judge who had reached the age of seventy (after serving at least ten years) and had failed to retire. Cummings had taken his discovery over to the White House, suggesting to Roosevelt that this principle might be applied now to the Federal judiciary—*including the Supreme Court*. Thus the Court would be enlarged to a maximum of fifteen members, Roosevelt would have a chance to nominate as the new members men who would not torpedo progressive legislation, and there would be no necessity for a Constitutional amendment. The whole thing would be done simply as a part of a mere plan for the provision of a larger and more alert judiciary.

Cummings had suggested other methods too of meeting the situation, but this one met with Roosevelt's immediate delight—a delight not decreased by the fact that there would be in it a well-concealed joke on Justice McReynolds. "That's the one, Homer!" cried the President, and straightway Cummings went to work upon it.

Not until January was well advanced, apparently, was anyone else except Solicitor-General Stanley Reed (and perhaps one or two subordinates in the Department of Justice) let in on the secret; then—according to Joseph Alsop and Turner Catledge—the plan was shown to Judge Rosenman and Donald Richberg; a little later it was shown to Tom Corcoran and perhaps two or three other intimate Presidential advisers. (Corcoran, for one, disliked it because of the indirection with which a major matter of governmental policy was attacked; he had been working on a quite different plan.) The rest of the Cabinet and the Congressional leaders, as we have seen, were completely in the dark. Very much on his own responsibility, the Presidential quarterback gave the signal for the boldest of trick forward passes.

That not all the players on the team relished making interference for such a play was immediately apparent. As Hatton Sumner, chairman of the House judiciary committee, walked away from the meeting at the White House he remarked grimly to his colleagues, "Boys, here's where I cash in my chips." He was thereafter in opposition. And although the Presidential message made public at noon that day was innocent-looking to the last degree—it argued that "the personnel of the Federal judiciary is insufficient to meet the business before them," spoke of the tendency of judges to continue on the bench "in many instances far beyond their years of physical or mental capacity," and argued that "a constant and systematic addition of younger blood will vitalize the courts and better equip them to recognize and apply the essential concepts of justice in the light of the needs and the facts of an ever-changing world" —a previously amenable Congress began at once to show signs of scattered but rising insurgency. Nor did there come from the country at large that overwhelming shout of approval which would have swept the plan to victory.

The reason was that three minority groups of voters combined in disapproval of the plan. First there was the large anti-New-Deal group who were ready to leap savagely upon any Roosevelt measure. Second, there were people who, however adverse their opinion of the Supreme Court of 1937, had a sharp emotional bias against interfering with the Court as an institution. Third, there were those who did not mind seeing the Court interfered with but thought the Roosevelt scheme too breezily disingenuous, and were offended at the idea of treating a grave governmental issue as a mere matter of arterial hardening. Even at the outset these three groups added up to make a majority; and they were enlarged by subsequent events.

A group of wily Republican strategists in the Senate managed to persuade ex-President Hoover and other Republican leaders outside Congress to muffle their protests, knowing that if the Court plan were allowed to take on the color of a party issue the Democrats would rally round the flag. These Republican strategists were happy to let Senator Burton Wheeler, a Democrat, be the shining leader of the opposition. Then Chief Justice Hughes was persuaded to write a letter to Senator Wheeler explaining that the Supreme Court was keeping up with its calendar and thus undermining the implication that the "nine old men" could not get through their work. Most effective of all, the Court itself had a sharp attack of prudence.

If anybody had supposed that the black-robed gentlemen of the Court were not very human—that the processes of the Court were impersonal and unpolitical, an Olympian matching of the text of an Act with the text of the Constitution—he was due for a shock in March and April, 1937. Realizing that a series of rejections of liberal laws would strengthen the Roosevelt attack, the Court suddenly turned as mild as any sucking dove. It upheld the Railway Labor Act and the new version of the Frazier-Lemke Farm Mortgage Moratorium Act. It reversed itself upon minimum wages for women and children, upsetting the decision which had so embarrassed Governor Landon at the time of his nomination less than a year before. More remarkable still, it upheld the Wagner Labor Relations Act by a vote of 5 to 4, Justice Roberts moving quietly from the die-hard group into the liberal group, and thus confounding those industrialists who had cheerfully expected the National Labor Relations Board to be blown into oblivion. A little later the Court upheld the Social Security Act. The climax came when Justice Van Devanter resigned, thus giving Roosevelt the chance to make his first appointment to the Court—and presumably to convert what had been usually a narrow anti-New-Deal majority into a narrow liberal majority.

All these moves weakened the Roosevelt side in Congress. "Why run for a train after you've caught it?" remarked Senator Byrnes after he heard the news of the Van Devanter resignation. An eloquent fireside chat by the President over the radio early in the battle over the bill had not started the snowball of public opinion rolling; a *Fortune* poll made during the spring indicated that only about one-third of the voters were definitely in favor of the plan. But the President would consider no compromise. The battle in Congress became more bitter. Not until June 3 did the President give ground. On that day he saw Senator Joseph T. Robinson, the Democratic leader (who was in an agony of embarrassment because he had long since been promised a seat on the Supreme bench, and the Van Devanter seat was now vacant, and nothing had been done about filling it) and agreed to let Robinson work out whatever compromise seemed necessary. But by this time the factions in Congress had become so ugly-tempered that even a compromise would be difficult to obtain.

Furiously, belligerently, exhaustingly, Robinson labored week after week as June gave way to July and the Washington heat became more sullen and Senatorial tempers became more frayed—until at last he came to the end of his elderly strength. On the morning of July 14 the Senator's maid became uneasy when he did not appear for breakfast. She looked in his bedroom and in the bathroom, did not see him and rang for the elevator boy to ask whether the Senator had gone out. He had not. The frightened maid returned with the elevator boy to the apartment. They found the Senator sprawled dead upon the bedroom floor—out of sight of the door—with a copy of the Congressional Record lying beside his outstretched hand. Roosevelt's strongest musterer of Senatorial votes had gone down in the battle.

Eight days later came the end of the inevitable Presidential retreat, when Senator Logan rose and moved to recommit the Supreme Court bill to the judiciary committee in order that this committee might substitute for it a bill providing for certain changes in the Federal judiciary but not touching the Supreme Court.

"Is the Supreme Court out of it?" asked Senator Johnson of California.

"The Supreme Court is out of it," replied Senator Logan.

"Glory be to God!" exclaimed Johnson.

Thereupon the motion to recommit was passed, 70 to 21. The Supreme Court bill was definitely beaten.

Still the President had not moved to fill Justice Van Devanter's seat. On August 12 he did so—and sprung another surprise. For on the nomination form which he sent by messenger to the Senate he had filled in in his own hand the name of Hugo L. Black of Alabama—a liberal Senator whose enthusiasm for the New Deal had been constant. Black's legal experience had been so limited that leaders of the legal profession were outraged at his selection, but Roosevelt counted on the nomination going through because Black was a Senator and his colleagues would hesitate to oppose him. He was right: the Senate consented. Many Senators, already embittered by the Court plan fight, were further angered, however; and in a few weeks a new storm broke. The Pittsburgh *Post-Gazette* produced what looked like substantial documentary proof that many years before, when the Ku Klux Klan had been strong in Alabama, Black had joined it. A member of the Supreme Court, guardian of the civil liberties of America, was shown to have been a member of an organization whose business it had been to promote racial and religious intolerance!

The outcry was terrific. Justice Black had gone to England; virtually besieged there by newspaper men, he refused to say a word. Not until the first of October, when he had returned to the United States, did he break his silence. On that evening he spoke over the radio from the living room of his friend, Claude E. Hamilton, Jr., in Chevy Chase; and millions of Americans heard him, in his soft Southern voice, confess that he had joined the Klan "about fifteen years ago," that he had "later resigned" and "never rejoined," and that he had "no sympathy whatever with any organization or group which, anywhere or at any time, arrogates to itself the un-American power to interfere in the slightest degree with complete religious freedom." The new Justice's concern for civil liberties was so apparent in his discourse that thereafter the storm of protest at his appointment died to a rumble.

Soon afterward Black took his seat on the bench, there to occupy a position considerably to the left, politically, of even the liberal justices already sitting. Now there was a definite liberal majority on the Court—which was later to be reinforced when the seats vacated by Justices Sutherland and Brandeis, who resigned, and Justice Cardozo, who died, were filled by the appointment of Solicitor-General Reed, Chairman William O. Douglas of the Securities and Exchange Commission, and Felix Frankfurter, long a behind-the-scenes adviser to the President. The Court's new inclination to look with a favorable eye upon the extension of Federal power became a settled trend.

Had Roosevelt, then, really lost his campaign? In one sense he had won: the Court no longer stood in his way. There was more than political ingenuity to his claim, in 1939, that he had attained his ultimate objective despite the defeat of his plan for reaching it. Yet in another sense he had lost. Many members of Congress hitherto glad to meet his wishes had been left sore and vindictive by the pressure put upon them to vote for a measure thrown at them as the Court plan had been; and there were also Senators who were piqued at the Black incident, feeling that they had somehow been tricked into endorsing an appointment which later brought them embarrassment at home. When, a year later, Roosevelt tried to bring about the defeat at the polls of various Senators who had voted against the Court plan, these wounds were further inflamed. There was nothing new about the attempt of a President to reward his loyal supporters and eliminate his disloyal ones—although the Roosevelt offensive of 1938, to which the opposition press attached the opprobrious term of "purge," was unusually bold and inclusive—but to make the vote upon the Supreme Court plan the test of loyalty was galling. The offensive failed. In friendships within Congress, in prestige within and without Congress, the President had suffered. In this sense the campaign over the Supreme Court had been for him a costly defeat.

§ 5

Sometimes the historian wishes that he were able to write several stories at once, presenting them perhaps in parallel columns, and that the human brain were so constructed that it could follow all these stories simultaneously without vertigo, thus gaining a livelier sense of the way in which numerous streams of events run side by side down the channel of time. The chronicle of American life during the spring and summer of 1937 offers a case in point. The drama of insurgent labor and the drama of Roosevelt against the Court were being played simultaneously, and all the while other disturbances and excitements were distracting our attention to other stages, other currents of tendency were flowing alongside these roaring torrents of change. How to give any sense of the multiplicity and heterogeneity of events without endless interruptions of what must, if anybody is to be able to read it, be an orderly and consecutive narrative?

It was on the showery evening of May 6, 1937—while the CIO was getting ready for the strike in Little Steel and Administration emissaries were coaxing Congressmen to vote for the Roosevelt Court plan—that the great German airship Hindenburg, nosing toward the mooring mast at Lakehurst to complete its first transatlantic flight of 1937, suddenly became a torch flaming in the dusk, and the cheerful inconsequentialities that poured out of American radios were broken into by staccato reports of the horror on the New Jersey plain. Down went the hopes which had built a mooring mast on the Empire State Building and had risen high as the Hindenburg made crossing after crossing safely in 1936. Now the future of transatlantic lighter-than-air transport looked black indeed. Within a few weeks, as if to point the contrast, Pan-American clippers and Imperial Airways flying boats were making survey flights between Britain and America in preparation for the inauguration of a regular passenger service.

During those same months of 1937 the armies of Francisco Franco were besieging Madrid, the farce of "nonintervention" was permitting Mussolini to help him, American liberals were "eating lunch against Franco" (in Elmer Davis's phrase), and American Catholics were arguing that Franco's offensive was a holy crusade against communist hordes which burned churches and slew priests.

In midsummer (just as the Supreme Court plan was coming to defeat in the Senate) the Japanese began a systematic attack upon China, thus adding a new major invasion to the lengthening list of international aggressions; soon Japanese bombs were falling in Shanghai and Americans were wondering whether the United States would have to choose between the loss of all its traditional privileges in China—and perhaps the lives of oil salesmen and missionaries—and war with Japan. What would happen if a stray bomb should hit Admiral Yarnell's flagship on the Whangpoo? And ought American women to wear lisle stockings on behalf of suffering China?

No picture of the America of the spring and summer of 1937 would be fully revealing which was not a montage of innumerable and varied scenes. It would show Walter Reuther and Richard Frankensteen, officials of the United Automobile Workers, being slugged and kicked and thrown bodily down on the concrete floor of a street overpass beside the Ford factory at River Rouge by "loyal employees," who according to the testimony of observers were hired thugs of the Ford "Service" organization. (Thus was the "American system" defended.) It would show American living rooms littered with books of reference and public librarians distracted by the fury of contestants in the Old Gold Puzzle Contest. (That picture of two women saying "All London is now sporting the wide-awake hat!" and "Do you know that Palmerston quits today as Foreign Sec?"—could the answer to that be Jenny Lind? And those two people picking oxeye daisies—would that be Sitting Bull or Morgan Dix?)

It would show Leon Henderson, the burly economic adviser of the WPA, becoming worried by the rising trend of prices, concocting a memorandum entitled "Boom or Bust," and communicating his fears of a business collapse to Secretary Morgenthau, who in turn communicated them to the President; whereupon the President issued a warning to the effect that certain prices—notably that of copper—were too high. (Henderson was right: trouble was coming, nor could such a statement avert it.)

It would show Americans bent over their newspapers as they devoured another series of installments of the royal romance that had so entranced them the preceding December: Wallis Warfield Simpson's divorce being declared absolute on May 3, 1937; the Duke of Windsor rushing from his

Austrian retreat to join her in France; their wedding taking place at Monts, France, on June 3; while, during the month's interval, the Duke's brother George was crowned King at Westminster with pomp and circumstance. "Yes, I set my alarm clock for five in the morning and listened to the whole coronation on the air and I could hear the crowds cheering as the King and Queen went by in the golden coach." "Wallis may not have got to be Queen, but that trousseau was *something.*"

The montage of American life in the spring and summer of 1937 would include endless other pictures: glimpses of Dust Bowl drought victims climbing into their jalopies to seek a newer world in the orchards of California; Joe Louis knocking out Jim Braddock at Chicago and becoming the titular heavyweight champion of the world (though not for another year would he bring down Max Schmeling); Edgar Bergen leaping into national popularity as he and his dummy Charlie McCarthy became features of the Chase and Sanborn radio hour in May, 1937, and shortly made it the most popular program of all. (Bergen had been almost unknown before he appeared at the Rainbow Room in New York on November 11, 1936. He made such a hit there that on December 17 he went on the air. Within a few months he was a national celebrity. Was there any area of American life, except the entertainment area, where success could come so swiftly?)

The montage would show Amelia Earhart Putnam flying from New Guinea toward Howland Island, never to be seen again, though the Navy searched the Pacific rollers long and hard; visitors to New York running through the theatre advertisements and trying to make up their minds whether to see "You Can't Take It With You" or "Brother Rat" or "Room Service," or Maurice Evans in "King Richard II"; a private car bearing northward from Ormond Beach the body of John D. Rockefeller, dead at the age of ninety-seven;

men and women in darkened movie theatres visiting the
peaceful gardens of Shangri La with Ronald Colman in
Frank Capra's screen version of *Lost Horizon*, or listening
to Jeanette MacDonald and Nelson Eddy in "Maytime";
bright billboards (donated by Outdoor Advertising, Inc., to
the National Association of Manufacturers' campaign against
labor-union influence) flaring with pictures of happy workmen over the title, "The American Way"; and Carolina
students working out the steps of "The Big Apple," a modified square dance which would presently break the monot-
ony of fox-trotting for hundreds of thousands of their agile
contemporaries.

The montage would show American women putting on
the oddest-looking peaked hats and openwork hats that had
balanced on feminine heads for many a year. And, as the
stock-market ticker stopped at noon on Saturday, August 14,
1937, it would show brokers debating whether Steel at 121
and Chrysler at 118⅝ were still attractive purchases, or
whether it might be a sensible idea to play a bit safe for a
time.

It would have been a distinctly sensible idea to play safe.
For the Recession of 1937-38 was at hand.

§ 6

When it came, it came fast—and apparently out of a clear
sky.

Toward the end of August, 1937, the stock market sold
off and business showed signs of slackening. After Labor
Day the retreat became sharper. Stocks went down fast and
far. On the morning of October 19 the market seemed near
demoralization, with support for some stocks apparently
quite lacking and selling orders pouring in from all over the
country; the tape lagged twenty-five minutes behind the

trading, and when at last the gong rang for the closing, the total of transactions had come to 7,290,000 shares—the biggest total since the collapse of the New Deal Honeymoon bull market in the summer of 1933. All through the autumn of 1937 the decline continued. Only the fact that speculation previous to August had been moderate and well-margined, with the SEC watching carefully to prevent manipulation, kept the annihilation of values from having disastrous consequences outside the exchanges. Meanwhile business operations contracted steadily and rapidly. Not until the end of March, 1938, did the stock market touch bottom; not until May did business do so. Never even during the collapse of 1929-32 had the industrial index shrunk at such a terrific rate.

Look first at what happened to the prices of some leading stocks in the space of only seven and a half months:

	Closing Price on August 14, 1937		Low Reached in March, 1938
American Telephone & Telegraph went from	170⅞	to	111
Chrysler	from 118⅝	to	35⅜
General Electric	from 58⅜	to	27¼
General Motors	from 60⅛	to	25½
New York Central	from 41½	to	10
U. S. Steel	from 121	to	38
Westinghouse E. & M.	from 159½	to	61¾

Then see what happened to our familiar measure of the state of business in general, the Federal Reserve Board's adjusted Index of Industrial Production. (Do you recall its previous ups and downs? Its high of 125 in 1929, its low of 58 in 1932 and of 59 in the bank-panic month of 1933, its rush up to 100 during the New Deal Honeymoon, its decline to 72 as the Honeymoon ended, and its wobbling rise thereafter?) At the end of 1936 the index had touched 121, which looked distinctly promising. As late as August, 1937, it stood at 117. Then it ran downhill, month after month, until by May, 1938, it had sunk to 76. *In nine months it had lost just about two-thirds of the ground gained during all the New Deal years of painful ascent!*

What had happened? During the latter part of 1936 and the early part of 1937 there had taken place sharp increases in the prices of goods—some of them following increases in wages during the CIO's offensive, some of them affected by armament orders from Europe, many of them accentuated by a general impression, among business men, that "inflation" might be coming and that one had better buy before it was too late. The price of copper—which you will recall especially disturbed the President—had jumped in five months from 10 cents a pound to 16. Business concerns had been accumulating big inventories. When the time came to sell these goods at retail to the public, the purchasing power to absorb them just was not there.

For new investment still lagged; and what was more, the government spending campaign, which had kept pumping new money into the economic system, had been virtually halted. During the summer of 1937, Henry Morgenthau, the Secretary of the Treasury, had persuaded the President to make a real attempt to balance the budget; and although it did not yet seem to be quite in balance, nevertheless when one took into account the Social Security taxes which were being levied (and were not counted on the credit side of the budget, being set apart in a separate account), the government was for a time actually taking in from the public more than it paid out.

Result: the goods which were piled up on the shelves moved slowly. Business men became alarmed and cut production. Two million men were thrown out of work in the space of a few months—and became all the less able to buy what was for sale. The alarm increased, for men well remembered what a depression was like and were resolved to cherish no false hopes this time. The vicious spiral of deflation moved with all the more rapidity. Thus out of that apparently clear sky—no great speculative boom in stocks or real estate, no tightness in credit, no overexpansion of capacity for making capital goods (in fact, not nearly enough expansion)—came the Recession of 1937-38.

It brought its ironies. Precisely a year after the beginning of the great sit-down strikes in General Motors, the president of the Corporation announced that about 30,000 production men were to be laid off immediately, and the remaining men would be reduced to a three-day week. What price CIO gains now? (If you had visited a General Motors dealer and seen the used cars accumulated on his hands, you would have realized why the Corporation had to stop glutting the market.)

Another irony was provided by the collapse of values on the New York Stock Exchange. Eight years before, when prices were tumbling, Richard Whitney had walked out on the floor and stemmed the panic by offering to buy Steel at 205; now Richard Whitney, deeply in debt, was misappropriating trust funds in the frantic attempt to save himself from bankruptcy. On Tuesday, March 8, 1938, just as trading for the day was beginning, President Gay of the Exchange mounted the rostrum and, as the gong rang to halt the brokers, read the amazing announcement that Richard Whitney & Company were suspended for "conduct inconsistent with just and equitable principles of trade." A few weeks later the hero of the 1929 panic, having confessed his all-too-obvious guilt, was on his way to Sing Sing.

Early the following winter—in December, 1938—the metropolis provided an even more extraordinary business scandal. F. Donald Coster, head of the reputable drug house of McKesson & Robbins, was discovered not only to have doctored the books of its crude drug department to the extent of many millions of dollars, but actually to be an ex-convict named Philip Musica who had changed his name and appearance and had successfully conducted a long masquerade as a respectable corporation official. When the police were closing in upon him, Coster-Musica gave this almost unbelievable episode its final touch of melodrama by committing suicide in his fine house at Fairfield, Connecticut. Again Wall Street was shaken, as men asked one another how bankers and accountants could have been so easily fooled. The Musica scandal, however, had no such overtones of significance as the collapse of Whitney. For Whitney had been the leader of the Old Guard of the Exchange. With his downfall during the Recession crumbled the last opposition to a reorganization of the Exchange in accordance with the wishes of Chairman William O. Douglas of the Securities and Exchange Commission. Soon the Exchange had a new paid President—a young man who had not even been acquainted with any member of it when he arrived in New York in 1931! Verily the old order had changed.

There was irony, too, in the earnest effort of Administration leaders to remain calm and hopeful-looking as they issued statements predicting an early upturn, while the economic landslide was roaring downhill. Hadn't there been another Administration, not so many years before, which they had ridiculed for doing much the same thing?

As the Recession deepened, there rose angry voices from the business community and the conservative press. The whole thing was the Administration's fault. This was a "Roosevelt Depression." With malicious glee they quoted a previous boast of the President's, made while the business indices were climbing: "We planned it that way." Well, this was what his planning came to. Especially they blamed the undistributed profits tax—a curious measure which was proving one of the less successful bright ideas of the Administration and which stirred the business world to particular wrath.

"Five years ago, with magnificent courage and resoluteness of purpose, President Roosevelt gave the financial and business communities of the nation an invigorating hope that banished fear," wrote David Lawrence on March 28, 1938. "Today, the same man has aroused in the financial and business communities a fear amounting almost to terror and a distrust which has broken down the morale of the whole economic machinery. . . . What Mr. Roosevelt has done—and I believe he has not done it intentionally—is to break down the spirit and faith of the business and financial world in the actual safety of a citizen's property and his savings. To strike down this bulwark of the whole economic system is to breed panic and fear of indescribably dangerous proportions."

Strong words—yet they were not unrepresentative of business opinion generally. So obsessed had many business men become with their *idée fixe* that nothing the Administration could do would mollify them. On November 10, 1937, Secretary Morgenthau, in a speech before the New York Academy of Political Science, announced that the Administration would do everything possible to balance the budget. His audience appeared half-pleased, half-amused, and wholly unconvinced. (The Morgenthau speech, as it happened, had been carefully revised and approved by the President.) Addressing Congress at the beginning of 1938, Roosevelt spoke in cordial terms of the need for co-operation between government and business. There was no resulting uprush of "confidence." At that moment the President was making a deliberate effort to pursue a conservative and conciliatory course, conferring with big business men and calling a conference of little business men—which turned into a virtual riot. No friendly gesture seemed to have any real effect.

It is true that there was a contest of policy going on inside the Administration ranks. Certain men of the well-defined liberal group which Joseph Alsop and Robert Kintner called the "New Dealers"—including among others Tom Corcoran, Ben Cohen, Leon Henderson, Herman Oliphant

of the Treasury, and Solicitor-General Robert H. Jackson—
had composed speeches for delivery by Jackson in which
the blame for the Recession was laid upon "monopolies"
and "the sixty families" (meaning that they blamed the
controllers and managers of the great corporations for pushing up prices by tacit agreement and then, when goods
could no longer be sold at these prices, slowing production
and throwing off workers lest their profits be unduly cut).
They had encouraged Secretary Ickes to make a similar
speech. But these speeches had been written without express
Presidential authorization, and the young New Dealers had
been risking their jobs and their influence in thus expressing
their private opinions. What happened was that jittery business men read these New Deal speeches, listened to the
calmer utterances of the President, and decided that no
blandishments from Washington meant anything.

For this fact the impulsiveness of a President who seemed
smilingly unaware of inconsistencies among New Deal pro-
nouncements was partly to blame; indeed, the President
commended Ickes for his "sixty families" speech on the eve
of composing his own appeal for co-operation. Nevertheless
it was true that as 1937 turned into 1938 Roosevelt was
trying to balance the budget and to refrain from proposing
measures which would frighten business men unduly; that
the conservative business community, in its wrath, seemed
oblivious of the attempts being made to appease it; and
that slowly the Administration leaders were becoming convinced that no policy of retrenchment and appeasement
would bear fruit.

All the while the New Dealers were urging a resumption
of deficit spending, and on April 2—as things were getting
worse and worse—the President threw up the sponge. At
lunch on the train from Warm Springs to Washington he
told Harry Hopkins and Aubrey Williams that he was ready
to abandon the budget-balancing effort and go in for heavy

spending again. On April 14 he went on the air to explain that he was asking Congress to appropriate three billion dollars for relief, public works, housing, flood control, and other recovery efforts.

That spring the legislation went through Congress, and simultaneously business began to show faint signs of improvement. In the latter half of June the stock market sprang to life. Recovery began again.

Economists might disagree as to whether the recovery was stimulated by the spending or was a mere coincidence, but among the young New Dealers there was no doubt at all. Look at the industrial index, they argued. It did no good to try to appease business; it did a lot of good to spend. Q.E.D.

The young New Dealers now rode high (so high, in fact, that in the autumn of 1938 they ventured into the comparatively unfamiliar field of politics and persuaded the President to make a dolefully unsuccessful attempt to defeat the Democrats in Congress who had voted against his Court plan). But the Administration as a whole had been struck a very heavy blow by the Recession. Meeting a new economic crisis, it had disclosed itself as neither able to generate "confidence" in business men nor to concoct any new and effective measures of recovery. The best it could do was to take down from the shelf a bottle of medicine to which it had been addicted for years—pump-priming.

§ 7

It had been a proud President who stood before the Capitol in the rain in January, 1937, and declared his intention to paint out the picture of "one-third of a nation ill-housed, ill-clad, ill-nourished." His pride had come before a fall. During a subsequent year and a half of friction and Recession his prestige in Congress had been sorely weakened; his economic policies had been tried in the balance and found wanting; the hateful picture of unemployment and poverty had been altered, if anything, for the worse.

Was the New Deal, then, played out?

Perhaps; but if so, the fact was becoming obscured by the approach of a new sort of crisis which would cause the citizens to look upon their country and its government with new eyes. For now the American skies were being slowly darkened by storm clouds rolling in from Europe.

Chapter Twelve
THE SHADOW OF WAR

§ 1

STUDIO NINE was a room "about the size of an average family living room." In it stood three desks and an old army cot with an army blanket. On each desk there was a microphone, and before one of these microphones sat a gray-haired man, wearing ear-phones. He was talking quietly in a crisp, precise voice. He looked tired and a bit disheveled, as if he had just risen from the rumpled cot. As he talked, he kept one eye on a plate-glass window, beyond which, in an adjoining room, sat a man watching him from behind a panel of instruments and occasionally signaling to him with a wave of the hand. From time to time other men would steal into the room, shove sheets of paper under his nose, and depart; he would glance at the sheets of paper and talk on, his crisp articulation unimpeded.

He was talking to millions of Americans—nobody knew how many. To hear what he had to say, girls in strapless evening dresses stilled their debate over whether to put their hair up for the winter season; lawyers turned from discussing Judge Pecora's declaration of a mistrial in the case of James J. Hines, whom District-Attorney Thomas E. Dewey of New York was attempting to convict as the "man higher up" in metropolitan racketeering; politicians laid aside the fascinating topic of the failure of President Roosevelt's attempt to "purge," in the Democratic primaries, the men who had failed to join his offensive against the Supreme Court in 1937; literary critics paused in their talk of what would become of Thomas Wolfe's mountains of manuscripts, now that he was dead; families in gray tenements stopped arguing about the chances for a reconciliation between the still hostile CIO and AF of L; actors and actresses interrupted their conjectures about the rising success of the hilarious Broadway production, "Hellzapoppin." For what the man in Studio Nine was telling these people seemed of more vital importance just then than anything else in the world.

The time was the latter part of September, 1938; the man was H. V. Kaltenborn, news commentator for the Columbia Broadcasting System; and Studio Nine was his headquarters at the center of the Columbia plexus in New York. He was interpreting the up-to-the-instant news of the Czechoslovak crisis in what he called "Yirrup," that crisis which was revealing to all the world what happens when an irresistible force meets a conciliatory body.

Ever since September 12 Kaltenborn had kept vigil day and night in Studio Nine, snatching sleep briefly on the army cot. Not until September 30—the day when Neville Chamberlain, just returned from Munich, came to the window of No. 10 Downing Street and said to the cheering crowd below, "I believe it is peace for our time"—would the Kaltenborn vigil end; not until he had delivered, in 18 days, a record total of 85 extempore broadcasts.

Kaltenborn was by no means the only interpreter of European affairs during those September weeks; every broadcasting system, every radio station was hurling news and interpretation into the ether. The names of Hitler, Henlein, Benes, Hodza, Chamberlain, and Daladier screamed persistently from front-page headlines, recurred in page after page of newsprint, sounded in the half-intelligible chanting of the men selling extras on the streets. In New England on the afternoon of September 21 a tropical hurricane struck without warning (the New York weather prediction that morning had been "Rain and cool today.

Tomorrow cloudy, probably rain, little change in temperature"). The hurricane ripped seashore villages into kindling wood or swamped them under tons of roaring water, it laid fine groves of trees in lines on the ground, made rivers out of the streets of cities, derailed trains, blocked highways, broke off communication by telephone and telegraph, and took an estimated 682 lives. Yet even in New England, when householders repaired from their darkened houses to their automobiles to listen over their automobile radios (uncrippled by the storm) and find out how wide-ranging was this havoc that had separated them from the rest of the world, the twist of the dial brought them into the midst of the man-made hurricane that was raging in Europe.

Out of the night came the familiar refrains of "A Tisket, a Tasket" . . . then, as the dial turned, a bit of comedy on the Rudy Vallee hour . . . and then, as the dial was twisted again, a voice swelling forth in the midst of a sentence: . . . "town of Godesburg where Prime Minister Chamberlain held a second historic conference with Chancellor Hitler. The effects of that meeting already have brought reactions from world news centers. Now, tonight we'll attempt first to receive a broadcast direct from Prague, the capital of Czechoslovakia, where Maurice Hindus, well-known authority on Central European affairs, has been observing the day's happenings. We take you now to Prague." A pause, while the mind leaped the Atlantic in anticipation; then another voice: "Hello, America, this is Prague speaking. . . ."

How the world had shrunk! In July, 1914, when Karl von Wiegand of the United Press had cabled a mere 138 words from Berlin to New York on the Austro-Hungarian ultimatum to Serbia—one of the grave events which produced the World War of 1914-18—he had been admonished for wasting cable tolls. Now, in September, 1938, the news of

NEW YORK

Tribune

LATE CITY EDITION

OCTOBER 1, 1938

New York City and Vicinity

Britain and Germany in Compact Never to Fight Each Other Again; Nazi Troops Cross Czech Border

Hitler's Vanguard Passes Austro-Czech Frontier at 1 A. M., an Hour After Deadline He Had Fixed

General Settlement Expected in Berlin

Deal on Spanish War, an Air Pact and Limit on Arms Due, Plus 4-Power Accord Sought by Italy

By The Associated Press

BERLIN, Oct. 1 (Saturday).—The first contingent of German troops crossed the Czechoslovak frontier near Aigen, Upper Austria, early today, starting the Nazi occupation of territory granted to Chancellor Adolf Hitler by the four-power Munich accord.

The gray-clad German infantry-men marched over the border shortly after 1 a. m. (7 p. m. Eastern standard time, Friday), little more than an hour after the midnight deadline Hitler had set for his occupation.

An infantry battalion, numbering about 600 men, advanced along several roads from Aigen to take possession of posts immediately behind the Czechoslovak frontier in southwestern Czechoslovakia. It was explained this movement was regarded as merely a vanguard operation, reconnoitering the terrain and preparing for the main army of occupation to march in later today, taking over the first of four districts granted to Hitler by the Munich pact.

The main body of troops, 30,000 men, assembled along the border of

Herald Tribune radio photo—Acme
Prime Minister Chamberlain at Heston Airdrome yesterday

Czechs, Bowing to Munich Pact, Get an Ultimatum From Poland

Warsaw Demands Evacuation of Teschen Today; 'We Want to Fight,' Prague Crowds Reply to Plan; 50,000 Non-Nazis Flee Sudetenland

Chamberlain Reveals New Pact of Friendship to Crowds Wildly Cheering Him on Return Home

Tells Them He Won 'Peace With Honor'

'I Believe It Is Peace for Our Time,' He Asserts; Later Parley Expected to Give Reich Colonies

By Joseph Driscoll
From the Herald Tribune Bureau
Copyright, 1938, New York Tribune Inc.

LONDON, Sept. 30.—Prime Minister Neville Chamberlain, returning tonight to receive a grateful welcome from hundreds of thousands of peace-loving Britons, brought from Munich not only the four-power agreement which authorizes Nazi Germany to take over Czecho-slovakia's Sudetenland by gradual stages, but an Anglo-German pact of friendship, by which the two nations resolve never to go to war against each other and to settle all disputes by consultation and negotiation.

When his American Lockheed airliner brought him back to English soil at Heston Airport this afternoon Chamberlain received his first hearty welcome, which was followed by stirring street scenes the like of which had not been equaled in London since Armistice Day, 1918. The Prime Minister responded by reading, for the benefit of the newsreels and television apparatus, the text of the peace pact to which he and Hitler had affixed their signatures.

"PEACE" AFTER MUNICH, 1938
From the front page of the New York Herald Tribune, October 1, 1938

ENTENTE CORDIALE, JUNE, 1939
The King and Queen of England at Hyde Park with President and Mrs. Roosevelt
and Mrs. James Roosevelt (center)

another grave event in the same part of the world—the sub-
mission of Czechoslovakia to dismemberment—stood in the
very center of American attention. Not until 1930 had
there been such a thing as a world-wide news broadcast;
now one could hear, in quick succession, voices from London, Paris, Berlin, and Prague, and millions of Americans
were hanging on every word.

Far back in the distance, already, seemed those lively
events of the earlier part of the summer of 1938 which had
so captured the public mind: Joe Louis knocking out Max
Schmeling at the Yankee Stadium in the first round—
actually before some radio listeners had got tuned in on the
fight; Howard Hughes flying round the world in the incredible time of 3 days, 19 hours, 8 minutes, 10 seconds;
the "wrong-way" pilot, Douglas Corrigan, starting in an
antiquated plane from Long Island "for California" and
fetching up in Ireland, to return and be feted in America,
still wearing his smile and his brown leather jacket; the
demented John Warde tying New York traffic into knots as
he stood for eleven hours on a narrow ledge on the seven-
teenth floor of the Hotel Gotham, contemplating his leap
to suicide. Even American events and problems of real significance were being thrust into the background. The hesi-
tant upward progress of the business indices, as a nation
still beset by large-scale unemployment tried to come back
from its Recession; the application of the new wages-and-
hours act; the still-unsolved farm problem; the perennial
headache of relief—all these things seemed to fall away into
unimportance as Hitler demanded the Sudetenland, Chamberlain flew to Berchtesgaden and Godesburg with his
furled black umbrella, and the heads of four nations met at
Munich to sign and seal the destruction of Czechoslovakia.
The war clouds from Europe were blotting out the American landmarks one by one.

§ 2

The chain of events which had dragged foreign problems into the forefront of American attention was a curious one, full of kinks.

At the beginning of the decade the United States had seemed to be drifting from a policy of national isolation toward a policy of acting in concert with other nations to maintain world peace. To be sure, there was no popular disposition to enter the League of Nations or to make foreign commitments, but there was a tendency in the State Department to come as close to doing this as public opinion would permit. In 1931, when Japan, seeing the European powers preoccupied by the Depression, seized its happy opportunity to invade Manchuria, it was Henry L. Stimson, Hoover's Secretary of State, who led the chorus of international condemnation. An American representative sat at Geneva as an "observer" while the League of Nations discussed Japan's offense; Secretary Stimson proclaimed that the United States would not recognize the Japanese conquest; he also sought to invoke the Nine-Power Pact against Japan, only to be rebuffed by Sir John Simon on behalf of Britain. Nothing that the League could or would do, none of the outcries of disapproval from Europe or America, stopped Japan; the first great breach in the post-war system of territorial arrangements was successfully completed—but not for lack of active interest on the part of the American government. America was in the thick of the diplomatic battle throughout. Its policy in 1931 was far from being isolationist.

The next great act of international aggression did not come for several years, and in the meantime the relations between the United States and the outside world went into a new crisis—this time economic. During the early Depression years, as nation after nation in its agony had lifted tariffs, devalued currencies, and otherwise dammed the international currents of trade and financial exchange in its attempts to save itself, the government at Washington had looked on in alarm. It was true that we had laid new bricks on top of our own tariff wall in 1930, but of course we considered our own tariff a purely domestic matter; we felt differently when other countries did such things. It was axiomatic in the minds of Hoover, the Treasury officials, the financial experts of Wall Street, and dominant American opinion generally that barriers to commerce must be removed, that the international gold standard was sacrosanct, that there could be no real American recovery without world recovery. But then came the New Deal—and the shoe was on the other foot. For now *we* wanted to do things which might upset international monetary and trade relations.

At first few people foresaw the impending clash of policies. President Roosevelt, to be sure, in his first inaugural in 1933, said explicitly that "our international trade relations, though vastly important, are in point of time and necessity secondary to the establishment of a sound national economy"—but had he not already appointed as his Secretary of State Cordell Hull, an inheritor of Woodrow Wilson's world-mindedness, and a passionate devotee of the stimulation of international trade by tariff reduction? Roosevelt, to be sure, took the United States off the gold standard, to the confusion of foreign currencies—but was he not simultaneously inviting foreign delegates to come and discuss measures of international economic co-ordination? Not even Roosevelt himself realized how sharp a collision he was headed for. He cheerfully entered into the preliminary plans for an economic conference to be held in London, in June, 1933, and sent to this conference, with inadequate instructions, a delegation headed by Secretary Hull which at once began arranging for the stabilization of currencies. A bit later, fearing that the United States might be tied into a hard-and-fast agreement for stabilization just as the inflation boom was lifting prices and delightfully stimulating business in America, Roosevelt sent to London his chief brain-truster, Assistant Secretary of State Raymond Moley, to restrain the delegates. But it was not until Moley had arrived in London that Roosevelt, becoming more and more entranced with the idea of prosperity through currency manipulation, decided abruptly that the conversations at London must not be allowed to endanger his domestic plans. When Moley agreed to a rather mild statement approving of stabilization in general principle, the President suddenly pulled the floor out from under everybody—Hull, the delegation, Moley, and for that matter the whole London conference—by refusing to have anything done about stabilization at all. An impulsive man had resolved the conflict between economic nationalism and economic internationalism by throwing his weight belatedly and without notice on the national side—to the utter discomfiture of his representatives.

After that—or rather after the experiment in gold-buying which followed it—the United States returned gradually to the ways of international economic facilitation. Secretary Hull doggedly carried on as if nothing had happened. He was permitted to get his reciprocal tariff bill enacted in 1934, and under it to ease the flow of goods between the United States and various other countries. In due course Secretary Morgenthau and the chiefs of British and French finance stabilized the currencies of Britain, France, and America. The adventure in economic isolation appeared to be over, though it had left its scars.

In the meantime, too, an olive branch had been held out to Latin America. In his first inaugural Roosevelt had proclaimed a "good neighbor" policy. To show the Latin

Americans that this was no mere phrase, the United States took its troops out of Nicaragua, did away with those parts of the Platt Amendment that had permitted intervention in Cuba, and assured the nations south of the Rio Grande that it interpreted the Monroe Doctrine as a doctrine of co-operation and mutual aid, not as a doctrine of domination. Such was Secretary Hull's patent sincerity that the assurance was on the whole well taken. Toward the end of the decade the United States was better liked and better trusted in most of Latin America than ever before.

But long before that the smashing of international frontiers had begun again. In 1935 Mussolini invaded Ethiopia in extremely cold blood. Britain and France and the League could or would do nothing effective to discipline Italy, and Mussolini was not stopped. Early in 1936 Adolf Hitler, whose attempt to engineer a Nazi coup in Austria had failed in 1934, entered the Rhineland—and was not stopped. Later in the same year the Spanish Revolution broke out; Mussolini, and Hitler too, began using the Spanish Revolution for their own imperial ends—and were not stopped. In 1937, the Japanese attacked China—and were not stopped. In March, 1938, Hitler swept into Austria—and was not stopped. And as the summer and spring of 1938 wore on, he began confidently polishing his knife for Czechoslovakia.

At the time when this series of crises began, American public opinion was perhaps more isolationist than at any time since before the World War. By 1935 the "revisionist" view of the World War of 1914-18 had become the majority view. According to this version there had been guilt on both sides, not simply on the German side, and the United States had been unhappily sucked into participation in the war by British propaganda and by its economic stake in an Allied victory. As late as April, 1937, a Gallup poll on the question "Do you think it was a mistake for the United

States to enter the World War?" drew a Yes from 71 per cent of those polled. In 1935 Walter Millis's *Road to War,* which presented the American decision of 1917 as a lamentable tragedy, became a best seller, influential among the highbrows. Several books and magazine articles drew sensational attention to the part played by munitions-makers in fomenting wars; and simultaneously the Nye committee of the Senate embroidered the same theme in a long investigation, showing up the unholy profits of American arms manufacturers from 1915 on, exposing the pretty little deals made by munitions salesmen abroad, and dragging Morgan partners to Washington to answer an implied charge that they had schemed to get the United States to fight Germany in 1917 in order to pull their chestnuts out of the fire. The picture of war as a horror into which the innocent common people were lured by the machinations of scienceless bankers and big business men was the more readily accepted because the general public still had a very lively memory of the failure of such men to lead the country out of the valley of Depression, and of the shoddy conduct of many bankers and big business men as laid bare in the investigations of 1933.

It must be remembered, too, that in 1935 the American radicals were nearly all hotly anti-war. Nor was there, then, any widespread American fear that the dictators in Europe might actually harm the United States from the outside; when people spoke of "the fascist menace" in 1935, most of them meant the menace of an American fascist movement, which they variously imagined as being led by Roosevelt, or by somebody like Huey Long, or perhaps by an army officer supported by big business. So general was the belief that America must hoe its own row, and take preventive measures in advance so that it could not be seduced into hostilities, that in a Gallup poll taken in the fall of 1935 no less than 75 per cent of the voters thought Congress should get the approval of the people in a national vote before declaring war.

In this very isolationist state of mind, the country welcomed the passage by Congress in 1935 of a Neutrality Act which decreed that when war broke out anywhere, Americans must not sell munitions to either of the belligerents. The Neutrality Act was at once applied to the Italian-Ethiopian conflict.

But the Administration—and the permanent staff of the State Department—did not like compulsory neutrality. They wanted the United States to be free to use its diplomatic influence in international affairs and they felt that a blanket law might be embarrassing in some unforeseen circumstance. They liked to play along with the British in foreign policy, and the Neutrality Act might hobble them. When the Spanish Revolution broke out, they fell in with the British scheme for non-intervention (a scheme which notoriously failed to prevent Mussolini from intervening in behalf of Franco) and pushed through Congress a strange act which applied the neutrality principle to the Spanish dissension, despite the fact that this was not a war between nations but a rebellion against a government recognized by the United States. When, a little later, Japan went into China, the Administration wobbled this way and that, first telling all Americans to leave China or remain at their own risk, then proposing to defend Americans in China, and *never applying the Neutrality Act at all!* They were able to do this by taking advantage of a loophole. The Act as passed in revised form in 1937 provided that the mandatory ban on shipments of munitions should take effect either when war was declared or when the President "found" that a state of war existed. Neither Japan nor China declared war—and the President failed to "find" that a state of war existed, though the Japanese were blasting at China with everything they had.

Presently the Administration departed still further from the isolationist idea and the idea of compulsory neutrality. In a speech at Chicago in October, 1937, Roosevelt said that "the moral consciousness of the world . . . must be aroused to the cardinal necessity . . . of putting an end to acts of aggression," added that an "epidemic of world lawlessness" was spreading, and that "when an epidemic of physical disease starts to spread, the community approves and joins in a quarantine of the patients in order to protect the health of the community against the spread of the disease." This looked like intervention against the aggressive nations with a vengeance. Later in 1937, in a letter to Governor Landon, Roosevelt insisted that "we owe some measure of co-operation and even leadership in maintaining standards of conduct helpful to the ultimate goal of general peace." When the American gunboat *Panay* was sunk by Japanese bombers early in 1938, the Administration made much of the incident, though it had occurred in the interior of a country at war and the *Panay* had been convoying Standard Oil tankers—in other words, had been engaged in just the sort of enterprise which the neutrality advocates of 1935 had sought to eliminate as a possible *casus belli*. At about the same time the Administration used its political influence with Congress to bury in committee the Ludlow Resolution which would have required a national referendum to get the United States into war; this measure, it said, would "cripple any President in the conduct of our foreign relations." Clearly the intention was to give full defense to American rights in China—even the right to convoy tankers with our own gunboats close to a battlefront; to impress the Japanese with the extent of American disgust at their behavior; and in general to use American influence wherever possible to keep aggressive nations within bounds.

Such a policy offered such a sharp contrast with what

public opinion had wanted in 1935 that it might have been expected to lead to general public condemnation of President Roosevelt and Secretary Hull. It did not—though the "quarantine" speech required some quick and deft explaining. There was grumbling, but never enough to prevent the continued nullification of the Neutrality Act. The basic reason was that American public opinion, too, was shifting ground. With each new crisis, American dislike of Hitler, Mussolini, and the Japanese war lords was becoming sharper.

It is not, to be sure, clear that there was any great weakening of the underlying preference for "keeping out of foreign entanglements" on the part of the great mass of the American people, particularly in the interior of the country. A study of the Gallup polls from 1935 to 1938 gives no sure evidence of any such shift. But informed and audible opinion, especially on the Eastern seaboard, had undeniably altered. Influential Republicans like Governor Landon and ex-Secretary Stimson stood back of the President in his anti-aggressor moves. Specialists in foreign affairs like the members of the Council on Foreign Relations felt strongly that America must uphold the "democracies" against the "dictatorships." And radical opinion had changed almost unrecognizably.

The communists had shifted from an anti-war policy to an anti-fascist policy and had become almost as warlike as the Daughters of the American Revolution. Back in 1934, Earl Browder (who became the communist candidate for President in 1936) had declared, "The only way to fight war is to begin by fighting the war-makers in our own land. . . . The Roosevelt Administration is carrying on the greatest war program ever seen in peace time." When Roosevelt made his "quarantine" speech in 1937, on the other hand, Browder applauded it as a "declaration of a positive peace policy." The half-somersault executed by the American

Student Union, a somewhat leftist youth organization, offered a perfect illustration of the general change in radical and liberal thought: at its meeting at the end of 1936 it had endorsed the Oxford pledge "not to support any war which the government may undertake"; at the end of 1937 it called for "immediate steps to restrain fascist aggression, . . . American leadership in naming aggressors, employing embargoes against aggressors, and organizing these efforts through international collaboration," and it urged "repeal or modification of the present Neutrality Act so as to discriminate between aggressor and attacked and to give aid to the latter." Young men and women who in 1934 and 1935 had spoken scornfully of war as a device for the enrichment of capitalists were by 1937 and 1938 making bonfires of silk stockings to express their detestation of Japan. Still they did not want war, but they were militantly taking sides in foreign quarrels.

In some respects, too, general public opinion was changing. The Gallup polls showed a swelling majority in favor of a larger American navy, army, and air force. When in February, 1938—just before Hitler's conquest of Austria—the Gallup poll-takers propounded the question, "If Germany and Italy go to war against England and France, do you think we should do everything possible to help England and France win, except go to war ourselves?" the vote came out Yes, 69 per cent. (If the issue had been differently phrased, there might not have been such a heavy affirmative vote; nevertheless the two-thirds majority was impressive.)

Still the great majority of Americans were earnestly anxious to keep out of war. But as the Hitler advance continued, crisis by crisis, more and more people began to feel that it menaced America too, that deliberate non-participation in foreign quarrels would be difficult and might be morally wrong. Then, almost on the heels of Hitler's

Austrian coup, came his Czechoslovak coup of September, 1938, and shook America from end to end.

§ 3

A feeling of insecurity and apprehension, a feeling that the world was going to pieces, that supposedly solid principles, whether of economics or of politics or of international ethics, were giving way under foot, had never quite left thoughtful Americans since the collapse of Coolidge-Hoover prosperity in 1929 and 1930. It had been intense during the worst of the Depression, had been alleviated somewhat as business conditions improved, and had become more acute again as the international aggressors went on the rampage (and as, simultaneously, the United States slid into the Recession). The Munich crisis of September, 1938, produced a new attack of nerves.

Whether the strange incident of the Orson Welles broadcast should be considered a manifestation of this attack of nerves cannot be proved one way or the other—but at least it is significant that at the time a great many observers thought that it was one. On the evening of Sunday, October 30, 1938—a month after Munich—Orson Welles of the Mercury Theatre gave, over the Columbia Broadcasting System, a scheduled radio dramatization of an old fantasy by H. G. Wells, *The War of the Worlds*. To make it vivid, he arranged it to simulate a current news broadcast. After an announcer had clearly explained the nature of the program, a voice gave a prosaic weather forecast; then another voice said that the program would be continued from a hotel, with dance music; shortly this music was interrupted by a "flash" to the effect that a professor at "Mount Jennings Observatory," Chicago, reported seeing explosions at regular intervals on the planet Mars; then the listeners were "returned" in orthodox radio fashion "to the music of

Ramon Raquello . . . a tune that never loses favor, the popular 'Star Dust' "; then came an interview with an imaginary Princeton professor, with more information about disturbances on Mars—whereupon a series of further "news bulletins" described the arrival of Martians in huge metal cylinders which landed in New Jersey. The broadcast gathered speed, bulletin following bulletin. More Martians landed—an army of them, which quickly defeated the New Jersey State Militia. Presently the Martian attack was vividly described as being general all over the United States, with the population of New York evacuating the city and Martian heat-rays and flame-throwers and other diabolical devices causing terrific destruction, till all was laid waste.

Despite the announcer's introduction, despite the fact that this was a scheduled program, that one needed only to twist a dial to hear the reassuring voice of Charlie McCarthy, that all names given were fictitious, that the program was once interrupted in the routine manner for an explanatory station identification, and that in numerous respects the "news" given out was preposterous on its face, the following remarkable reactions to the program took place:

All over the country, people called up newspapers or the police in wild panic to find out what to do. (The *New York Times* alone received 875 calls; the Associated Press had to send out an explanatory bulletin to its member papers.) In many communities terror-stricken people rushed out of their houses and milled about in the streets, not quite sure whether they were being attacked by Martians or by Germans, but sure that destruction was on the way and they must flee somewhere. In Newark, New Jersey, several families, convinced that a "gas attack" had begun, put wet cloths on their faces and tried to pack all their belongings in a car; the traffic was jammed for blocks around. A woman in Pittsburgh prepared to take poison, crying, "I'd rather die this way than that!" A woman in Indianapolis rushed into a church screaming, "New York destroyed; it's the end of the world. You might as well go home to die. I just heard it on the radio," and the church service came to a hurried end. When a church service in New Jersey was similarly interrupted, the congregation prayed for deliverance from catastrophe. A man in the Bronx section of New York rushed to the roof when he heard the news and thought he saw "the smoke from the bombs" drifting over the city. In a town in the State of Washington the electric-light service was interrupted during the broadcast, convincing listeners that the terror was close at hand, and women fainted.

So it went, with endless variations, all over the country. Even if only one person in twenty among those who heard the program took it at its face value, this credulous minority—together with the people whom they alarmed with their garbled stories of what they thought was happening—caused enough panic to serve as a remarkable case study in national hysteria.

But let us not argue whether the broadcast incident showed that people's nerves had been shaken by the September war scare. (Perhaps there was better proof of nerve strain in some of the observations made upon the incident. Dorothy Thompson, for example, in her syndicated column, called the episode "the news story of the century—an event which made a greater contribution to an understanding of Hitlerism, Mussolinism, Stalinism, anti-Semitism, and all the other terrorisms of our times than all the words about them that have been written by reasonable men," and said that it "cast a brilliant and cruel light upon the failure of popular education." That was pretty tall talk.) There was other and more reliable evidence of mounting apprehension. Throughout the United States in the winter of 1938-39 there was a marked upsurge of anti-Semitism, noticeable even in Western towns where Jews were few, and even in the behavior of men and women who had no use for Hitler. Father Coughlin's anti-Semitic broadcasts did much to accelerate this sort of uneasy scapegoat-hunting. Among many liberals there was manifest a new and lively fear of Nazi influence within the United States; people who all their lives had laughed at red scares and had made light of the Russian connections of the Communist Party saw nothing to laugh at in Nazi propaganda in America and cried out that organizations with German connections must be investigated and broken up. Dinner-table conversations turned to the alarming increase in German trade with Latin America (which actually was no larger, relatively, than in 1913 and was less than half as great as United States trade with Latin America) and to the ominous question whether Nazi planes operating from South American bases could not quickly smash the Panama Canal and destroy American cities. Many lovers of peace had become obsessed with a sense that the United States, along with the rest of the world, was on its way to an inevitable doom. "When war breaks out in Europe, we'll be in it in six months—nothing on earth can stop it." The best that sanity seemed able to offer by way of reply was, "If in 1929 our best thinkers thought capitalism was triumphant, and in 1933 they thought communism was becoming triumphant, and in 1938 they think fascism is becoming triumphant, what will they think in 1943?"

All the while the Administration was quickening its efforts to make American influence felt by upholding the British and French, excoriating Hitler, and trying to impress him with the idea that if he went on he might have America against him. When in November, 1938, there were new and cruel German attacks on Jews, the American Ambassador at Berlin was called home "for report and consultation"; he did not return. Roosevelt said that the news from Germany had "deeply shocked public opinion in the United States." The American delegation at the Lima Con-

ference in December sought strenuously to line up the
Latin American nations against interference by European
dictators—and met with a limited success. In his annual
message to Congress in January, 1939, Roosevelt called for
American unity in the face of foreign threats to free institutions, and for a heavy increase in American armaments—
which was granted him. Pointedly he said (and he might
have added "Berlin papers please copy") that there were
"many ways short of war, but stronger and more effective
than mere words, of bringing home to aggressor governments the aggregate sentiments of our own people." Later
that month a Douglas attack plane crashed at Los Angeles,
and soon it was discovered that the passenger in this plane
built to United States Army specifications had been a Frenchman; obviously France was being permitted, with the Administration's blessing, to order good new American fighting planes. Then the President held a long secret session
with the Senate Committee on Military Affairs, and after
this meeting came senatorial rumors—which were sharply
denied—that the President had said that if war came, America's frontier would be in France.

On Easter Sunday, as he left Warm Springs, Roosevelt
called out to the crowd in the station, "I'll be back in the
fall if we don't have a war"; he afterwards made it clear to
the press that "we" had been meant to include, however
vaguely, the United States. Secretary Ickes, long famed for
the deadliness of his epithets, and other members of the
Administration, were turning their rhetorical artillery upon
the German government. When in due course Roosevelt
issued a plea for peace to Hitler and Mussolini in mid-
April of 1939—an eloquent document to which Hitler replied, not in a letter, but in a belated speech of great
length, refusing guarantees—many observers felt that the
plea had been weakened in advance by too much loose anti-
Nazi talk by American officials.

Concurrently the pace of aggression in Europe was quickening. In January, 1939, Barcelona fell, and soon the Spanish Civil War was over: a fascist victory. In March Germany broke her promises at Munich, overran the rest of Czechoslovakia, and annexed Memel. In April Mussolini, not to be quite outdone, seized Albania. Then followed a pause; the news from Europe dropped for a time out of the American headlines. But already there had been a new intensification of the American dismay at these constant and frightening disturbances.

In March, 1939, a Gallup poll on the question "In case war breaks out, should we sell Britain and France food supplies?" had brought a Yes from 76 per cent of those polled; in April the question was repeated and the percentage jumped from 76 to 82. In March the further question "Should we sell them airplanes and other war materials?" brought a Yes from 52 per cent; in April the figure had gone way up to 66—a striking increase. True, only 16 per cent of those polled thought we should send the Army and Navy abroad to help England and France. But the great majority of Americans wanted to help somehow—and more than half of the Gallup voters expressed the ominous expectation (though not by any means the wish) that if war broke out America would be "drawn in."

Was the United States moving along that road to war which only a few years previously it had tried so hard to block off with red lights?

§ 4

On the morning of Sunday, April 30, 1939, the gates of the New York World's Fair were thrown open. The theme of the Fair was "The World of Tomorrow"; the opening ceremonies were held in a vast enclosure called the "Court of Peace." Could anybody in that throng of tens of thousands, gathered under a blue sky in which hung mountainous clouds, fail to reflect upon the question ironically posed by those two phrases?

Here, all about one, was the embodiment of the American dream, 1939 model. Bold modern architecture, sometimes severe, sometimes garish, but always devoid of the traditional classical or Gothic decoration, and glowing with color—offering the first chance most of the visitors had ever had to see what modern architects might do if the economic condition of the country let them go in for large-scale construction. Gardens, fountains, waterfalls leaping off buildings; music resounding everywhere; at night, the splendor of superb lighting. Miracles of invention and of industrial efficiency to goggle at. A sense of festival. Here every man could briefly feel himself, if not a king, at least the citizen of a gay and friendly country, the beneficiary of spotless industrial engineering, privileged to idle along the lagoons, to watch the fireworks flower in orange and blue and green, to see the trylon piercing the sky behind the young trees turned silver by the lights. Here General Motors and Remington Rand sat cheek by jowl with the WPA, Soviet Russia presented her delights to people who would presently compare them with Eastman Kodak's delights; in this fantastic paradise there were visible no social classes, no civil feuds, no international hates, no hints of grimy days in dreary slums, no depression worries. Here was a dream of wealth, luxury, and lively beauty, with coca-cola at every corner and the horns of the busses jauntily playing "The Sidewalks of New York."

Outside the gates was a nation one-third of whose citizens were still "ill-housed, ill-clad, ill-nourished," and a world from which the hope of true peace seemed to have passed forever. What would the real world of tomorrow hold for America?

Still the basic economic problem of America remained

unsolved. An uncertain climb out of the pit of the Recession brought the Federal Reserve Board's adjusted index up to 102 in August, 1939. But that was only a shade higher than the point it had reached during the New Deal Honeymoon; and still there were nine and a half million people unemployed, according to the estimates of the National Industrial Conference Board. The colossal enterprise of work relief was becoming every day more clearly a tragic makeshift, demoralizing, as the years dragged on, to many if not to most of those unfortunate enough to be dependent upon it. Though it had been generously conceived, had produced some fine achievements in the arts and some welcome civic improvements, and had at least kept millions of men and women from the extremities of want and despair, nevertheless as a permanent institution the WPA offered an intolerable prospect—and it was getting to look all too permanent. The farm problem was still unsolved, despite Secretary Wallace's herculean efforts; instead of an ever-normal granary the United States seemed to be saddled with an eversubsidized granary. A kindly government could alleviate the lot of families forced off the land, but could not yet catch up with the tractor as it drove new families, east and west, into homeless migration. Fine things as well as foolish things had been done in Washington, but still the prosperity which had vanished in 1929 looked as unattainable as a rainbow.

Must America at last be reconciled to the dictum that as its population growth slowed up its economic growth must slow up too? Must it accept either a continuance of this twilight-prosperity, with the burden of carrying the unemployed becoming progressively greater, or else a grim deflation of prices and wages and debts till the labor surplus could become absorbed—a deflation which might be even less endurable than that of 1929-33? No one could relish either of those prospects. Well then—a war boom? No gain thus made could be lasting. A speculative boom? That, too, would carry with it the seeds of its own destruction. No healthy expansion of the American economy could be achieved without a steady flow of money into new investment (along with a maintenance of popular purchasing power), and this flow was still dammed.

What dammed it? That question could not be answered adequately without taking into account one of the most significant economic developments of the nineteen-thirties: the increased importance of the great corporations which I have called economic principalities. Everybody was aware that the power of the Federal government had grown enormously during the decade, until its fingers reached into every nook and cranny of the country. Everybody was aware that all manner of activities and enterprises which had been managed on an individual or small-group basis were now becoming socialized—until even that company of rugged individualists, the medical profession, found itself fighting a rear-guard action against the gradual advance of group medicine, even of state medicine. Not everybody was aware of the extent to which the general trend toward centralization, toward bigger and bigger units of social and economic action, was affecting business as well.

Gone since 1929, it was true, were the dizzy days when promoters merged companies into super-companies and super-companies into super-super-companies, when holding-company pyramids were built four and six and eight stories high, and little groups of men in Wall Street, playing with paper stock certificates, thought they were well on their way to the control of all American enterprise. Some of the pyramids had fallen down in the Depression, others had been at least partly razed by a disapproving government; and as for the rest, their days of skyscraping growth were over—for the present at least. The public wanted no more Insulls or Van Sweringens to flourish. Yet most of the great corporate structures which had been put together in the generation before 1929, and especially in the decade before 1929, still stood intact after the storm.

Not only that: it was these great corporations, generally speaking, which during the nineteen-thirties had been making whatever money was made in business. Look at these revealing figures from E. D. Kennedy's *Dividends to Pay*. In the year 1935 there were nearly half a million corporations in the United States, and they made, between them, a tidy profit of over a billion and two-thirds dollars—but if one omitted from the reckoning 960 of the biggest (the 960 companies, with stocks active on the New York Exchange, for which the Standard Statistics Company tabulated earnings) that collective profit turned into a deficit. In short, in 1935 the 960 big companies were, collectively, making a profit; the 475,000 or so smaller companies were, collectively, losing money. Mr. Kennedy was not able to show what happened in 1937 to the great mass of corporations because the government figures had not yet appeared, but he was able to trace the further fortunes of the 960 at the top, and his findings provided more illumination. Of all the money made in 1937 by these 960 aristocrats of business, well over a half— 60 per cent—was made by just 42 of them; and nearly a quarter—24 per cent—was made by a mere six of the very biggest. (You would like the names of these six? They were General Motors, American Telephone, Standard Oil of New Jersey, United States Steel, du Pont, and General Electric.)

Imagine yourself setting up a new company to compete against one of these giants or even a group of lesser giants, with their huge resources and their ability to maintain prices by mutual custom and business understanding if by no more devious means, and you will begin to understand one of the reasons why new investments did not flourish. Too many of the roads on which it might wish to proceed were already occupied by marchers able to keep the highway to themselves.

Parenthetically it should be added that the great principalities were now becoming less dependent upon the investment houses of Wall Street for capital; they could maintain and modernize and even expand their plants out of their own ample pockets. Perhaps the palmy days of the Wall Street bankers were over—not only because of government restrictions but also because the great principalities were becoming more powerful than the banks. Was it wholly irrelevant that during the last two or three years of the decade several big corporations, notably U. S. Steel and General Motors, moved in one way or another to reduce the authority of officers and directors who represented essentially Wall Street and the traditional power of capital, to increase the power of men who represented the active management, or to add directors who represented local business interests outside Wall Street? True, there was doubtless a political motive behind such moves. The managers of the principalities had waked up to the fact that they were in politics whether they wanted to be or not. "Public relations" were no longer a mere press-agent's job, but demanded the attention of at least a vice-president. The big corporations were spending millions to win popularity. Wall Street was not popular; why not go through the motions, at least, of casting it off? Nevertheless there may have been more to it than that. Perhaps the day was at hand when, figuratively speaking, Mr. Sloan would not call on Mr. Morgan; Mr. Morgan would call on Mr. Sloan.

The profits of these great principalities went into millions of American homes, for their cohorts of stockholders had never been so numerous. But to only a tiny minority of wealthy stockholders did enough money go to be potentially an important factor in new investment. This tiny minority, beset with taxes, were in no mood for gambles in the areas where the great principalities did not stifle competition. "Why take a chance?" they would say; "if we lose, we lose; if we win, the government will take most of it away." They preferred to keep their money invested in the principalities and in tax-exempt bonds, or even to hold it uninvested in cash. Give us a government that will free us from burdens and restrictions, they had been shouting, and you will see new investment burgeon. But the behavior of the business indices in 1938 and 1939, when the New Deal had certainly become less adventurous and more willing to conciliate capital, had given little indication that such would be the case. There was always some good reason why the burgeoning must be postponed: the man who in 1937 had sworn that the return of "confidence" waited only for the repeal of the undistributed profits tax lamented in 1938 and 1939 that new investment was being held back by the fear of war. The banks continued to be glutted with idle money.

There were other reasons, of course, why the money lay idle. Who, for example, would risk money in new building when costs were held so high—by crushing real-estate taxes, high prices for materials, high hourly wages for labor, antiquated and inefficient building methods, etc.—that no profit could be anticipated? Here the difficulty was not that a few great corporations monopolized the field, but that a multitude of suzerainties, large and small, and a multitude of frozen debts and unresolved Depression problems, prevented great corporations from entering the field at all with the economies of large-scale production. Yet on the whole the generalization appeared to stand. The highways of industry and trade were well filled with going concerns with which only big, well-heeled companies could compete, and the men who could afford to bring such companies to birth had no enthusiasm for the battle. They thought their troubles were mostly political; actually, the evidence suggested that they were mostly economic.

During 1938 and 1939 the government, through a Temporary National Economic Committee, set out to investigate the blocking of new investment, especially by the competition-stifling practices of the principalities (which for political reasons were referred to by the good old fighting term "monopolies"). Some of the New Dealers were studying the prospects for investments by the government itself to take up the slack. But the problem was thorny; and when in the spring of 1939 the President made a gesture in the direction of investment by the government—combining the idea with that of unemployment relief in what was called the Lending-Spending Bill—Congress threw the whole scheme out the window. (Not content with thus rebuffing Roosevelt, Congress cut the admirable Theatre Project out of the WPA and decreed that wage-rates for skilled workmen on the WPA should be cut, thus provoking a strike which the columnist Bugs Baer called the "mutiny on the bounty.") The 1940 elections were becoming visible to the naked political eye, ardent New Dealers were prophesying a third term for Roosevelt, Republicans and conservative Democrats were taking a rich delight in demolishing his domestic proposals, and the economic issues were becoming lost in the political shuffle.

Now at last it looked as if the New Deal was really through. It had played its cards and had no more new ones to offer—or, if it had them, it could no longer induce Congress to let it play them. The country was manifestly wearying of economic experiment; the Republican party had taken advantage of this weariness to make substantial gains in the 1938 elections. The social salvationists were losing their zeal for legislating prosperity. Now, like Roosevelt himself, they had become tense with excitement about foreign affairs and had half forgotten the dismal unsolved problems on the domestic front; they were either forming committees for the defense of freedom and tolerance against dictatorship, or breaking up into new alignments over the question whether America should stay out of war at all costs or come to the rescue of Britain and France. Yet still the secret of prosperity remained undiscovered.

For three and a half of the ten years since the Panic of 1929 the Hoover Administration had fought valiantly but vainly against disaster. For six and a half years the Roosevelt Administration had experimented and palliated, and had merely kept disaster at bay—to the tune of an increase of not far from twenty billion dollars in the public debt of the United States.

But was that all that could be said?

On the credit side of the national ledger there were certain entries to be made. *Item 1.* No revolution, no dictatorship born of the Depression had done away with the essential civil liberties of Americans. *Item 2.* The government in power had never willfully denied the principle stated in Roosevelt's second inaugural, that "we are determined to make every American citizen the subject of his country's interest and concern, and we will never regard any faithful law-abiding group within our borders as superfluous." Whatever sins were to be charged against the New Deal, at least it had done its task humanely. (This item loomed large in the eyes of men who looked abroad in 1939 and thought of the hordes of refugees seeking footholds where they would not be "regarded as superfluous.") *Item 3.* Despite all the miseries of the Depression and the recurrent fears of new economic decline and of war, the bulk of the American people had not yet quite lost their basic asset of hopefulness.

It was still their instinct to transform a suburban swamp into a city of magic and call it "The World of Tomorrow." In that world of tomorrow the show which they liked best of all and stood in hour-long queues to enjoy was the General Motors Futurama, a picture of the possible delights of 1960. They still liked to build the biggest dam in all creation and toy with the idea of the happy farmsteads it would water, the enormous engines it would drive, the new and better business it would stimulate. They still liked to stand with elbows on the fence at the edge of the farm and say, "Sooner or later I aim to buy those forty acres over there and go into this thing on a bigger scale." They still scrimped to give their sons and daughters "a better education than we ever had," feeling obscurely that a better education would be valued in the years to come.

A nation tried in a long ordeal had not yet lost heart.

§ 5

So one meditated as the summer of 1939 slipped by. But always now the meditation was interrupted by the recurring question: What will happen in Europe, and what will it mean to us here?

That question could hardly fail to be in the back of one's mind when, early in June, the King and Queen of England visited the United States. The Roosevelts tactfully made the most of this opportunity to cement the bonds of Anglo-American amity and erase whatever unfavorable memories lingered from *l'affaire Simpson*—and from Munich. Their reception of their royal guests was carefully arranged to be both dignified and heartily American, with more than a touch of the military.

When the King and Queen arrived in Washington—on a day of terrific heat which must have made the King's epauletted admiral's uniform almost intolerable—ten "flying fortress" bombing planes roared over the route of the procession to the White House, and the cars in which rode the King and the President, and the Queen and Mrs. Roosevelt, were preceded by sixty businesslike-looking baby tanks. After the state dinner that evening, there was a White

House concert the program for which included Negro spirituals, cowboy ballads, and square dances, with well-assorted solos: not only by Lawrence Tibbett but also by Marian Anderson, the great Negro singer—with Kate Smith contributing that perennial radio favorite, "When the Moon Comes Over the Mountain." Three days later, their Royal Highnesses picnicked with the Roosevelts at Hyde Park, and the King consumed hot dogs and beer. (He could have dodged the hot dogs, for the menu also included cold ham, smoked and plain turkey, and various salads, as well as baked beans and brown bread, doughnuts and ginger bread, cookies, coffee, and soft drinks—but he knew well that a hot dog eaten smilingly in America might be worth a dozen battleships.) When the guests boarded their train at Hyde Park that evening, the President clasped his hands together high over his head in democratic farewell and the crowd sang "Auld Lang Syne" and "For He's a Jolly Good Fellow."

Nor did Mrs. Roosevelt, in her amiable newspaper column "My Day," fail to take the American public into her confidence about her concern over the domestic arrangements for the visit—such as the care taken to provide the guests with early morning tea and with water chilled but not iced—and about those small mishaps which would cause every hostess who read of them to vibrate with sympathy—such as the fact that a butler entering the big library at Hyde Park with a tray of drinks slipped and dropped the tray with a crash.

The King and Queen in their turn were by universal consent cordial, unassuming, and engaging. The crowds both in Washington and New York were enormous and enthusiastic; in fact, Mrs. Roosevelt remarked in her column that during the procession in Washington she had been quite unable to explain to the Queen what buildings they were passing because the roars of applause drowned every word. No untoward incident marred the triumphal royal progress. Altogether, the visit was an almost incredible success.

A few weeks after this success, the President tried hard to get Congress to rewrite the Neutrality Act and do away with the mandatory ban on the export of arms and munitions to warring countries. Not yet, however, was Congress ready to take this leap. In a matter which might determine the issue of war or peace, a majority of the men on the Hill were still unwilling to yield to this volatile man who so firmly believed that Hitler must be stopped and that the United States must help stop him by making it plain that if he did not hold his hand he would have American planes and guns, if not American soldiers and sailors, to reckon with.

Wherever one turned, that summer, the thought of Europe followed.

The Transatlantic Clippers (41-ton planes with a wingspread of 152 feet) began carrying passengers from Long Island Sound to France and England—a potential link between allies, one asked oneself, or between belligerency and neutrality? The American submarine *Squalus* sank off Portsmouth in 240 feet of water, and 33 of her 59 men were rescued by diving bell—was it just a coincidence that a British submarine and a French submarine were lost at about the same time? *The Grapes of Wrath* lay upon the summer-porch table—and beside it lay *Days of Our Years, Inside Asia,* and *Not Peace, But a Sword,* all three of which took the American reader overseas. The long quarrel between the TVA and the Commonwealth & Southern utility system was moderated with the government's purchase of the Tennessee Electric Power Company's properties—and one realized that the hatred of Roosevelt which had burned for years in the hearts of big business men was already dying to embers. A salesman could still get orders by sending in a card which said

> If You Don't Give Me An Order
> I'll Vote For Him Again

but some of the once-indignant business men were even beginning to like Roosevelt now—for his foreign policy.

Prospective débutantes were wondering, that summer, who would succeed Brenda Diana Duff Frazier as the "glamour girl" of the new season; the idea of glamour (or "oomph" if you preferred) was now so ubiquitous that *Life* was calling Thomas E. Dewey "Republican Glamour Boy No. 1," and Attorney-General Murphy "New Deal Glamour Boy No. 1." The fashion experts were returning from Europe with the news that Paris said corsets and hour-glass figures. Summer vacationists were bending over their Chinese checkers; trying to emulate the swimming mermaids and mermen of Billy Rose's Aquacade; comparing Grover Whalen's financial troubles, as he tried to prevent the "World of Tomorrow" from going bankrupt, with the troubles of the managers of the San Francisco Fair; discussing Johnstown's speed on the racetracks; driving to the movies to see Robert Donat in "Goodbye Mr. Chips," or Bette Davis in "Dark Victory." Would all these everyday trifles of the 1939 summer season come back to memory, some day, as incidents of the happy lull before the storm?

One thing was almost certain. If war broke out in Europe, we should look back upon the day of declaration as the day when a line was drawn across our national life. Whatever strange form the war might take, whatever might be America's relation to it, it would bring America new problems, new alignments, new hopes and fears.

But surely there wouldn't be war. Things were really rather quiet in Europe, on the surface, in July and early August. And if Hitler should make a new crisis over Danzig and the Polish corridor, surely somebody would back down before it was too late. Somebody always had.

§ 6

The storm moved up late in August.

First, like a rumble of premonitory thunder, came the report that von Ribbentrop was to fly to Moscow to sign a German-Russian agreement. Then came the agreement itself; it was proclaimed in streamer headlines in the papers of August 24:—

GERMANY AND RUSSIA SIGN 10-YEAR NON-
AGGRESSION PACT; BIND EACH OTHER NOT
TO AID OPPONENTS IN WAR ACTS;
HITLER REBUFFS LONDON; BRITAIN
AND FRANCE MOBILIZE

That announcement sent ideas, expectations, and assumptions reeling the world over. In America, the supposed experts on world affairs stumbled for a foothold in reality as their logical premises fell away from under them. The communists performed quick ideological contortions as they saw the party line coming to a hairpin turn. Business men decided not to put in that buying order yet awhile, to wait till the shape of things was clearer; steamship officials debated the canceling of sailing dates; the stock market hesitated, sold off a little, wobbled uneasily. Americans went again to their radios for last-minute European bulletins.

Days of negotiations, mobilizations, frantic efforts for settlement, threats and counter-threats—then, very early on the morning of September 1, Hitler's armies marched into Poland.

It had begun. But still there was a question hanging in the air—what about Britain and France?

All that day—it was a Friday—the question remained not quite answered, and all the next day too. It traveled along with Labor Day week-enders departing for their three-day holiday, burned in their minds even on the golf links and the bathing beaches.

The answer was delivered at last on Sunday morning, September 3—ten years to a day from that hot September 3 of 1929 with which this chronicle opened. Over the radio came from London the voice of Neville Chamberlain, an infinitely unmartial voice, speaking in tones low and tired and sad:—

"This morning the British Ambassador in Berlin handed to the German government a final note stating that unless we heard from them by eleven o'clock that they were preparing at once to withdraw their troops from Poland, a state of war would exist between us. I have to tell you that no such undertaking has been received and in consequence this country is at war with Germany."

With those sentences, spoken so quietly thousands of miles away, an era ended for America and another one began.

Appendix

SOURCES AND OBLIGATIONS

In the Appendix to *Only Yesterday* I spoke first of all of my debt to Robert S. Lynd and Helen Merrell Lynd for "the extraordinarily varied and precise information collected in *Middletown*," of which I had "made frequent use"; and I added, "I do not see how any conscientious historian of the Post-war Decade could afford to neglect this mine of material." *Mutatis mutandis,* I must now say the same thing of their *Middletown in Transition* (Harcourt, Brace, 1937). I have quoted from it more frequently in the present volume than from any other source, and have leaned more upon it than the number of quotations would suggest.

In writing my first four chapters, I have made much use of *The Hoover Administration, A Documented Narrative,* by William Starr Myers and Walter H. Newton (Charles Scribner's Sons, 1936), and *Hoover Off the Record,* by Theodore G. Joslin (Doubleday, Doran, 1934). These two books, one formal, the other informal, both have proved helpful for reference and quotation, partisan though they are. Similarly I have found the five volumes of *The Public Papers and Addresses of Franklin D. Roosevelt* (Random House, 1938) of great value for the New Deal period. Two other books which came out while mine was in preparation have been useful to me at many points and would be even more useful to writers who could take fuller advantage of them than I was able to: the splendid *America in Midpassage,* by Charles A. Beard and Mary R. Beard (Macmillan, 1939), and Raymond Moley's detailed and searching first-hand account of the New Deal, *After Seven Years* (Harper, 1939). Needless to say, I have made constant use of the successive volumes of the *World Almanac,* and especially the Chronology which appears in it annually and is invaluable to anyone engaged in a project of this sort; and also the files of the *New York Times* in the New York Public Library.

My other sources—books, newspapers, magazines, and ideas and anecdotes and observations picked up throughout the decade—have been so voluminous that it would be wearisome to recite them all. But certain sources I should like to mention either by way of explanation or to express special obligation, and these I shall arrange chapter by chapter for convenience:

In Chapter I ("Prelude: September 3, 1929") the quotations from Gilbert Seldes are from "Talkies' Progress," in *Harper's Magazine*, September, 1929. The paraphrase of F. C. Mills is based on a quotation from him in *Middletown in Transition*, pp. 53-54. The late George W. Wickersham very kindly wrote me shortly before his death and showed me a copy of the Commission minutes for September 4, 1929. From newspaper data, Calvin Coolidge did not move to his larger house in Northampton until 1930, although William Allen White's biography of him would seem to imply an earlier move. The 1929 data about Dr. Francis E. Townsend are based on a letter from Old Age Revolving Pensions, Ltd.; about "Amos 'n' Andy" and Edgar Bergen, on information kindly supplied through Julian Street, Jr., when he was with the NBC; about Garnet Carter and Hervey Allen, on letters from them; about Pearl Buck, on a letter from Richard J. Walsh. For these letters I am grateful.

In Chapter II ("Exit Prosperity") the polls of the National Economic League are from reproductions of them in *The Folklore of Capitalism*, by Thurman W. Arnold (Yale University Press, 1937). The quotation of Denna Frank Fleming is from his book, *The United States and World Organization, 1920-1933* (Columbia University Press, 1938), p. 325. The item about Roosevelt and Farley at election time, 1930, is drawn from James A. Farley's book *Behind the Ballots* (Harcourt, Brace, 1938). Henry Pratt Fairchild's population estimate is from an article by him, "When the Population Levels Off," in *Harper's Magazine*, May, 1938. The concluding pages of this chapter repeat (with some revisions) passages in a talk I gave at Bennington College, Commencement, 1938, which was printed by the Catamount Press at North Bennington, Vt., with the title "In a Time of Apprehension."

In Chapter III ("Down, Down, Down") the item about William McC. Martin, Jr., he kindly gave me himself. The Roosevelt-Farley item is again from Farley's *Behind the Ballots* (see above). The details of my story of the Hoover moratorium are based chiefly on Myers and Newton, Joslin, and Mark Sullivan's article on "President Hoover and the World Depression" in the *Saturday Evening Post* for March 11, 1933. The Peter F. Drucker quotation was taken from the manuscript of his book *The End of Economic Man* (John Day, 1939). The National Credit Corporation item was drawn from *Three Years Down*, by Jonathan Norton Leonard (Carrick & Evans, 1939), a lively and useful, if bitter, account of the years 1929-33 to which I am also indebted for several items about the effects of the Depression on individuals. The Kuznets figures on interest payments are from "National Income, 1929-32," by Simon Kuznets, which is Bulletin 49 of the National Bureau of Economic Research. The E. D. Kennedy figures are from his valuable book *Dividends to Pay* (Reynal & Hitchcock, 1939), pp. 16-17. The figures on domestic corporate issues are from *The United States, a Graphic History*, by Hacker Modley, and Taylor (Modern Age Books, 1937). The Croxton figures for Buffalo were cited in *The Christian Century*, December 28, 1932. My account of the Lindbergh case is in large degree based upon Sidney B. Whipple's exceptionally interesting and careful account in *The Trial of Bruno Richard Hauptmann* (Doubleday, Doran, 1937), to which I am greatly indebted.

In Chapter IV ("A Change of Government") the account of the Chicago Convention draws much from Farley's *Behind the Ballots* (see above); the incident of the Acceptance Address manuscript is from Raymond Moley's *After Seven Years* (see above). The Elmer Davis quotation is from "The Collapse of Politics" in *Harper's Magazine* for September, 1932. My account of the Bonus Army episode is based on a comparison of many versions, including especially Paul Y. Anderson's personal observations in *The Nation* for August 17, 1932. The farmer's remark to Mary Heaton Vorse is from her article, "Rebellion in the Corn Belt," in *Harper's Magazine*, December, 1932. My description of a farmers' protest meeting follows the account of one in *We Too Are the People*, Louise V. Armstrong (Little, Brown, 1938), which is helpful also to an understanding of relief problems. For Hoover's unsmiling demeanor see *42 Years in the White House* by Irwin Hood Hoover (Houghton Mifflin, 1934). My account of Hoover and Roosevelt in the interregnum is based largely on a comparison of the versions Myers and Newton, Joslin, Moley, Farley, and others. In my account of the bank crisis I have used *28 Days: A History of the Banking Crisis*, by C. C. Colt and N. S. Keith (Greenberg, 1933).

In Chapter V ("New Deal Honeymoon") the beginning of Roosevelt's Inaugural is taken from the *New York Times* for March 5, 1933; the version given in *The Public Papers and Addresses of Franklin D. Roosevelt* omits the "national consecration" clause. The quotations from letters embodying plans for recovery are actual quotations from letters I was kindly shown in the NRA files at the Department of Commerce. The genesis of the NRA is based on many accounts, including chiefly "Whose Child is the NRA?" by John T. Flynn in *Harper's Magazine* for September, 1934. Jonathan Mitchell's article, "The Versatility of General Johnson," appeared in *Harper's Magazine* for October, 1934.

In Chapter VI ("A Change of Climate") I have made use of a study of *Youth and Sex* by Dorothy Dunbar Bromley and Florence Haxton Britten (Harper, 1938), and at several points have used an especially interesting article on "Youth in College," *Fortune,* June, 1936, which was reprinted in *American Points of View,* edited by William H. Cordell and Kathryn Coe Cordell (Doubleday, Doran, 1937). On bootlegging after Repeal, I have used *After Repeal,* by Leonard V. Harrison and Elizabeth Raine (Harper, 1936). The Virginia book-burning was described in *Ken,* August 28, 1938. My mention of slot machines, pinball, etc., draws heavily from Samuel Lubell's article, "Ten Billion Nickels," in the *Saturday Evening Post,* May 12, 1939; of the Irish Sweepstakes, from an article by John J. McCarthy in *Harper's Magazine,* June, 1934; of "Bank Night," from "Bank Night Tonight," by Forbes Parkhill, *Saturday Evening Post,* December 4, 1937; of softball, from "Baseball's Precocious Baby," by Ted Shane, *American Magazine,* June, 1939. The Gallup poll on gambling was cited in the *New York Times* for November 27, 1938.

In Chapter VII ("Reform—and Recovery?") I have quoted from George R. Leighton's article, "In Search of the NRA," which appeared in *Harper's Magazine,* January, 1934. On relief, *Spending to Save,* by Harry L. Hopkins (W. W. Norton, 1936) is the source of some facts. On Huey Long I have drawn plentifully from *Huey Long, A Candid Biography,* by Forrest Davis (Dodge, 1935); the White House incident is from Farley's reminiscences (see above). On the Townsend Plan, many facts are from "The Old People's Crusade," by Richard L. Neuberger and Kelley Loe, *Harper's Magazine,* March, 1936.

In Chapter VIII ("When the Farms Blew Away") the opening quotation is from "Life and Death of 470 Acres," by R. D. Lusk, *Saturday Evening Post,* August 13, 1938. The map which I mention is in *Problems of a Changing Population,* National Resources Committee (May, 1938), p. 65. The Neuberger quotation is from *Our Promised Land* (Macmillan, 1938). On the changes in American agriculture I am especially indebted to Paul S. Taylor, from whose "Power Farming and Labor Displacement in the Cotton

Belt, 1937" (published by the U. S. Department of Labor and Bureau of Labor Statistics, serial No. R 737, Government Printing Office) I have quoted, and to Ladd Haystead's memorandum for Arthur Kudner, Inc., "The Farmer Looks at Himself." On farm tenancy, I am indebted to (and have quoted from) the chapter on "Labor in Evolving Economy" in the Beards' *America in Midpassage.* The Stuart Chase quotation on the flood of 1936 is from *Rich Land, Poor Land* (Whittlesey House, 1936), which was a helpful source also on government conservation measures.

In Chapter IX ("The Voice with the Smile Wins") the figures I have given on Federal deficits are net (after subtracting the amount paid out for statutory debt retirements); I have not attempted to go into the very intricate and debatable question of the extent to which the expenditures in these years represented in part money which should come back to the Federal government. In the discussion of Moley and Corcoran and Cohen I have used chiefly that illuminating little book, *Men Around the President,* by Joseph Alsop and Robert Kintner (Doubleday, Doran, 1939), and also Moley's *After Seven Years* (see above), checking the latter against the former. For many details in this chapter *In 1936,* by Alvin C. Eurich and Elmo C. Wilson (Henry Holt, 1937), came in handy.

In Chapter X ("With Pen and Camera Through Darkest America") the quotation from Malcolm Cowley is from an advance proof of the *New Republic* for November 8, 1939. My passage on Benny Goodman and swing leans heavily on "The Killer-Diller," by Frank Norris, *Saturday Evening Post,* May 7, 1938, and "No. 1 Swing Man," by Irving Kolodin, *Harper's Magazine,* September, 1939; the Toscanini-Chotzinoff item is from "Toscanini on the Air," *Fortune,* January, 1938; the figures on music appreciation are from an excellent summary, "Music Goes into Mass Production," by Dickson Skinner, *Harper's Magazine,* April, 1939. The data about centralized newspaper control are taken from John Cowles's chapter on "Journalism—Newspapers," in *America Now,* by 36 Americans, edited by Harold E. Stearns (Scribner's, 1938). On the movies, I have taken a number of facts from advance proofs of Margaret Farrand Thorp's fine survey, *America at the Movies* (Yale University Press, 1939).

In Chapter XI ("Friction and Recession") I have made extensive use, in the labor section, of Edward Levinson's valuable *Labor on the March* (Harper, 1938), and am also indebted to Herbert Harris for his *American Labor* (Yale University Press, 1939), another useful source. The account of the meetings between Lewis and Taylor is drawn from "It Happened in Steel," in *Fortune*, May, 1937. My account of the Supreme Court battle follows pretty closely three fine articles by Joseph Alsop and Turner Catledge in the *Saturday Evening Post* for September 18, September 25, and October 16, 1937, entitled "The 168 Days" (later published in book form). The Leon Henderson item is from *Men Around the President* (see under Chapter IX); and I have also leaned somewhat on that book in my account of the Administration shifts of policy during the Recession.

In Chapter XII ("The Shadow of War") the quotation of the international broadcast is from bound volumes of the Columbia Broadcasting System's Broadcasts, at the New York Public Library. As to Studio Nine, I have drawn on H. V. Kaltenborn's *I Broadcast the Crisis* (Random House, 1938). My account of the London Economic Conference of 1933 naturally makes use of Moley's detailed narrative in *After Seven Years*. In this chapter I have made much use of the Gallup public-opinion polls on foreign affairs, as handily collected for reference in F. S. Wickware's "What the Polls Say," in *Harper's Magazine*, September, 1939; such polls sometimes seem to indicate more than they actually do (for much depends on the wording of the questions) but they at least help to show trends, especially when the same question is asked at intervals. E. D. Kennedy's book, from which I have drawn figures on corporate earnings, I have already cited above (under Chapter III).

I cannot list all the people who have been good enough to help me in one way or another, but I should like especially to thank the William Zuills of Orange Grove, Bermuda, for their thoughtful hospitality while I was at work on the opening chapters; and, for assistance of various sorts, Letitia C. Rogers, Oliver Ellsworth Allen, Margaret MacMullen, Charles W. MacMullen, Cathleen Schurr, the David Cushman Coyles, Charles C. Colt, John A. Kouwenhoven, Paul S. Taylor, George R. Leighton, Luther H. Gulick, Remley J. Glass, Daniel I. McNamara, Julian Street, Jr., Deems Taylor, Florence Alonso, and the staff of the New York Public Library (especially in the Newspaper Room and the Economics and Sociology Division). My wife, Agnes Rogers Allen, is to be thanked above all—for helpful ideas and criticism and for much hard work on behalf of this project.

F. L. A.

New York City
November 10, 1939

INDEX